Sanctuary in Ireland
Perspectives on Asylum Law and Policy

Sanctuary in Ireland
Perspectives on Asylum
Law and Policy

Edited by Ursula Fraser and Colin Harvey

IPA

INSTITUTE OF PUBLIC
ADMINISTRATION

First published in 2003
by the Institute of Public Administration
57–61 Lansdowne Road
Dublin 4
Ireland

ISBN 1 904541 04 6

British Library cataloguing-in-publication data
A catalogue record for this book is available
from the British Library

Cover design by Butler Claffey Design, Dún Laoghaire
Typeset in Garamond 10/11.5 by Carole Lynch, Sligo
Printed by ColourBooks Ltd, Ireland

Contents

Asylum applications in Ireland 1992-2003

1992	1993	1994	1995	1996	1997	1998	1999	2000	2001	2002	2003 (to 30 October)
39	91	362	424	1,179	3,883	4,626	7,724	10,938	10,325	11,634	7,158

Source: Office of the Refugee Applications Commissioner, www.orac.ie

Acknowledgements

The editors wish to acknowledge the diligence, co-operation and expertise of the contributors to this book. They are also very grateful for the assistance of the following: Eileen Brannigan; David Costello; Eleanor Edmond; Paul Farrell; P.J. Farrell; Frank Fraser; John Garry; Cabrini Gibbons; Nuala Haughey; Liam Herrick; Brian Ingoldsby; Bernie McGonagle; Marcus McMahon; Stephen O'Brien; Berenice O'Neill; Joan Roddy; Ivy Wong; Tony McNamara; Eileen Kelly; Hannah Ryan; Tom Turley.

Notes on Contributors

Cathryn Costello was Director of the Irish Centre for European Law from 2000 to 2003 and lecturer in European law at Trinity College Dublin Law School from 1998 to 2003. A barrister, her areas of specialisation include fundamental rights, equality issues, the European Community (EC) judicial system, asylum and immigration. She has published widely on fundamental rights and the EC courts. In Autumn 2003, she took up a senior research fellowship in public and EC law at Worcester College, Oxford.

Suzanne Egan is a member of the Irish Human Rights Commission and has been a lecturer in international and human rights law at University College Dublin since 1992. She is a qualified barrister and holds a Master of Laws degree from Osgoode Law School in Toronto. Prior to lecturing at UCD, she was the legal supervisor of an independent research centre on refugee law and policy in Canada (1989-1991) and a research assistant at the Law Reform Commission in Ireland (1991-1992). She is a founding member of the Refugee Protection Policy Group, an independent group of lawyers, academics and other experts working in the field of refugee law and policy. She has published widely in the area of human rights and, particularly, with regard to refugee law and policy.

Harry McGee is political editor with the *Irish Examiner*. He has worked with the *Sunday Tribune*, *The Sunday Press*, RTE, the *Connaught Tribune* and was editor of *Magill*. He is a qualified barrister.

Siobhan Mullally lectures in human rights and public international law at the National University of Ireland, Cork. She previously taught at the University of Peshawar, Pakistan, and the University of Hull in England. In 1999 Siobhan was a visiting fellow at the Harvard Human Rights Program. She has participated in human rights missions in Kosovo, Pakistan and Afghanistan. She has written extensively on refugee issues.

Donncha O'Connell is a qualified barrister and lecturer in law at the National University of Ireland, Galway, where he teaches constitutional law, European human rights law and legal systems. From 1999 until 2002 he was the first full-time Director of the Irish Council for Civil Liberties. He was appointed the Irish member of the EU Network of Independent Experts on Fundamental Rights established by the European Commission in 2002. He also teaches human rights, on a part-time basis, at the Law School, Trinity College Dublin.

Peter O'Mahony was an aid worker in the developing world from 1983 to 1996. Having first worked with Concern for four years in Bangladesh, he was field director for the Save the Children Fund in Morocco, Mali and Somaliland. Since 1999 he has been Chief Executive of the Irish Refugee Council, an NGO working to influence Ireland's policy on asylum seekers and refugees.

Pia Prütz Phiri, a Danish national, began her international career working for the EU before joining UNHCR in 1984. For the nineteen years she has worked with UNHCR, she has held posts in Zambia, Turkey, Nordic and Baltic states, southern Africa and Kenya. She holds a Masters degree in law from Copenhagen University and studied international relations and French in the Sorbonne University, France. She has been Representative of UNHCR's Representation in Ireland since July 2000.

Bill Shipsey is a senior counsel practising at the Irish Bar. He has appeared in numerous asylum and refugee cases over the past twenty years. He is a past chairperson of the Free Legal Aid Centres and Amnesty International. He founded a volunteer refugee legal service in the early 1990s, a precursor to the Legal Aid Board Refugee Legal Service. He is currently Chair of 'Art for Amnesty' and the Irish Hospice Foundation and he is President of the Amnesty International (Ireland) Foundation.

Ciara Smyth is a lecturer in law at the National University of Ireland, Galway, where she teaches contract law and legal systems. From 2001 to 2003 she worked for the United Nations High Commissioner for Refugees Representation in Ireland, training personnel involved in refugee status determination. She was legal officer with the Irish Commission for Prisoners Overseas and also spent two years at the Ministry of Foreign Affairs in Cambodia. She holds an LLM in human rights and conflict resolution from the Queen's University, Belfast.

Siobhan Stack is a graduate of the National University of Ireland, Cambridge University and the Honourable Society of the King's Inns. She was formerly a lecturer in law at University College Dublin. Called to the Bar in 1995, she is now a practising barrister working in asylum law and other areas.

The editors

Ursula Fraser studied law at Trinity College Dublin, was called to
the Irish Bar in 1995, and was awarded an MLitt at Trinity College
in 2000, writing on the temporary protection of asylum seekers in
international and EU law. She has worked as a legal officer with
the Irish Refugee Council and advocacy officer at the European
Council on Refugees and Exiles in Brussels. She has also worked
for Amnesty International Irish Section and the United Nations
High Commissioner for Refugees. She has lectured in international,
EU, and human rights law for Boston University and Trinity College.
She is presently advising NGOs in West Africa on refugee and
human rights issues.

She has written *Asylum Law and Policy In Ireland – A Critical
Guide* (2000, Amnesty International), *Ireland and the European
Asylum Debate* (with Michael Lindenbauer, 2000, Practice and
Procedure); 'Judicial Review in Ireland', in *No Welcome Here –
Refugees and Asylum Seekers in Ireland and Britain* (2001,
Regency Press, Belfast); *Not in my Back Yard: Reforming the
Asylum System* (2003, Open Democracy, London).

Colin Harvey was born and educated in Derry, Northern
Ireland. He attended St Columb's College, Derry, has an LLB
(Lancaster) and a PhD (Nottingham). He is now Professor of
Constitutional and Human Rights Law, School of Law, University of
Leeds. He has previously taught at the University of Wales,
Aberystwyth; Queen's University Belfast; the University of
Michigan; and Adam Michiewicz University, Poznan, Poland. He
was refugee co-ordinator for Amnesty International Irish Section
1998-2000 and a member of the Executive of the Committee on the
Administration of Justice in Northern Ireland 1999-2000. In 1999 he
was a visiting professor at the Refugee and Asylum Law Program,
Faculty of Law, University of Michigan.

He has published extensively in academic and more popular
formats on issues of human rights law and politics. His publications
include *Seeking Asylum in the UK: Problems and Prospects* (2000,
Butterworths); *Special Issue on Social Democracy: Canadian
Journal of Law and Jurisprudence* (2004, forthcoming); *Human
Rights in the Community* (2004, Hart Publishing, forthcoming);
*Human Rights, Equality and Democratic Renewal in Northern
Ireland* (2001, Hart Publishing); *Voices, Spaces and Processes in
Constitutionalism* (with Jo Shaw and John Morison, 2000,
Blackwell Publishers).

Foreword

For most Irish people the concept of asylum is a new one. Until comparatively recently the matter rarely arose as a live public issue, largely because Ireland, for a variety of reasons, mainly geographic and economic, attracted few asylum seekers. One result of this was an absence of any public consciousness on the issue.

That is no longer the case. The number of those seeking asylum rose from thirty-nine in 1992 to almost 12,000 in 2002. This has brought with it, not a crisis, but a range of problems – cultural, political, social, administrative, economic and logistical. Moreover, these problems were visited on a people with no folk memory, no past administrative experience of dealing with asylum seekers, and for the most part, no proper awareness of the forces which turned people into refugees or drove them, in desperation, to seek asylum far from home. To make matters even more difficult, all this was happening in a country with no real experience of, or exposure to, racial and cultural diversity. The political science text books had for decades stressed the homogeneity of Irish society in the Republic, white, Catholic and nationalist and, in this, the text books reflected the reality.

As the numbers of those seeking asylum rose, it quickly became clear that the government and its agencies were taken unawares by the extent and complexity of the problem. Initially there was denial, then an element of floundering and confusion, but gradually a series of systems began to emerge. The administration did react. Resources, and significant resources at that, were made available; attempts were made to tackle the problem in a structured and rational way. The reality, however, was not always co-ordinated, not always adequate, not always enough and, in some instances, ill-advised and counterproductive.

It would be easy to seek to apportion the blame for what happened, but the fact was that for everybody involved there was a learning curve, the breaking down of old unexamined attitudes, the coming to terms with the strange and the unknown. And there were the problems created by those who sought to exploit the fears and uncertainties of ordinary, decent people, whether it was for political gain, media sales or just plain nastiness.

Asylum has now been a major fact of Irish life for over a decade. We have had time to draw breath, to examine those things that have worked and those things that have not. We have had time to learn from our own mistakes and to learn from the examples of others. We have had time to realise that many asylum seekers have a real and positive contribution to make to an increasingly multicultural society.

This book represents a particularly valuable contribution to the ongoing debate on asylum. It exposes many of the misunderstandings that have bedevilled the debate up to now, seeks to bring clarity to the language and terminology of that debate, examines the evolution and context of asylum law and puts our law and practice into the context of international standards and European development. This is a particularly important aspect of the debate, emphasising the critical importance of aspiring to the best international practice in all we do. These opening chapters set the framework for the rest of the book, which manages to be analytical, seriously practical and helpfully prescriptive. There is no shrillness, no rushing to judgement, but what we do get is a deeply principled and comprehensive approach to the many difficult issues which face all sides in this debate.

In spite of sometimes lurid media headlines, Ireland does not have an asylum crisis. It does however have – not one, but several – problems with aspects of the asylum system. None of these problems is insurmountable, but virtually all are capable of exacerbation if tackled in the wrong way, or if not tackled at all.

This book examines these problems soberly, calmly and objectively. For policy makers, politicians and media especially, it deals trenchantly with past mistakes and failed policies while pointing clearly to the choices and decisions ahead. Ursula Fraser and Colin Harvey, along with the contributors to this book, are to be congratulated on producing what will become a landmark publication on this subject.

Maurice Manning
President
Human Rights Commission

CHAPTER 1

Introduction

Colin Harvey and Ursula Fraser

D uring 1992, thirty-nine people claimed asylum in Ireland. This figure rose to 11,634 in 2002. Ireland has also witnessed significant demographic changes due to the arrival of migrant workers and returned emigrants and it is estimated that one in five non-nationals living in Ireland is an asylum seeker.[1] The increase in asylum numbers has presented Ireland with specific challenges throughout all sectors of society.

In the early nineties, many Irish people were unfamiliar with the concept of asylum. Although some had an idea of what it meant to be a refugee, the image often conjured up was one of desperate and hungry mass movements of people. Although that image is not totally unjustified, as television scenes in Bosnia and Kosovo have shown, it is not the complete picture. Not all asylum seekers are forced to flee in situations of mass panic leaving everything behind. Many plan their escape carefully and spend time and money trying to plan for their future in a new country. In Iraq, for example, when Saddam Hussein was in power, citizens had to be extremely careful when trying to leave. Most countries, however, have more relaxed approaches to their departing citizens and so planning does not have to be so precise.

The Irish government has a history of affording protection in crisis situations. People fleeing the Hungarian uprising were invited to Ireland in 1956, Chileans came in 1973 and 1974, Bosnians in the early 1990s and Kosovars in 1999. The arrival of these groups caused little controversy because of the controlled and orchestrated manner with which their arrival was handled. In the mid 1990s, however, asylum seekers started to arrive in Ireland spontaneously – and in growing numbers. This caught many people off guard. Initially, local voluntary groups sprang up to assist asylum seekers to settle into towns and communities and their efforts were augmented by the growth of a structured

---

[1]   Address by the Minister for Justice, Equality and Law Reform, Michael McDowell TD, at a conference, Developing Anti-racism Awareness at a Local Level, on 9 October 2002 (www.justice.ie).

non-governmental sector to assist asylum seekers who were unfamiliar with accommodation, education and health care facilities. The Irish governmental response to spontaneous asylum seekers was a slower one. Due to lack of staff to deal with asylum issues in the Department of Justice, Equality and Law Reform, many asylum seekers were stalled in a legal limbo waiting for years for a decision on their application.[2] Other departments had similar staffing difficulties. The Refugee Act 1996 finally became operational in November 2000 and a comprehensive asylum procedure was established which improved the situation. The offices of the Refugee Applications Commissioner and the Refugee Appeals Tribunal were set up at this time, two statutorily independent bodies vested with the responsibility of adjudicating on all asylum applications in the state. Their establishment has greatly increased efficiency in the asylum procedure.

The asylum debate in Ireland, like elsewhere, has been fraught with misunderstandings. The misuse of terminology is especially pervasive. In the Irish context, and in all countries with formal asylum procedures, an 'asylum seeker' is a person who flees his or her country to seek protection due to persecution, or fear thereof, arising from religion, political views, membership of a social group, nationality or race. An asylum seeker, if s/he can prove to the satisfaction of the asylum authorities that his or her reasons for flight are among these categories, may be granted 'refugee status'. Refugee status carries with it economic and social rights akin to those of Irish citizens. Asylum seekers, however, are entitled to lesser rights (for example, they do not have the right to work).

This book examines the evolution and content of asylum law and policy in Ireland. The aim is to provide a guide to selected aspects of law and practice and to place this in the context of international standards and European developments. Chapter 2 outlines aspects of refugee law and human rights at the international level. Colin Harvey emphasises the continued relevance of international law and principles. While sophisticated national asylum laws and other domestic legal principles exist, he suggests that international law retains its significance in assessing State practice.

Chapter 3 describes in detail the laws and policies of the European Union on asylum. Cathryn Costello describes the asylum and immigration legislative programme of the European Union as the EC's most ambitious and extensive. She focuses on deflection of asylum seekers, temporary protection and burden sharing, a uniform asylum system, and removal policies. As well as offering a formal account of the legal

---

[2]   In 1996, there were four people in the asylum division of the Department of Justice, Equality and Law Reform. As of June 2003, approximately 640 staff are involved in asylum and immigration work at the Department.

and institutional framework of the EU, this chapter demonstrates the effect of more subtle forces of official interaction that enable viewpoints and practices to be shared between member states. The European Convention on Human Rights 1950 (ECHR) is a landmark piece of human rights legislation drafted after the atrocities of World War II. Chapter 4 looks at how the judgments handed down by the European Court of Human Rights have impacted on the rights of asylum seekers. This has proved a rich source of case law for refugee lawyers and, as Suzanne Egan shows, will have an impact in Ireland. Laws and policies in other jurisdictions on direct provision, dispersal, accelerated procedures and detention have all been scrutinised by the European Court of Human Rights with mixed results for asylum seekers.

Chapter 5 describes the procedure for claiming asylum in Ireland. The Refugee Act 1996 is the basic legal framework for the asylum process in Ireland. Due to changes in domestic asylum policy and legislative developments at the EU level, the Refugee Act has undergone significant amendment. Ursula Fraser charts the origins of and changes to the asylum procedure in Ireland and pays particular attention to the Immigration Act 2003, which represents the most significant overhaul of Irish asylum procedures to date.

Chapter 6 outlines the involvement of the office of the UN High Commissioner for Refugees (UNHCR) in the Irish asylum process. Written by Pia Prütz Phiri, the chapter explains Ireland's unique situation vis-à-vis the rest of Europe with regard to refugee protection. UNHCR has been actively involved in Irish asylum affairs since the mid-1980s and its activities include training, legal advice, monitoring the asylum process, capacity-building of non-governmental organisations, refugee integration and resettlement. The detail of Ireland's financial, and other, contributions to UNHCR for its global refugee work are also included.

It is sometimes claimed that asylum seekers travel to Ireland because it is a 'soft touch', in terms of welfare benefits and possibilities for integration into Irish society. Chapter 7 casts a critical eye on the social, economic and legal entitlements of asylum seekers. In particular, Peter O'Mahony analyses the place of dispersal and direct provisions in the history of Ireland's asylum policy. The government introduced the direct provision and dispersal policies in response to the shortage of accommodation in the greater Dublin area, to avoid the 'ghettoisation' of asylum seekers and to fall into step with European Union member states that have introduced similar policies. All accommodation costs for asylum seekers are paid for directly by the state in accommodation centres around Ireland, plus miscellaneous exceptional payments where necessary. In this chapter, it is argued that in spite of these benefits, some gaps in state-support services remain which have led to the social exclusion of asylum seekers and to the continued need for voluntary agencies to compensate. This chapter also questions the legal basis for the direct provision policy and its compatibility with Ireland's equality laws.

Taking a more microscopic look at the asylum process, Chapter 8 examines the use of accelerated procedures within the normal asylum process. The Irish asylum procedure, like its European counterparts, allows for the 'fast tracking' of certain asylum claims in order to deal with less meritorious asylum claims in a speedy fashion. The use of accelerated procedures in Ireland has diminished in recent years. However, due to the provisions of the Immigration Act 2003, it appears that such practices will be re-ignited, in particular for asylum applications from countries deemed safe. Siobhan Mullally cautions against the use of accelerated procedures where they circumvent legal safeguards. She points out the risk that over-emphasis on credibility issues can overlook the substantive merits of asylum claims.

Chapter 9 examines how the Irish courts have played a role in shaping the asylum process. Judicial review to the High Court and, exceptionally, the Supreme Court is the final avenue of appeal open to asylum seekers to challenge various aspects of the administrative process. Siobhan Stack and Bill Shipsey examine the procedural obstructions that face asylum seekers and the State during the judicial review process. The chapter also looks at the tests that the High Court applies in asylum-related judicial review cases (for example, whether the authorities are under a duty to give reasons for their assessments) and recent cases are drawn upon for illustration.

Chapter 10 charts the media response to asylum seekers in Ireland. Although the media displayed some sympathy for the plight of asylum seekers in the early 1990s, there ensued a radical shift in reporting, with misinformation, myth-building and exaggeration fuelling the confusion which already abounded. Hatred on radio phone-in talk shows and derogatory descriptions of asylum seekers as 'scroungers' in the press became commonplace. The media has been generally unsympathetic to asylum seekers and refugees when referring to them as a group, but reporting has been kinder when focused on individuals, particularly where racist abuse is involved. As Harry McGee notes, certain sections of the Irish media have tended to reflect government policy and public attitudes in a largely unquestioning manner with very little reporting on the circumstances that compel asylum seekers to leave their countries. The overall impression is that asylum has not been given full and fair consideration in the media. Although some editorial decisions continue to be responsible, a preference for sensationalist approaches tends to subsist.

'Abuse' of the asylum process is a much discussed topic. It is regularly asserted that most asylum seekers are not in need of protection and that they use the asylum process simply to access Ireland to seek a better life. There is no doubt that this does occur. This is partly explained by the fact that few cases are successful: in 2002, refugee status was granted in 14 per cent of cases where recommendations were made. Chapter 11 explains why this figure is so low by noting the limitations of the refugee definition. Ursula Fraser demonstrates the need for a complementary protection scheme to compensate for its strict requirements. Ireland has a very limited form of complementary protection and if such a scheme was formally established, it would lead to a rise in the percentage of people granted protection. The percentage is unlikely to rise significantly, however, based on the experience of other countries, although prospects are a matter of speculation. Another form of protection, namely temporary protection, is also described in this chapter. This describes the emergency protection that can be provided when there is a sudden mass influx of asylum seekers to the European Union. Considerable progress has been made at the European Union level to set up a temporary protection legal structure which could be triggered in such a situation. Discussions on this form of protection heated up in the lead up to military action in Iraq but because the projected refugee flow did not transpire, the European Union did not need to invoke such a scheme.

Finally, in chapter 12, Donncha O'Connell and Ciara Smyth examine the constitutional rights for citizens whose family members are not Irish. In particular, they evaluate the Supreme Court judgment of January 2003 where it was held that the state has a right to deport the non-national parents of children born in Ireland. As a result, the legal status of thousands of families is now in question. O'Connell posits that the matter may ultimately be settled by a referendum but, in the meantime, a political consensus will need to be carefully crafted in order to avoid an opportunistic reduction of the complex issues involved to one of race.

Ireland has witnessed a significant rise in the numbers of people seeking asylum. Successive Irish governments have introduced laws and policies to deal with a variety of challenges arising from their arrival. The aim of this edited collection is to provide the reader with greater insight into the challenges faced by government, Irish citizens, non-governmental organisations and asylum seekers over the last decade and those that remain to be solved in future decades.

CHAPTER 2

Refugees, Asylum Seekers and International Human Rights Protection

Colin Harvey

Introduction

The movement of refugees is by its nature an international issue. Human displacement does not respect borders. If protection is not available in her state of origin, and she has the necessary resources, then flight across the border is often the only option left to the displaced person. This international phenomenon has attracted an international legal and political response. Asylum is now a major policy issue at the national, regional and international levels. The difficulty is that it is frequently classified alongside security threats and transnational criminality. The image is created of asylum as a risk to legal and political order. This negative construction of asylum contrasts markedly with the humanitarian origins of the institution.

International law offers specific protection to the refugee and creates standards of general applicability which include the plight of refugees and asylum seekers. This body of law is significant for several reasons. It confirms that refugees do not depend entirely on national legal systems for a source of legal guarantees. International law offers standards which national legal systems can be measured against. The existence of international legal standards does not, of course, mean that they can be applied directly in national law. This depends on how the national legal system receives international standards. Care must also be taken to discover whether the state has signed and/or ratified the relevant international convention. Nevertheless, international law is an indispensable framework within which to locate the treatment of refugees and asylum seekers.

The aim in this chapter is to note the relevance of international law and indicate the standards which are useful for refugees and asylum seekers. The focus is on international treaty law, and no attempt is made here to examine the disputes surrounding the state of customary international law in this area. Detailed developments in Irish law and practice are examined in other chapters. The intention is to provide a brief overview of the international legal standards only and to suggest why they are relevant to refugee protection. First, I examine the legal protection of refugees in international law. Secondly, I highlight key aspects of international human rights law. Finally, I refer to the significance of regional human rights protection.

The focus on international law in this chapter should not be interpreted as neglect of the fundamental significance of national legal systems. Refugees and asylum seekers still rely ultimately on the reception they receive at the national level. The purpose of international legal standards, in my view, is to assist in the improvement of national practices by setting down minimum standards to be complied with.

Refugees and international law

Before considering refugee law I will make two points about international law. First, it is essential to know whether the state has signed the relevant international convention. This may seem an obvious point. However, a state is not bound in international law by a treaty it has not signed. The position with respect to the applicability of rules in customary international law is different.

Secondly, the status of international law in the national legal system under consideration is also important. Is the state monist or dualist? Ireland is a dualist state, which means that an international convention must be given effect in national law before it can be used by an individual. This rather simplistic explanation will suffice for the purpose of this chapter, but things are not quite as straightforward in practice. International instruments can have an influence in national legal systems which goes beyond their formal status in national law.

The 1951 Convention relating to the Status of Refugees[1] (as amended by the 1967 Protocol relating to the Status of Refugees)[2] remains the primary international instrument governing the protection of refugees. The relevance of the 1951 Convention has increasingly been questioned in recent years. However, it retains its significance. This is primarily because the 1951 Convention contains a definition of refugee status and specific guarantees which result from recognition. The status-granting dimensions of refugee law are of particular importance because of the security this may bring to the experience of human displacement.

States have tended to insist on gaining a precise answer to the question: Who is a refugee? The reason is connected to established concerns about state sovereignty. States demand the power to set out clearly who will be entitled to enter their territory and who will be

---

[1]   189 UNTS 150, entry into force 22 April 1954.
[2]   606 UNTS 267, entry into force 4 October 1967.

permitted to become a citizen. Forced displacement raises concerns for states because of its potentially unpredictable nature. States have therefore sought clarity in determining who they will be prepared to offer protection to. Refugee law arose as a mechanism to address these state concerns while at the same time recognising the humanitarian needs of displaced persons.[3] Refugee law was created as a mechanism for the provision of 'international protection'; it does not, for example, concentrate on addressing the root causes of refugee movements. The 1951 Convention, like all such international instruments, is a compromise. The reasons (state interest and humanitarianism) which inspired states to draft it do not appear to have eroded. From the perspective of the individual, the root causes of forced displacement still exist. Therefore, such international legal protection remains important. In addition, there is nothing to prevent a state taking a more generous approach to refugee protection and going beyond the protection obligations established in existing international standards.

Law, by its very nature, reduces complexity. Refugee law makes the complex phenomenon of forced displacement manageable for states. It does so in a way which both includes and excludes. This fact of exclusion may be lamented, but it is an inherent aspect of all attempts at legal definition (some people will qualify, others will not). The reason is again that states demand precision and that the law reflect a commitment to selective protection of the forcibly displaced. States do not accept responsibility for providing protection to all those who seek it. As a result, the legal definition of refugee should not be confused with the popular usage of the term.

The 1951 Convention defines a refugee as someone who

> owing to a well-founded fear of being persecuted for reasons of race, religion, nationality, membership of a particular social group or political opinion, is outside the country of his nationality and is unable or, owing to such fear, is unwilling to avail himself of the protection of that country.[4]

The definition has to be interpreted as a whole but it has distinct elements. There are thousands of legal cases which tackle the meaning of this definition. Guidance is available from the UNHCR and at the regional level the EU is involved in an attempt to develop a common approach. The aim here is not to survey this material. I want instead to highlight the central elements of the definition as set out in the 1951 Convention.

First, the individual must be outside her state of origin. The 1951 Convention does not protect internally displaced persons. This is not because the internally displaced are any less deserving. The position

---

3   Hathaway, James C. (1991), *The Law of Refugee Status*, Butterworths: Toronto.
4   Article 1 A(2).

reflects a core aspect of international law's respect for the sovereignty of states. However unrealistic in practice, in theory the internally displaced remain within the jurisdiction, and therefore under the protection, of their state of origin. Modern developments relating to humanitarian intervention have made the position of the internally displaced less stark. As a group, they have received increased international attention. The fact that they have not crossed the border does make a material difference, however, to the international legal standards which may be applied.

Secondly, the state of origin must be unable or unwilling to provide protection. Refugee law is a surrogate form of 'international protection'. If the state of origin is willing and able to provide protection then there is no need for the individual to seek refuge elsewhere. There may be, for example, another area within the state where protection can be offered on a humane basis. Refugee law offers formal acceptance of the reality that the citizen-state bond can break down to such an extent that protection is required elsewhere.

Thirdly, the individual must have a 'well-founded fear of persecution'. There are three aspects to this. She must have a fear, which is a subjective state of mind. This fear must then be shown to be well founded. Thus the subjective aspect meets the objective conditions which give rise to the fear. While both elements are taken seriously in the guidance provided by the UNHCR it is hard to escape the conclusion that the objective test will always trump the subjective state of mind of the applicant. It is difficult to understand how a state could organise an effective refugee status determination system if it did not.

The 'well-founded fear' must relate to treatment that amounts to persecution. There is no agreed definition of persecution. However, one useful suggestion is that it should be defined 'as the sustained or systemic violation of basic human rights demonstrative of a failure of state protection'.[5] This link to human rights law is important because it connects refugee protection to the denial of core human rights and thus forges a close connection between these two bodies of law. International law provides much assistance in determining what are 'core human rights'.

Fourthly, the 'well-founded fear of persecution' must be for a 'Convention reason'. Some states, such as Ireland, have opted to be more generous by expanding on the grounds through legislation. The 'Convention reasons' are, however, exhaustive, they are not intended to be merely illustrative of possible reasons for persecution. The debates which continue over the grounds will be familiar to any lawyer. Should the grounds be interpreted purposively in order to keep them in touch with progressive developments in human rights

---

[5] Hathaway above n. 3, p. 105.

law? In other words, should the focus be on modern trends in human rights rather than the minds of the drafters of the 1951 Convention? How does this fit with the aim of creating a nexus between the fear of persecution and civil and political status? Can the grounds be developed expansively and do clear limits exist to this progressive interpretation? These matters have been extensively analysed in case law from a range of jurisdictions and in academic commentary. There is evidence to suggest a willingness on the part of some states (or perhaps more accurately the judiciary within the states) to contemplate a more purposive approach which keeps refugee law in touch with the development of human rights law.

Even if an individual brings her application within the definition set out above she still may not be entitled to refugee status in international law. The 1951 Convention permits the exclusion of a person from refugee status. The exclusion clauses are contained in Article 1F of the 1951 Convention.

> The provisions of this Convention shall not apply to any person with respect to whom there are serious reasons for considering that:
> (a) he has committed a crime against peace, a war crime, or a crime against humanity, as defined in the international instruments drawn up to make provision in respect of such crimes;
> (b) he has committed a serious non-political crime outside the country of refuge prior to his admission to that country as a refugee;
> (c) he has been guilty of acts contrary to the purposes and principles of the United Nations.

With more intense interest in tackling transnational criminality and international terrorism, the exclusion clauses are now part of a wider debate.[6] Exclusion from refugee status is distinct from the question of whether a person may be lawfully returned to his state of origin. The result is that, in international law, the situation may arise where a person is excluded from refugee status but still cannot be returned to her state of origin for human rights law reasons.

The 1951 Convention contains a range of guarantees. The Article 33 prohibition on *refoulement* is the one that is widely known and discussed. It provides:

> 1) No Contracting State shall expel or return (*refouler*) a refugee in any manner whatsoever to the frontiers of territories where his life or freedom would be threatened on account of his race, religion, nationality, membership of a particular social group or political opinion.
> 2) The benefit of the present provision may not, however, be claimed by a refugee whom there are reasonable grounds for regarding as a

[6]   Hathaway, James C. and Harvey, Colin J. (2001), 'Framing Refugee Protection in the New World Disorder', 34 *Cornell International Law Journal* 257-320.

danger to the security of the country in which he is, or who, having been convicted by a final judgment of a particularly serious crime, constitutes a danger to the community of that country.

Article 33 obliges state parties not to return a refugee *in any manner whatsoever* to the conditions described in the provision. The explicit attempt to cover any means used to return an individual suggests that the provision is intended to protect refugees from the multiple methods states adopt. The provision is not absolute. It leaves open the notion of permissible *refoulement* in national security cases or when serious criminality is in issue. The reference to 'reasonable grounds for regarding' does not suggest an exacting standard and the provision reflects the security fears that existed at the time the Convention was drafted.

In addition to the principle of *non-refoulement,* the Convention accords entitlements on: non-discrimination (Article 3); religion (Article 4); personal status (Article 12); access to courts (Article 16); employment (Article 17); housing (Article 21); public education (Article 22); social security (Article 24); free movement (Article 27); travel documents (Article 28); and expulsion (Article 32). Article 31 of the Convention recognises the fact that refugees may enter a state without the required documentation and thus be in breach of the immigration laws of the state. If the refugee presents herself without delay to the authorities, and provides a good cause for illegal entry, then state parties are obliged not to impose penalties. The purpose of Article 31 is to acknowledge that refugees often need to flee by irregular means. If they do so, they should not be punished for it.

Unlike the international human rights instruments that came later, the 1951 Convention does not have a committee mandated to monitor compliance. The UNHCR is the organisation tasked with providing a supervisory role. It does not, however, function as an individual complaints mechanism. Its work has steadily expanded in recent decades and it is now not only involved with refugees but with internally displaced persons.

The 1951 Convention (Article 35) obliges state parties to co-operate with the UNHCR:

1. The Contracting States undertake to co-operate with the Office of the United Nations High Commissioner for Refugees, or any other agency of the United Nations which may succeed it, in the exercise of its functions, and shall in particular facilitate its duty of supervising the application of the provisions of this Convention.

2. In order to enable the Office of the High Commissioner or any other agency of the United Nations which may succeed it, to make reports to the competent organs of the United Nations, the Contracting States undertake to provide them in the appropriate form with information

and statistical data requested concerning:
(a) the condition of refugees,
(b) the implementation of this Convention, and
(c) laws, regulations and decrees which are, or may hereafter be, in
force in relation to refugees.

The UNHCR has undertaken a variety of roles. Its work is governed by
the Statute of the Office of the UNHCR 1950. Article 1 provides:

1. The United Nations High Commissioner for Refugees, acting under
the authority of the General Assembly, shall assume the function of
providing international protection, under the auspices of the United
Nations, to refugees who fall within the scope of the present Statute
and of seeking permanent solutions for the problem of refugees by
assisting Governments and, subject to the approval of the Governments
concerned, private organizations to facilitate the voluntary repatriation
of such refugees, or their assimilation within new national communities.
In the exercise of his functions, more particularly when difficulties arise,
and for instance with regard to any controversy concerning the international status of these persons, the High Commissioner shall request
the opinion of the advisory committee on refugees if it is created.

2. The work of the High Commissioner shall be of an entirely non-
political character; it shall be humanitarian and social and shall relate,
as a rule, to groups and categories of refugees.

The expansion of the role of the UNHCR has raised both internal and
external debates about its future. These debates are not of direct
concern to this chapter. The Conclusions of its Executive Committee
provide significant guidance on ongoing issues in refugee protection.
Their value rests not only in the substance of the Conclusions, but
because the Committee is composed of states. Ireland is a member of
the Executive Committee along with sixty other states. The UNHCR has
provided a wealth of guidance on the interpretation and application of
refugee law. It remains an authoritative voice in relation to ongoing
debates on refugee protection.

International human rights law

The development of the international law of human rights is one of the
more remarkable legal legacies of the twentieth century. The transformation of human rights into international law, and the widespread
acceptance of these legal standards, has impacted on the development
of the international community. As Antonio Cassese states:

Today the human rights doctrine forces States to give account of how they
treat their nationals, administer justice, run prisons, and so on. Potentially,

therefore, it can subvert their domestic order and, consequently, the traditional configuration of the international community as well.[7]

Cassese might also have added reference to the implication for the treatment of refugees. The international law of human rights, with its focus on the entitlement of 'the person' to rights, and not just citizens, has direct consequences for the protection of refugees. This is the case even when direct reference is not made to this group. This result is due primarily to the work of the UN human rights treaty monitoring bodies in interpreting and applying general norms of human rights law.

An examination of the rules of refugee law must include some reference to international human rights law. As noted above, international human rights law continues to have an impact on the progressive development of refugee law through the ongoing interpretation of the definition. It also provides protections which supplement refugee law in increasingly valuable ways.

States have never been prepared to accept the idea of an individual right to be granted asylum. The Universal Declaration of Human Rights 1948[8] provides for a right to seek asylum from persecution.[9] The word 'receive' was removed from an earlier draft of the Universal Declaration and, one might say: never to return again. The United Nations Declaration on Territorial Asylum 1967[10] marked a shift towards placing the right firmly in the hands of the state. It provides (Article 1):

1. Asylum granted by a State, in the exercise of its sovereignty, to persons entitled to invoke article 14 of the Universal Declaration of Human Rights, including persons struggling against colonialism, shall be respected by all other States.

2. The right to seek and to enjoy asylum may not be invoked by any person with respect to whom there are serious reasons for considering that he has committed a crime against peace, a war crime or a crime against humanity, as defined in the international instruments drawn up to make provision in respect of such crimes.

3. It shall rest with the State granting asylum to evaluate the grounds for the grant of asylum.

The weight of effort within the human rights community has been on the prevention of return (or more simply, ensuring that removal is prohibited in prescribed circumstances) rather than guaranteeing a right to enter. The right to seek and enjoy asylum should not, however, be downplayed; in an age of containment policies and prevention discourse it remains highly relevant.

---

[7]   Cassese, Antonio (2001), *International Law*, Oxford University Press: Oxford, p. 349.
[8]   UNGA Resolution 217 A(III).
[9]   Article 14(1).
[10] UNGA Resolution 2312 (XXII).

The UN was not able to advance beyond this Declaration and no multilateral Convention has been adopted to secure a right to asylum. For reasons which I hope to have made clear above, states remain unwilling to move beyond the right of the individual to seek asylum. The debate has arisen again in the context of the development of a 'Common European Asylum System' in the EU. For example, the EU Charter of Fundamental Rights 2000 provides:

> The right to asylum shall be guaranteed with due respect for the rules of the Geneva Convention of 28 July 1951 and the Protocol of 31 January 1967 relating to the status of refugees and in accordance with the Treaty establishing the European Community.[11]

The reference to a right to asylum appears as an advance, but this is securely tied to the 1951 Convention and the established rules of EC law. The position remains that states are unwilling to agree to a 'right' of the individual to be granted asylum. However, with developments in human rights law, particularly the prohibition on removal, this absence of a specific legal right to be granted asylum is perhaps less troubling.

International human rights law supplements international refugee law in significant ways. In some instances human rights law offers more protection to the refugee and asylum seeker. It also remedies some of refugee law's more obvious gaps. Given the absence of an international supervisory mechanism for refugee law international human rights mechanisms are effectively the only way that the treatment of refugees and asylum seekers can be challenged at an international level.[12] It is commonplace now to refer to relevant international human rights standards in the refugee and asylum area.

Article 3 of the United Nations Convention Against Torture and other Cruel, Inhuman or Degrading Treatment or Punishment 1984[13] provides:

1. No State Party shall expel, return (*refouler*) or extradite a person to another State where there are substantial grounds for believing that he would be in danger of being subjected to torture.
2. For the purpose of determining whether there are such grounds, the competent authorities shall take into account all relevant considerations including, where applicable, the existence in the State concerned of a consistent pattern of gross, flagrant or mass violations of human rights.

---

[11] Article 18.
[12] For an examination of UN human rights treaty monitoring see Alston, P. and Crawford, J. (eds.) (2000), *The Future of UN Human Rights Treaty Monitoring*, Cambridge: Cambridge University Press.
[13] UNGA Resolution 39/46, 10 December 1984, entry into force 26 June 1987.

This provision has been interpreted by the UN Committee Against Torture in a number of important communications.[14] The Committee has also issued a General Comment on the Implementation of Article 3 in the Context of Article 22 of the Convention Against Torture.[15]

The United Nations Convention on the Rights of the Child 1989,[16] Article 2, provides:

1. State Parties shall respect and ensure the rights set forth in the present Convention to each child within their jurisdiction without discrimination of any kind, irrespective of the child's or his or her parent's or legal guardian's race, colour, sex, language, religion, political or other opinion, national, ethnic or social origin, property, disability, birth or other status.

In relation to refugee children, the Convention provides in Article 22:

1. State Parties shall take appropriate measures to ensure that a child who is seeking refugee status or who is considered a refugee in accordance with applicable international or domestic law and procedures shall, whether unaccompanied or accompanied by his or her parents or by any other person, receive appropriate protection and humanitarian assistance in the enjoyment of applicable rights set forth in the present Convention and in other international human rights or humanitarian instruments to which the said States are Parties.

The UN Committee on the Rights of the Child has offered important guidance on the meaning of these provisions.

The International Covenant on Civil and Political Rights 1966[17] does not directly refer to refugees. Its provisions are, however, relevant. Articles 7 and 9, in particular, are applicable to the plight of the asylum seeker who is threatened with removal and/or detention. The UN Human Rights Committee has also clarified in its General Comments the significance of the Covenant for 'aliens' generally.[18]

These are not the only instruments of importance in international law. The International Convention on the Elimination of All Forms of Racial Discrimination 1966[19] is also of direct relevance and its monitoring body (the Committee on the Elimination of Racial Discrimination) again plays a role in developing the existing standards.

---

[14] *H.I.A. v. Sweden* Comm. No. 216/2002; *M.V. v. Netherlands* Comm. No. 201/2002; *U.S. v. Finland* Comm. No. 197/2002; *V.N.I.M. v. Canada* Comm. No. 119/1998; *Tala v. Sweden* Comm. No. 43/1996; *Kisoki v. Sweden* Comm. No. 41/1996; *X v. The Netherlands* Comm. No. 31/1995; *Alan v. Switzerland* Comm. No. 21/1995.

[15] UN Committee Against Torture, General Comment 1, 21 November 1997.

[16] UNGA Resolution 44/25, 20 November 1989, entry into force 20 September 1990.

[17] UNGA Resolution 2200A (XXI), 16 December 1966, entry into force 23 March 1976.

[18] See General Comment 15 (twenty-seventh session 1986); General Comment 20 (forty-fourth session 1992).

[19] UNGA Resolution 2106 (XX), 21 December 1965, entry into force 4 January 1969.

International law, human rights and regional refugee protection

Regional developments are increasingly significant in refugee protection. The EU is often cited due to the attempts to agree a common approach. The advancement of refugee law through regional innovation is important, but it must also comply with the international standards mentioned above. The OAU Convention on the Specific Aspects of Refugee Problems in Africa 1969[20] is a useful example of a more expansive regional approach to the refugee definition. Article I provides:

> (2) The term 'refugee' shall also apply to every person who, owing to external aggression, occupation, foreign domination or events seriously disturbing public order in either part or the whole of his country of origin or nationality, is compelled to leave his place of habitual residence in order to seek refuge in another place outside his country of origin or nationality.

The reference to events seriously disturbing public order is echoed to some extent in the Cartagena Declaration on Refugees 1984.[21]

> ... in addition to containing the elements of the 1951 Convention and 1967 Protocol, includes among refugees persons who have fled their country because their lives, safety or freedom have been threatened by generalized violence, foreign aggression, internal conflicts, massive violation of human rights or other circumstances which have seriously disturbed public order.

This definition acknowledges the direct role of internal conflict in the generation of mass movements of people. It reflects a definition which captures well some key factors in the current processes of human displacement.

Regional human rights mechanisms also offer protection to refugees and asylum seekers. The European Convention on Human Rights 1950 and its Protocols are the best example. There is no reference to refugees or asylum in the European Convention. Despite this the European Court of Human Rights has interpreted Convention rights to make them directly applicable to the plight of the asylum seeker.[22] The Inter-American and African regional mechanisms are also significant in the development of effective human rights practice at the national level.[23]

---

[20] Goodwin-Gill, G. (1996), *The Refugee in International Law*, 2nd edn, Oxford: Oxford University Press, pp. 429-434.
[21] Goodwin-Gill above n. 20, pp. 444-448.
[22] See the chapter in this volume by Suzanne Egan.
[23] Cassese above n. 7 pp. 366-368.

Conclusion

International law provides a set of minimum standards to be met by states. Even in refugee law, with its focus on the award of a status, much is left to the state to decide. The determination of refugee status is primarily a matter for national legal systems. States may opt for a more generous national standard and are not bound in international law to any uniform approach which means they must only comply in a minimal way. States may go further than the minimum standards which international law provides. It is essential that due regard is paid to the established rules of international human rights law and their progressive development. The purpose of this is to secure more effective national level protection. This is not only relevant to asylum seekers. Often neglected is the fact that the full implementation of international human rights law would reduce considerably the root causes of forced displacement.

CHAPTER 3

EU Asylum Law and Policy

Cathryn Costello

Introduction

This chapter aims to evaluate European Union asylum policy and policymaking processes (Section I). In so doing, the chapter examines the evolving legal and institutional[1] framework, seeking in particular to identify the relationship between the EU and the member states in the process of policy elaboration. While this is largely a formal legal account, emphasis is also placed on more subtle forces, whereby the processes of official interaction at European level result in the development of shared values, viewpoints and practices. Through this emphasis the section seeks to dispel the misperception that 'more Europe' means less national power, and instead illustrates the enhancement of national executive power through European mechanisms, as national executives escape national parliamentary and judicial accountability. In light of this discussion, Ireland's optional participation in European asylum policy will be considered.

The chapter also provides an overview of legislative achievements in this area since the entry into force of the Treaty of Amsterdam on 1 May 1999 (Section II).[2] The legislative programme in this area is currently the EC's most ambitious and extensive. Although progress

---

[1] 'Institutions' throughout is defined not in its strict legal sense but, more broadly, as 'rules, norms, conventions and discursive frameworks that shape human interaction'.

[2] The European Union (EU) is the over-arching structure which formally came into being in 1992 as a result of the Maastricht Treaty (or Treaty on European Union (TEU)). The EU is based on a three-'Pillar' structure: the first is the European Communities 'Pillar', the second is the Common Foreign and Security 'Pillar' and the third is the Justice and Home Affairs 'Pillar'. To break it down further, the first Pillar comprises the three European Communities, namely the European Community (EC), the European Coal and Steel Community (ECSC) and the European Atomic Energy Community (Euratom). The three European Communities have separate founding treaties. The Treaty of Amsterdam, which came into force in May 1999, is not a founding treaty as such but is rather directed at amending the TEU and the founding treaties establishing the European Communities. In repect of the latter, most changes were made to the Treaty establishing the European Community (EC Treaty) by the Treaty of Amsterdam.

has been limited and patchy, it is nonetheless possible to detect the contours of an emerging EC asylum and immigration policy. The section focuses on measures to deflect asylum seekers, temporary protection and burden sharing, an attempt to create a uniform asylum system and removal policies.

Finally the place of asylum law in the Future of Europe debate will be considered (Section III). The impact of the draft Constitutional Treaty for the European Union and the EU Charter of Fundamental Rights on asylum law and policy will be examined.

SECTION I: European Union Asylum Policymaking

1 The legacy of intergovernmentalism

The 1957 Treaty of Rome instigated a process aimed towards the creation of an advanced form of economic integration, a common market in which not only products (goods and services) but also the factors of production (labour and capital) would be liberalised. The original economic rationales underlying the common and internal market could have, and arguably should have, embraced migration of at least those so called 'third country nationals' within the territory of the member states. As factors of production, their labour movements should also have been liberalised. However, early on it became clear that such an interpretation was not acceptable to most member states, and the issue of the movement of third country nationals was viewed as originally escaping Community context.[3]

---

[3] The exception related to the free movement of services, where the original Treaty provided for the extension of the freedom to non-nationals (Article 49(2) EC). However, this is not to suggest that existing EC rules do not affect the position of third country nationals. In fact there is a disparate set of rights which third country nationals derive from Community law. As family members of mobile economic actors of Community nationality, third country nationals have long come within the scope of Community law. In addition, the posted workers directive benefits nationals of third countries. Of increasing importance, various association agreements grant certain mobility rights to nationals of parties to those agreements. For a discussion of these rights see Staples H., *The Legal Status of Third Country Nationals in the EU* (Kluwer Law International, 1999); Hedemann-Robinson M., 'An Overview of Recent Legal Developments at Community Level in relation to Third Country Nationals resident within the European Union, with particular relevance to the caselaw of the European Court of Justice' (2001), *CMLRev* 325. Thus for example the EC/Turkey Agreement grants rights to work to Turkish nationals in the EU and the various Agreements with Central and Eastern European states grant rights of establishment. In many instances, these rights are directly effective. See, for examples, Case C-63/99 *R v. Secretary of State for the Home Department, ex parte Gloszczuk* [2001], ECR I-6369; Case C-257/99 *R v. Secretary of State for the Home Department, ex parte Bartoki and Malik* [2001] ECR I-6557; Case C-235/99 *R v. Secretary of State for the Home Department, ex parte Kondova* [2001] ECR I-6427 – the European Court of Justice (ECJ) held that the establishment provisions of the Association Agreements with Poland, the Czech Republic and Bulgaria were directly effective. Other bilateral

At the time of the Single European Act, much debate surrounded the question of whether the internal market provision (Article 14 EC) would entail the abolition of internal border controls for third country nationals.[4] Several member states strongly objected to any such interpretation, in particular the UK.[5] Due to these conflicts, those member states in favour of the abolition of border controls (being Belgium, the Netherlands, Luxembourg, France and Germany) set up the Schengen system in 1985, which dissipated the pressure to abolish internal border controls under Article 14 EC. The Schengen system operated outside the constitutional constraints of the E(E)C. It was however envisaged that the Schengen system would operate as a 'laboratory' or 'engine' to push border politics back onto the Community agenda.[6] The Schengen *acquis* evolved into a complex legal and institution apparatus, comprising the Schengen Agreement,[7] the Schengen Implementing Convention,[8] various Accession Protocols[9] and many decisions and declarations adopted by the Schengen Executive Committee, as well as acts of bodies on which the Executive Committee conferred implementing powers.[10]

---

[3] *contd.* agreements, for instance those with Morocco and Tunisia, contain a reference to liberalisation of the provision of services in the context of the General Agreement on Trade in Services (GATS). The focus of this paper is not on these established areas, important as they are in practice, but on the competence and scope to develop a coherent policy in the area of immigration and asylum.

[4] As it happens the ECJ has now confirmed this restrictive interpretation of Article 14 EC and that the provisions on non-discrimination on grounds of nationality do not embrace third country nationals. Case C-378/97 *Wijsenbeek* [1999] ECR I-6207; Case C-230/97 *Awoyemi* [1998] I-6781.

[5] See the Declaration attached to the Single European Act at the insistence of the UK to the effect that the abolition of border controls did not affect national sovereignty regarding the movement of third country nationals.

[6] Wiener, Antje, 'The Embedded *Acquis Communautaire*. Transmission Belt and Prism of New Governance', (1998), *European Law Journal* 294.

[7] Of 14 June 1985. This agreement aimed to create a framework to abolish border controls on goods and persons between participating states.

[8] The Schengen Implementing Convention was signed in 1990, but did not enter into force until 26 March 1995. It sets out detailed provisions on the abolition of border controls, the application of common external border controls, police co-operation and measures on responsibility for processing asylum claims (now dealt with under the Dublin Convention/Regulation).

[9] The original Schengen Agreement 1985 was signed by Belgium, France, Germany, Luxembourg and the Netherlands. Over the next seven years, all other EU member states joined, with the exception of the UK and Ireland.

[10] For a discussion of the contents of the *acquis* see the House of Lords, Select Committee on the European Communities, Twenty-first Report, *Defining the Schengen* Acquis, 27 March 1998, available at <www.publications.parliament.uk /pa/ld199798/ldselect/ldeucom/087xxi/ec2101.htm>. The report notes the uncertainty that surrounded the contents of the *acquis* for some time, stating that the decisions of the Schengen bodies 'would appear to comprise some 3000 pages. There is as yet no definitive list or version, though it is hoped to agree one soon. The Government has agreed to deposit copies of the full *acquis* in both Houses, once the *acquis* has been definitively established,' (at para. 4). Later the same year, on 8 September 1998,

The 1992 Treaty on European Union (TEU) created a new area of intergovernmental activity in the Third Pillar, which included asylum and immigration. Under the TEU, the Third Pillar was characterised by a cumbersome five-tier intergovernmental process. Various non-binding measures were adopted thereunder, which were criticised for their dilution of international human rights standards.[11] The only significant binding measure was the Dublin Convention,[12] dealing with the allocation of responsibility for processing asylum claims, and introducing the notion of burden sharing into EU asylum policy. Although in some instances, these measures were poorly implemented at national level,[13] a very strong network effect was evident in the exchange of information, construction of common terms such as 'safe country of transit', common visas list, and the generalisation of certain policy instruments, such as carrier sanctions (penalties on airlines, ferry companies etc for transporting individuals who seek to enter a state without proper authorisation). At the implementation level, a range of interactions were evident including operational co-operation between border police, liaison officers, data exchange and technological co-operation in areas such as fingerprinting of asylum seekers and document fraud. The pre-Amsterdam era has thus had lasting agenda-setting effects, despite significant legal and institutional changes introduced by the Treaty of Amsterdam. From a governance perspective, the legacy of intergovernmentalism is pernicious. The era has been characterised as one whereby national ministers in the Justice and Home Affairs (JHA) Council created an institutional framework marred by lack of 'coherence, consistency, democratic accountability, respect for the rule of law and for human rights, and effectiveness'.[14] This is explicable by the fact that

---

[10] *contd.* the Committee published a further report entitled *Incorporating the Schengen* Acquis *into the European Union*, available at <www.publications.parliament.uk/pa/ld199798/ldselect/ldeucom/139/8072801.htm>.

[11] The measures included the London Resolutions on a Harmonised Approach to Questions Concerning Host Third Countries, 30 November 1992; London Resolution on Manifestly Unfounded Applications for Asylum, 30 November 1992; London Conclusions on Countries where there is generally no serious risk of persecution, 30 November 1992; Council Resolution on minimum guarantees for asylum procedures, 20 June 1995; Council Resolution on burden-sharing with regard to the admission and residence of displaced persons on a temporary basis, 25 September 1995; Joint Position of 4 March 1996 defined by the Council on the basis of Article K3 of the TEU on the harmonised application of the definition of the term 'refugee' in Article 1 of the Geneva Convention.

[12] Convention determining the state responsible for examining applications for asylum lodged in the member states of the European Communities [1997] OJ C254/1.

[13] Peers, Steve, *Mind the Gap! Ineffective member state Implementation of European Union Asylum Measures* (ILPA 1998).

[14] Kostakopoulou, T., 'The "Protective Union": Change and Continuity in Migration Law and Policy in Post-Amsterdam Europe' (2000), *Journal of Common Market Studies*, 497, 498. See further, Collinson, S., *Beyond Borders: West European Migration Policy Towards the 21st Century* (RIIA, 1993); O'Keeffe, D., 'Recasting the Third Pillar' (1995), *CMLRev* 893; Bieber, R. and Monar, J., *Justice and Home Affairs in the European Union: The Development of the Third Pillar* (EUI, 1995).

European integration and the process of Europeanisation allowed member state national executives to overcome institutional constraints that they are faced with at the domestic level.[15]

The Treaty of Amsterdam is a milestone in European integration in that it marked the communitarisation of asylum policy[16] and the integration of the Schengen *acquis*[17] into the EU and EC Treaties, providing an opportunity for more transparent and accountable institutional arrangements and greater policy coherence. It provides for the establishment of an 'area of freedom, security and justice'. Within five years of the Treaty of Amsterdam coming into force (ie five years from 1 May 1999) the Council must adopt measures defining:

- the member state responsible for examining an asylum claim
- minimum standards on the reception of asylum seekers
- minimum standards on the qualification of third country nationals as refugees and beneficiaries of subsidiary protection
- minimum standards on procedures for granting and withdrawing refugee status
- minimum standards for giving temporary protection.

Measures must also be adopted (though not within five years) on burden-sharing between member states. However, as outlined in Sections I2 (i) and I2 (ii) below, there are several remaining peculiarities of EC asylum policymaking, reflecting a strong intergovernmental flavour. In addition, judicial control of this area remains weak (Section I2 (iii) below).[18]

Furthermore, the communitarisation of asylum policymaking was not accompanied by a fundamental rethinking of the underlying premises.[19] Although communitarisation coincided with the consecration of a new

---

[15] Thielemann, E., 'Explaining Stability and Change in European Asylum Policy', paper presented at the American Political Science Association Annual Meeting, San Francisco, 30 August – 2 September 2001, 9.

[16] 'Communitarisation' refers to the fact that asylum (together with visa, immigration and civil judicial co-operation) issues were brought under the European Community Treaty, in the form of the new Title IV EC. These issues went from being 'Union' to 'Community' competences.

[17] An exposition of the challenges of that effort is outside the scope of this work, but see J. de Zwaan, 'Opting Out and Opting In: Problems and Practical Arrangements under the Schengen Agreement', 1 (1998) *Cambridge Yearbook of European Legal Studies*. See also the House of Lords Select Committee on the European Communities Reports, above n. 10.

[18] For a general discussion, see S. Peers, 'Who's Judging the Watchman? The judicial system of the area of freedom, security and justice' (1998) *Yearbook of European Law*.

[19] Thus Kostakopolou argues, 'The Community has adopted from the member states' own discourse on the "securitization" of migration and asylum policy ... and the concomitant identification of possible sources of insecurity: the notion of freedom, security and justice is based on the assumption that migration is a security threat which must be effectively controlled and reduced'. Kostakopoulou, T., 'The "Protective Union": Change and Continuity in Migration Law and Policy in Post-Amsterdam Europe', (2000) *Journal of Common Market Studies*, 497, 508.

overarching objective for the EU, the creation of an 'area of freedom, security and justice',[20] the security dimension has dominated. For example, the mutual dependence between the migration issues under Title IV EC and criminal matters under the remaining parts of the Third EU Pillar is emphasised throughout the Treaty.[21] The references to 'freedom' and 'security' immediately beg the question 'whose'? That of asylum seekers who are forced to undertake perilous covert journeys to reach the relative safety of the EU? Or 'ours', the affluent and comfortable citizens of the Union, from the perceived security threat of unmanaged migration? The Treaty suggests the latter. The penultimate phrase of the Preamble to the Treaty on European Union refers to free movement of persons 'while ensuring the safety and security of their peoples, by including provisions on justice and home affairs in the Treaty'. Similarly Article 29 TEU refers to the need 'to provide citizens with a high level of safety within an area of freedom, security and justice'. It has been suggested that this posits the security of Community nationals *from* threats posed by third country nationals.[22] While one should not over-estimate the determinative force of such Treaty language, the underlying assumptions in such a politics of exclusion and inclusion at the supranational level are worrisome. In this respect, Crowley has stated,

> [T]here is perhaps no *inherent* difficulty in an area of 'freedom, security and justice'; once, however, 'security' has been defined by reference to a protean threat attached, even vaguely, to a group of people not susceptible to precise legal definition, the erosion of freedom by considerations of security becomes depressingly likely.[23]

2 Features of post-Amsterdam EC asylum policymaking

i) Lawmaking procedures

Title IV EC has created EC competence in the area of asylum and immigration. However, the Title's institutional features set it apart from normal EC mechanisms. During the transitional period of five years, member states, as well as the European Commission may make proposals. After the transitional period, the Commission's right of initiative becomes exclusive, but it must examine requests from the member states.

---

[20] Defined as an area in which the free movement of persons was to be assured in conjunction with appropriate measures with respect to external border controls, immigration, asylum and the prevention and combating of crime.
[21] Article 61 EC, Article 31(e) TEU.
[22] Guild, E., 'Primary Immigration: The Great Myths' in Guild, E. and Harlow, C. (eds), *Implementing Amsterdam: Immigration and Asylum Rights in EC Law* (Hart Publishing, Oxford, 2000).
[23] Crowley, J., 'Differential Free Movement and the Sociology of the Internal Border' in Guild, E. and Harlow, C., *op cit*, 25.

The second important aspect of the lawmaking framework is that unanimity is required in the Council for the adoption of measures, and the European Parliament is merely consulted. During the transitional period the only measures which may be adopted by qualified majority voting (QMV) are those concerning the list of countries whose nationals must be in possession of visas when crossing external borders and those whose nationals are exempt from that requirement and a uniform format for visas.[24] After the transitional period the Council may subject all or some of the areas under Title IV to the co-decision procedure with QMV in the Council and extend the powers of the ECJ.

The 2001 Treaty of Nice (ECN)[25] made some changes in this regard. In keeping with an aim of the Intergovernmental Conference (IGC) in 2000 to make QMV the lawmaking method throughout the Community pillar, several aspects of Title IV will be subject to QMV. However, in many cases this is a qualified transition. Article 62(2)(a) ECN provides that measures on the crossing of external borders may be adopted by QMV, where the Council decides unanimously to do so. Article 62(4) ECN provides that measures on freedom of travel for nationals of third countries will be subject to QMV as from May 2004. Article 63(1) ECN provides that common rules on asylum will be subject to QMV, but only once the common rules and basic principles have been set out. Finally, Article 63(3)(b) ECN provides that immigration rules will be subject to QMV, again after 2004. However, these changes must also be assessed in light of the opt-outs of Ireland, the UK and Denmark under Title IV, discussed in Section 13 below.

In the context of the dominance of the Council of lawmaking in this area, a number of Council working groups, with both information sharing and policy elaboration functions, have emerged. These include the High Level Working Group on Asylum and Migration;[26] the Asylum Working Party;[27] the Working Party on Migration and Expulsions; SCIFA working group (Strategic Committee for Immigration, Frontiers and Asylum)[28] and many others. In effect, this means that national civil servants from justice departments are the main players in the policy-making process. While at national level, one expects the views of justice ministers and officials to be tempered by cross-cabinet

---

[24] Article 62(b)(i) and (iii).

[25] The Treaty of Nice was signed on 26 February 2001 and came into force on 1 February 2003.

[26] In December 1998, the High Level Working Group on Asylum and Migration was established to produce action plans on the root causes of migration. It comprises high level officials from ministries of justice/home affairs and foreign affairs and Commission and Council officials.

[27] The Asylum Working Party gathers officials from the ministries responsible for asylum in order to discuss proposals in the asylum field.

[28] This committee's role is to draw up strategic guidelines for matters relating to immigration, external borders and the right to asylum.

deliberations, with other concerns (such as human rights and foreign policy) the EU processes are characterised by a dense network of like-minded officials, with a strong cross-border agenda-setting role. The EU agenda is thus not dominated by distant Eurocrats (ie Commission officials) but rather by *national* bureaucrats who are engaged in constant policy iteration, amplifying restrictive tendencies in national policies, often untempered by 'normal' national political accountability.

ii) Administrative co-operation

As well as lawmaking processes with a strongly intergovernmental bent, administrative co-operation and information exchange in this field is dense and highly institutionalised. The Schengen Information System (SIS) became operational in March 1995. This extensive database is housed in Strasbourg. The SIS database is backed up by Bureaux in each state that provide on request more detailed information/ intelligence. It is supplemented by the little-known SIRENE[29] database which permits the exchange of additional information, such as fingerprints and photographs, to that held on the SIS, as well as facilitating the 'free standing' exchange of police information. Current proposals would extend the range of information held in the system considerably beyond the immigration field.[30] The operation of the SIS has been subject to much criticism, particularly because it may be difficult to challenge non-admission and deportation decisions based on information contained therein.[31]

A further information-exchange system is Eurodac, which entered into force on 15 January 2003. This database collates fingerprints of asylum seekers and assists in the implementation of the Dublin Convention. The Centre for Information, Discussion and Exchange on Asylum (CIREA) aims to gather, exchange and disseminate information and compile documentation on all matters relating to asylum. CIREA was replaced in July 2002 with a new European network of asylum specialists (EURASIL). Its task is to gather information and share expertise on asylum policy. While many of these co-operative structures are necessary in order to make any common policy a reality, disquiet must be expressed in relation to the absence of political and judicial accountability.

---

[29] This stands for 'Supplementary Information Requests at the National Entry'.

[30] Initiative of the Kingdom of Spain with a view to adopting a JHA Council Decision concerning the introduction of some new functions for the Schengen Information System, in particular in the fight against terrorism [2002] OJ C160/1.

[31] See, for example, the report by the UK human rights group JUSTICE, *The Schengen Information System: a human rights audit*, available at <www.justice.org.uk>. This report is discussed by Colvin, M., 'The Schengen Information System: a human rights audit', (2001) *EHRLR* 271. For discussion focusing on judicial control in one member state, see Guild, E.,'Adjudicating Schengen: National Judicial Control in France', (1999) *European Journal for Migration and Law* 419.

iii) Legal constraints and control

The asylum policy area, although characterised by novel institutional mechanisms, is already the subject of much EU and international legal regulation, including norms of *jus cogens*, such as *non-refoulement*.[32] The norm-setting capacity of the EC is thus shaped by this existing body of law, notwithstanding the fact that the Title IV competence allows only the setting of minimum standards. Any just and legal asylum and immigration policy must respect existing international obligations. In the area of asylum, the principal instrument is the 1951 Geneva Convention on the Status of Refugees (the Refugee Convention) and the 1967 Protocol, Article 1 (definition of refugee) and Article 33 (protection against non-refoulement) which form part of customary international law. Article 63 (1) TEC acknowledges that EC asylum policy should be framed in accordance with the Refugee Convention. Other relevant international provisions include Article 3 of the 1950 European Convention on Human Rights and Fundamental Freedoms; Article 7 of the 1966 International Covenant on Civil and Political Rights; Article 3 of the 1984 UN Convention against Torture and other Cruel, Inhuman or Degrading Treatment or Punishment and Article 22 of the 1989 Convention on the Rights of the Child.

Despite the normative superiority of the existing precepts of refugee law, Title IV EC is characterised by an absence of adequate judicial control mechanisms. The preliminary reference procedure,[33] the main avenue for holding member states to their Community law bargains, and for testing the validity of Community legislative measures, is significantly restricted under this Title. The ECJ's role under Article 68 EC is confined. Only national courts and tribunals 'against whose decisions there is no judicial remedy under national law' are empowered to refer and indeed are obliged to refer only if they consider that a decision on the question is necessary to enable them to give judgement. As the Court itself has opined in a policy statement issued during IGC 2000,[34] such a restriction is undesirable from the point of view of procedural economy and securing the uniformity of EC law. In particular it is impossible to reconcile with the *Foto-frost*[35] jurisprudence that national courts may not deem EC acts to be invalid and are consequently

---

[32] Article 33(1) of the Refugee Convention states that 'No Contracting State shall expel or return ("refouler") a refugee in any manner whatsoever to the frontiers of territories where his life or freedom would be threatened on account of his race, religion, nationality, membership of a particular social group or political opinion'.

[33] The general preliminary reference procedure is enshrined in Article 234 (ex 177) EC. However, a different variant of the procedure applies under Title IV EC, in Article 68 EC.

[34] Court of Justice of the European Communities, *The Future of the Judicial System of the European Union – Proposals and Reflections* (1999).

[35] Case 314/85 *Foto-Frost v. Hauptzollamt Lubeck-Ost* [1987] ECR 4199.

obliged to a make preliminary reference where a decision on the invalidity of an EC measure is necessary in order to allow them to give judgement. Thus, for example it has been suggested that the provisions of the Treaty in Title IV are incompatible with Community general principles on effective judicial control.[36] In addition, interpretative rulings may be sought by the Council, Commission or member states under Article 68(3) TEC, subject to the caveat that the ECJ's rulings in this context 'shall not apply to judgments of courts or tribunals of the member states which have become *res judicata*'.[37]

iv) External dimension

It is self-evident that immigration and asylum have an external dimension, in that they concern the rights and status of the 'other', in this context defined as 'third country national'. However, the policy area is now characterised by particularly strong institutionalised co-operation with third countries, taking many forms. For example, Readmission Agreements to facilitate deportations have become a key policy tool. Co-operation with countries of origin and transit has been developed as reflected in the Commission's Communication on Integrating Migration Issues in the EU's Relations with Third Countries[38] and the action plans of the High Level Working Group on Asylum and Migration. In addition, the transplanting asylum regimes eastwards throughout Central and Eastern Europe has been ongoing.[39] A further external dimension is discussed below, the emerging policy trend in favour of 'external processing'. Viewed together, these initiatives reflect a strong emphasis on policies of non-admission and non-arrival, as detailed below at Section II*1* below.

3 Ireland's optional participation

Ireland, the UK and Denmark have opted out of the Schengen Integration Protocol and Title IV EC. The opt-out of the UK and Ireland has its origins in a particular British conception of border politics and general reluctance in the UK in relation to the participation in European policies.[40] The argument often propounded is that the British

---

[36] Ward, A. 'The Limits of the Uniform Application of Community Law and Effective Judicial Review' in Kilpatrick, C., Novitz, T. and Skidmore, P. (eds), *The Future of Remedies in Europe* (Oxford, Hart Publishing, 2000).

[37] *Res judicata*, in summary, provides that a valid and final judgment by a competent court on a claim precludes a second action by the same parties on that claim or any part of it.

[38] COM 2002 703 final, 3 December 2002.

[39] For a detailed overview, see Byrne, R., Noll, G. and Vedsted-Hansen, J. (eds), *New Asylum Countries? Migration Control and Refugee Protection in an Enlarged European Union* (Kluwer Law International, 2002).

[40] Wiener, Antje, 'Forging Flexibility – The British "No" to Schengen' (1999), *European Journal of Migration and Law* 441.

conception of internal security depends on strict border control, with internal liberty thereby guaranteed. In contrast, the 'continental system' depends less on border control and more on internal checks, exemplified in the use of national identity cards, which citizens must carry at all times. While the contrast is no doubt an overstated one, it does influence the construction of national interests in this area. Schengen's flanking policies are at times portrayed as an attempt to transplant the 'continental' system of internal controls to the UK and Ireland. However, the UK opt-out has not been without its critics. For example, the House of Lords Select Committee on the European Union has reported that it views the opt-out as unfeasible in the long term. In particular, its report pointed out that 'The EC Treaty, especially after Amsterdam, does not always make neat divisions between "immigration" measures (which the United Kingdom can choose not to opt into) and "Single Market" measures (by which the United Kingdom is bound)'.[41]

Ireland's opt-out is in turn attributed to the need to maintain the Common Travel Area between the UK and Ireland.[42] Accordingly, one of the principal considerations whether to take part in measures in the immigration area is the consequences of the measure for the common travel area. This is reflected in Ireland's *Declaration on Article 3 of the Protocol on the position of the United Kingdom and Ireland*, whereby Ireland undertook to exercise its right to opt in to Title IV measures 'to the maximum extent compatible with the maintenance of its Common Travel Area with the United Kingdom'. The Fourth Protocol to the Treaty of Amsterdam sets out the position of the UK and Ireland as regards Title IV EC. In effect, each state has three months from the date of the presentation of the proposal or initiative to the Council, to notify the President of the Council in writing of its wish to participate in the adoption of the measure.[43] Ireland can also opt to participate after a measure has been adopted.[44] In the asylum field, Ireland has opted in to the bulk of the measures on the table, but this is not so in relation to the common immigration policy.[45] In the asylum field, Ireland has opted into all but the Directive on Reception Standards and is only now opting into the Directive on Temporary Protection.

This was attributed by a senior official to the fact that it was not possible to opt in to deliberations within three months, because 'a

---

[41] Select Committee on the European Union, Thirteenth Report, *A Community Immigration Policy* (2001), see http://www.parliament.the-stationery-office.co.uk/pa /ld200001/ldselect/ldeucom/64/6414.htm

[42] For a general discussion, see Bernard, R., 'The common travel area between Britain and Ireland' (2001), *MLR* 64(6) 855.

[43] Article 3 of the Protocol.

[44] Article 4 of the Protocol.

[45] Response to parliamentary question posed by Conor Lenihan TD to the Minister for Justice, Equality and Law Reform, 12 February 2003.

major part of the period was during the recess of the Houses of the Oireachtas'. However, it was also stressed that 'The non-exercise of our option does not prevent our participation in discussions on the pro posals in the relevant Council Working Parties – and we are fully engaged in those discussions – as we have a right to participate by virtue of our Council membership.'[46] What appears inadequate, however, is a national debate and explanation for the exercise of these opt-ins. Under the provisions of Article 29(6) of the 1937 Constitution of Ireland, exercising such an opt-in requires the approval of both Houses of the Oireachtas.[47] Regrettably, the exercise of the opt-ins has not been the occasion of much debate at the national level.

SECTION II: The Contours of EU Asylum Policy Post-Amsterdam

The Tampere Summit[48] of the European Council held in October 1999 set the agenda for the realisation of the policy goals sets out in Title IV EC, which entered into force on 1 May 1999. The European Commission,[49] European Parliament[50] and European and national non-governmental organisations[51] all set out detailed policy papers which were submitted to the summit, which remain useful benchmarks for the evaluation of the development of EC policy in this area. The conclusions on the 'Common European Asylum System' [52] stressed the following elements:

- a clear and workable determination of the state responsible for the examination of an asylum application

---

[46] Costello, D., *Ireland and the Development of the Common European Asylum Policy*, paper presented at the Irish Centre for European Law Conference on Refugee Law, 2 March 2002.

[47] 'The State may exercise the options or discretions provided by or under Articles 1(11), 2(5) and 2(15) of the [Treaty of Amsterdam] and the second and fourth Protocols set out in the said Treaty but any such exercise shall be subject to the prior approval of both Houses of the Oireachtas.'

[48] Special Meeting of the European Council on the Establishment of an Area of Freedom, Security and Justice, Tampere, Finland, 15-16 October 1999.

[49] Commission Working Document, *Towards Common Standards on Asylum Procedures* (March 1999) SEC (1999) 271 final.

[50] European Parliament *Report on the Action Plan of the Council and Commission on How Best to Implement the Provisions of the Treaty of Amsterdam on an Area of Freedom, Security and Justice* (18 March 1999).

[51] European Council on Refugees and Exiles (ECRE), European Network Against Racism, Migration Policy Group, *Guarding Standards – Shaping the Agenda* (April 1999) (hereinafter 'ECRE – Guarding Standards'); Irish Refugee Council, *Recommendations on Asylum Policy to the Special Meeting of the European Council on the Establishment of an Area of Freedom, Security and Justice, to be held in Tampere, Finland on 15-16 October 1999*, Dublin, 3 September 1999.

[52] For a critical appraisal, see Egan, S., 'European Asylum Policy: Reflections on the Tampere Conclusions' (2000) *Irish Human Rights Review*, 168.

- common standards for a fair and efficient asylum procedure
- common minimum conditions of reception of asylum seekers
- the approximation of rules on the recognition and content of refugee status.

These were to be followed by

- measures on subsidiary forms of protection offering an appropriate status to any person in need of such protection
- a common asylum procedure
- a uniform status for those who are granted asylum valid throughout the Union.

Also stressed was the need to complete work on the temporary protection measure and Eurodac.[53] Finally, under the heading 'Management of migration flows', the Tampere Conclusions stress issues such as trafficking,[54] border controls,[55] and readmission agreements.[56] In order to maintain the legislative impetus in this area, the Commission prepares a biannual scoreboard to track progress in the creation of the 'area of freedom, security and justice'. Since the summit, the following features have emerged in the common EU asylum policy:

1 Deflection
2 Temporary protection and burden sharing
3 Uniform system
4 Removal.

1 Deflection

One of the key features of European asylum policy is deflection.[57] While the European Union itself has not employed the most dramatic form of deflection – interdiction of vessels – it nonetheless pervades asylum policy. Many forms of deflection are evident – one is the creation of various mechanisms to make entry to the asylum process more difficult. Another entails shifting of the burden towards other states, which may take various forms. A number of 'deflection' tools are outlined in this section.

---

[53] Conclusions 14-17.
[54] Conclusions 22 and 23.
[55] Conclusions 24 and 25.
[56] Conclusion 27.
[57] Noll, G., *Negotiating Asylum: The EU Acquis, Extraterritorial Protection and the Common Market of Deflection* (Martinus Nijhoff Publishers, 2000).

a) Pre-entry deflection measures

i) Visa policy

Since 1995, a common EC regulation has determined which third country nationals require visas in order to enter the EU.[58] The list is informed by fears of illegal immigration[59] and, in practice, this means countries from where many asylum seekers arrive are targeted.[60] While this harmonisation may appear benign from the point of view of the asylum seeker, when viewed together with other policy instruments, it becomes apparent that the effect of the visa regime is to render entry to the EU most difficult. In particular, provisions on carriers' liability and trafficking seek to restrict the only remaining entry route for many asylum seekers – the illegal one.[61]

ii) Carriers' liability

Carriers' liability refers to the imposition of financial penalties on carriers (airlines, ferry companies etc) for transporting individuals who seek to enter a state without proper authorisation. In many instances, this can include stowaways. The deflection aim is clear – by their nature, such policies deter carriers from granting passage to individuals where any doubt hangs over the legality of their entry to the state of destination. Two fundamental human rights objections may be raised. First, this ignores the fact that very often it is the 'genuine' refugee that will be unable to arrange legal entry to the receiving state. The Refugee Convention itself contains an implicit acknowledgment that many asylum seekers are forced to have recourse to illegal means of entry.[62] Second, such policies transfer the responsibility for determining the

---

[58] Council Regulation 2414/2001 of 7 December 2001 amending Regulation 539/2001 listing third countries whose nationals must be in possession of visas when crossing the external borders of the member states and those whose nationals are exampt from that requirement [2001] OJ L327/1.

[59] The Preamble provides that 'risks relating to security and illegal immigration should be given priority consideration when the said common list is drawn up' (Paragraph 3).

[60] See, for example, the analysis of Gregor Noll, *Negotiating Asylum: The EU Acquis, Extraterritorial Protection and the Common Market of Deflection* (Martinus Nijhoff, 2000), 166.

[61] For detailed studies on this phenomenon, see Noll, above n. 57; Morrison, J. and Crosland, B., 'The Trafficking and Smuggling in Refugees: The end game in European asylum policy?' UNHCR New Issues in Refugee Research, Working Paper No. 39, April 2001, available at <www.unhcr.ch/refworld/pubs/pubon.htm>. Christian, B.P., 'Visa Policy, Inspection and Exit Controls: Transatlantic Perspectives on Migration Management', (1999) *Georgetown Immigration Law Journal* 1.

[62] Article 31(1) of the Refugee Convention states 'The Contracting State shall not impose penalties, on account of their illegal entry or presence, on refugees who, coming directly from a territory where their life or freeedom was threatened in the sense of Article 1, enter or are present in their territory without authorization, provided they present themselves without delay to the authorities and show good cause for their illegal entry or presence'.

legality of entry to the carrier – a private actor with no interest other than reducing its exposure to risk of financial penalty.

Carriers' liability measures are central to EC deflection policies. In June 2001, a Directive on Carriers' Liability was adopted, based on a French initiative.[63] The second recital to the Directive refers to the fact that the measure aims at 'curbing migratory flows and combating illegal immigration'. This may be read as a peculiarly frank admission that such measures curb all migration, including that of refugees. Nonetheless the subsequent recital contains the customary reference to the Refugee Convention. Ireland introduced carrier sanctions into Irish law by virtue of the Immigration Act 2003, signed into law in July 2003.

The core obligation, set out in Article 2 of the Carrier's Liablity Directive, requires member states to ensure that the obligation of carriers to return third country nationals provided for in the provisions of Article 26(1)(a) of the Schengen Convention shall also apply when entry is refused to a third-country national in transit if: '(a) the carrier which was to take him to his country of destination refuses to take him on board; (b) or the authorities of the state of destination have refused him entry and have sent him back to the member state through which he transited'. If this is not possible, in accordance with Article 3, carriers are obliged to cover the cost of return. Article 4 sets out requirements as to effective penalties.

iii) Combating trafficking

In December 2000, the Commission proposed a Framework Decision to combat trafficking in human beings,[64] which was adopted in July 2002.[65] Because this is a measure dealing with criminal sanctions, it is based on the Third Pillar of the Treaty on European Union. Accordingly, there is no applicable opt-out mechanism. The concept of trafficking turns on the exercise of force, deceit or abuse of authority with a view to exploitation, including sexual exploitation.[66] For certain aggravated forms of trafficking, the maximum penalty must be 'not less that eight years'.[67] Also currently proposed is a Directive on the short-term residence permit issued to victims of illegal immigration and trafficking in human beings who cooperate with the authorities.[68]

---

[63] Council Directive 2001/51/EC of 28 June 2001 supplementing the provisions of Article 26 of the Convention implementing the Schengen Agreement of 14 June 1985 [2001] OJ L187/45.

[64] COM(2000)854, [2001] OJ C324.

[65] [2002] OJ L203/1.

[66] Article 1. Member states are required to take the necessary measures to ensure that such acts are punishable.

[67] Article 3.

[68] Commission Proposal for a Council Directive on the short-term residence permit issued to victims of action to facilitate illegal immigration or trafficking in human beings who cooperate with the competent authorities [2002] OJ C126/393.

iv) Assisting illegal entry generally

The French government also proposed two related Directives on the facilitation of unauthorised entry, movement and residence, again building on measures taken in the Schengen framework.[69] The main provisions of the proposal are as follows:

- member states must take the necessary measures to ensure that the act of facilitating intentionally, by aiding directly or indirectly, the unauthorised entry, movement or residence in its territory of an alien who is not a national of a member state is regarded as an offence
- member states must take measures to ensure that participation, as an accomplice or instigator, in the facilitation of illegal immigration be considered to be an offence, as shall also the attempt to commit such an offence, and that such offences are punishable by effective, proportionate and dissuasive penalties
- each member state may exempt from criminal prosecution certain persons who are closely linked to the alien who has benefited from the aiding (ie a relative in the ascending or descending line, brothers and sisters and their spouses, his spouse or the person known to cohabit with him).

In the European Parliament, the rapporteur Ozan Ceyhun criticised the absence of any distinction between organised networks trading in human beings and humanitarian assistance and therefore suggested that 'for purposes of direct or indirect gain' be added to the definition of the offence.[70] At its plenary session, the Parliament finally rejected the initiative outright, by 242 votes against 203 and by 31 abstentions. Of course, as the Parliament is merely consulted in this area, the Council is free to ignore its view. The Council continues to debate the measure, but two key questions remain. Firstly the scope of the humanitarian exemption (if any) and, secondly, the 'minimum maximum sentence' to apply (six and ten years are being considered). Also on the table is a German initiative on illegal immigration networks.[71]

---

[69] Initiative of the French Republic with a view to the adoption of a Council Directive defining the facilitation of unauthorised entry, movement and residence (10675/2000 – C5-0427/2000 – 2000/0821(CNS)); initiative of the French Republic with a view to the adoption of a Council Framework Decision on the strengthening of the penal framework to prevent the facilitation of unauthorised entry and residence (10676/2000 – C5-0426/2000 – 2000/0820(CNS)). [2000] OJC253/1.

[70] A5-0315-2000, 25 October 2000

[71] Draft initiative of the Federal Republic of Germany for the adoption of a Council Resolution on member states' obligation to transmit information on illegal immigration and facilitator networks pursuant to an early warning system, 2 March 2001, Council Document 13165/1/00.

v) External Processing

In addition, the Danish Centre for Human Rights has prepared a detailed report on external processing for the European Commission, examining mechanisms to process asylum claims while asylum seekers are still abroad. The attractions of such an approach are manifold. The processing state will not necessarily bear the 'burden' of the asylum seeker's welfare. In addition, it may provide a better escape route, for those for whom being smuggled into the EU is financially or materially impossible. The report struggles to reconcile external processing and human rights concerns. The same cannot be said for another recent initiative in this area. In March 2003 the UK government proposed a variant of external processing, based on 'regional protection areas' and 'transit processing centres'.[72]

Partly in response to the UK proposal, the Commission issued a Communication entitled *Towards a more accessible, equitable and managed international protection regime*.[73] The Communication analyses the UK proposals and the UNHCR's views on arrangements in regions of origin. It then goes on to propose an EU approach. The objectives of external protection include a) the orderly and managed arrival of persons in need of international protection in the EU from the region of origin; b) burden and responsibility sharing within the EU as well as with regions of origin, enabling them to provide effective protection as soon as possible and as closely as possible to the needs of persons in need of international protection; and c) the development of an integrated approach to efficient and enforceable asylum decision-making and return procedures. While these objectives seem reasonable, the proposal of establishing 'a complementary mechanism for examining certain categories of applications lodged in or at the border of the EU' is dubious, particularly as it is linked to the establishment of 'closed processing centres' at particular locations.

It appears that this policy is being given serious consideration. It was discussed by the heads of state and government at the Thessaloniki European Council. On 15 July 2003, the Commission announced finance for studies and projects, worth EUR 13 million, that relate to enhanced protection of refugees in their regions of origin.

b) Post-entry deflection measures

Also employed are post-entry measures, aimed to preclude the requirement to examine the claims of asylum applicants in the member states.

---

[72] For criticisms by the British Refugee Council, see <www.refugeecouncil.org.uk/news/june2003/relea122.htm>.

[73] (COM(2003) 315 final) 23 June 2003.

i) Dublin Convention and Eurodac

The instrument for determining the member state responsible for examining an asylum claim was originally the Dublin Convention.[74] The operation of the Dublin Convention as a stand-alone instrument, unaccompanied by any definitional or procedural harmonisation of asylum law throughout the EU, has proven to be problematic both for applicants and indeed the member states themselves. The context within which it operates renders it an inappropriate and unfair mechanism in many cases.[75]

In July 2001, the Commission proposed a regulation establishing the criteria and mechanisms for determining the member state responsible for examining an asylum application lodged in one of the member states by a third-country national. The proposal is based on some of the reflections contained in the Commission staff working paper, *Revisiting the Dublin Convention: developing Community legislation for determining which state is responsible for considering an application for asylum submitted in one of the member states*.[76] Designed to replace the Dublin Convention, its innovative features include

- provisions on a member state's obligations vis-à-vis other member states when allowing illegal residents to remain on its territory
- a reduction in procedural deadlines
- extended deadlines for implementing transfers to the member state responsible so as to allow for the practical difficulties arising in connection with such transfers
- new provisions to preserve family unity.

The Dublin II Regulation was formally adopted in February 2003.[77]

---

[74] Convention determining the state responsible for examining applications for asylum lodged in one of the member states of the European Communities (15 June 1990) [1997] OJ C254/1.

[75] See for example Byrne, R. and Shacknove, A. 'The safe country notion in European asylum law', (1996) *Harvard Human Rights Journal*, 185.

[76] SEC (2000) 522, 21 March 2000. This document has been the subject of much commentary, including *ECRE comments on the European Commission staff working paper revisiting the Dublin Convention: developing Community legislation for determining which Member Sate is responsible for considering an application for asylum submitted in one of the Member States* (June 2000); *Revisiting the Dublin Convention. Some reflections by UNHCR in response to the Commission staff working paper* (January 2001); *Amnesty International's response to the Commission Staff Working Paper on Revisiting the Dublin Convention* (November 2000); *Caritas Europa/CCME/COMECE/ICMC/JRS Consultation on the Commission staff working document 'Revisiting the Dublin Convention'* (July 2000); *ILPA representations on the Commission staff working document 'Revisiting the Dublin Convention'* (June 2000).

[77] Council Regulation 343/2003 of 18 February 2003 establishing the criteria and mechanisms for determining the member state responsible for examining an asylum application lodged in one of the member states by a third-country national (2003) OJ L50/1.

Ireland opted into this measure[78] and it applies from 1 September 2003. The final regulation maintains the basic features of the Dublin Convention system. Changes relate to the applicable criteria and procedures. In brief, the existing four criteria for responsibility have been retained and supplemented by two new criteria, relating to unaccompanied minors (first criterion) and family reunion with asylum-seekers (third criterion, following the present criterion for family reunion with recognised refugees, which is essentially unchanged except for its optional extension to unmarried partners). The second criterion in the existing rules (issue of a visa or a residence permit) will be the fourth criterion, but is not significantly changed in substance. The third criterion (crossing the border irregularly) will be the fifth criterion, but responsibility will now terminate after twelve months, and will be transferred in the event of subsequent stay in the territory of another member state for five months.[79] Next, the sixth criterion (formerly the fourth) is the state responsible for controlling the entry of a non-visa national, with the wording of the existing Dublin rules retained (despite the Commission's initial proposal for amendments). Finally, as before, the default criterion is the member state where the asylum-seeker submitted his or her application.

Also of note in this context is the adoption of a controversial instrument on the fingerprinting of asylum seekers, aiming to ensure the efficacy of the Dublin Convention system. On 11 December 2000, the Council adopted the Eurodac Regulation.[80] This establishes a system for the comparison of fingerprints of asylum seekers. Both Ireland[81] and the UK opted in to this instrument, and Denmark has requested that a separate agreement be concluded between it and the Community in order to allow it to use the Eurodac system. The Eurodac system became operational on 15 January 2003.

ii) Readmission Agreements

Readmission agreements and clauses have become a key part of policy to secure the removal of failed asylum seekers and illegal immigrants, as is emphasised in the 2002 Commission Communication 'Integrating Migration Issues in the European Union's Relations with Third Countries',[82]

---

[78] Response to parliamentary question posed by Conor Lenihan TD to the Minister for Justice, Equality and Law Reform, 12 February 2003.

[79] Responsibility will also shift to such a member state under this criterion even if it cannot be shown whether or not the asylum-seeker initially crossed the external border of another member state irregularly.

[80] Council Regulation 2725/2000/EC of 11 December 2000, [2000] OJ L316/1. For analysis, see Brouwer, E., 'Eurodac: Its Limitations and Temptations', (2002) *European Journal of Migration and Law* 231.

[81] Response to parliamentary question posed by Conor Lenihan TD to the Minister for Justice, Equality and Law Reform, 12 February 2003.

[82] COM (2002) 703.

and several European Council Conclusions.[83] In December 1999, a text of future wording to be included in EC readmission agreements with third states was agreed.[84] To date, a number of readmission agreements have been concluded between the EC and particular countries. These include the readmission agreement between EC and the government of the Special Administrative Region (SAR) of Hong Kong, 27 November 2002. The agreement obliges the Hong Kong SAR to readmit both its present or former permanent residents, other persons to whom it has issued a visa or residence authorisation, and other persons who have entered the EU directly from Hong Kong. Equivalent obligations are placed upon EU states. Ireland has opted into this measure.[85] In addition, the Commission reached agreement on draft readmission treaties with Sri Lanka (May 2002) and Macao (October 2002), but these have not yet received the requisite approval from the Council. The Council has also granted the Commission negotiating mandates to conclude such agreements with Russia, Pakistan, Morocco (all September 2000), Ukraine (2002), Albania, Algeria, China, and Turkey (all 28/29 November 2002).

As well as stand-alone readmission agreements, the EC now also routinely includes readmission clauses in association and co-operation agreements. In this respect, the key provision is Article 13 of the 2000 Cotonou Agreement between the EU and the African, Caribbean and Pacific group of states (ACP).[86] Article 13(5)(i) of the Agreement

---

[83] The Tampere (October 1999) European Council conclusions included readmission among the elements of the 'area of freedom, security and justice'. It called for 'assistance to countries of origin and transit' partly in order to enable them 'to cope with their readmission obligations towards the Union and the Member States'. It also proposed that the Council use the powers conferred upon the EC by the Treaty of Amsterdam so as 'to conclude readmission agreements or to include standard clauses in other agreements between the European Community and relevant third countries or groups of countries ...' According to the Laeken conclusions (December 2001), 'European readmission agreements must be concluded with the countries concerned on the basis of a new list of priorities and a clear action plan. The European Council calls for an action plan to be developed on the basis of the Commission communication on illegal immigration and the smuggling of human beings'. The point was developed in the Seville conclusions (June 2002). These proposed that 'top priority' be given, *inter alia*, to 'speeding up of the conclusion of readmission agreements currently being negotiated and approval of new briefs for the negotiation of readmission agreements with countries already identified by the Council'. In the Seville conclusions, the European Council also 'urge[d] that any future co-operation, association or equivalent agreement which the European Union or the European Community concluded with any country should include a clause on joint management of migration flows and on compulsory readmission in the event of illegal immigration'.

[84] Council document 12134/1/99.

[85] Response to parliamentary question posed by Conor Lenihan TD to the Minister for Justice, Equality and Law Reform, 12 February 2003.

[86] [2000] OJ L317. The General Secretariat of the Council of the EU, acting for the Community, lodged its act of notification of ratification of the Agreement on 27 February 2003. It was due to enter into force on 1 April 2003, once the ratification procedure was completed by the requisite number of ACP states (ie 52 out of 77). See www.eu-oplysninger.dk/euidag/rapdi/PRES_03_60_0_RAPID.

contains an obligation to accept the readmission of nationals of the state in question found illegally on the territory of a state on the other side. Article 13(5)(ii) also provides for the negotiation in good faith of bilateral agreements 'governing specific obligations for the readmission and return of their nationals'. These agreements may also be extended to third country nationals and to stateless persons. Crucially, the trigger for that extension is that it be 'deemed necessary by any of the Parties'. Similar clauses have also been included in other recent agreements – for example, Article 46 of Association Agreement with Chile (OJ 2002 L 352/3, November 2002) and Article 76 of the Stabilisation and Association Agreement with Macedonia (Council doc 67206/01, March 2001)

The Commission Communication on integrating migration issues in the EU's relations with third countries highlights the difficulty of persuading other states to enter into readmission agreements. This is partly because the benefits of these agreements appear weighted in favour of the EU. It is also because of the costs of 're-integration' of a country's own nationals. Transit countries have special burdens, given the volume of persons involved and the difficulties with repatriating them to their own states. The Commission therefore wishes the EU to acquire greater 'leverage' over developing countries in relation to readmission. It proposes 'to provide a specific support for the preparation and implementation of the readmission agreements by third countries, aiming at increasing technical and financial assistance'. In states where readmission is likely to be especially costly, the EC and member states 'should be ready to consider supplementary types of incentives'. The limits on the incentives that may be offered are acknowledged.

c) Pre-emptive exclusion

A final exclusionary device should be noted – the so-called 'Spanish Protocol' to the EC Treaty inserted by the Treaty of Amsterdam.[87] It denies the right of EU nationals to apply for asylum in other EU member states, except in four specific circumstances. While the Protocol has its origin in Spanish concerns about Basque asylum applications in Belgium, its true significance will only become apparent in the current accession context, where many applicant states produce many asylum seekers, whose right to reside in the EU will be conditional, while their right to claim asylum is greatly restricted.

---

[87] Its full title is the 'Protocol on Asylum for Nationals of Member States of the European Union'.

2 Temporary protection and burden sharing

On 20 July 2001, a Directive on temporary protection in the event of a mass influx of displaced persons was formally adopted.[88] This marks the culmination of negotiations of over six years. Ireland is only now opting into this Directive and it is unclear why the Irish government did not opt into the discussions preceding its adoption.

The Directive establishes an EU mechanism and minimum standards for granting temporary protection. Temporary protection is defined as 'a procedure of exceptional character to provide, in the event of a mass influx or imminent mass influx of displaced persons from third countries who are unable to return to their country of origin, immediate and temporary protection to such persons, in particular if there is also a risk that the asylum system will be unable to process this influx without adverse effects for its efficient operation, in the interests of the persons concerned and other persons requesting protection'.[89] The Directive stipulates that a mass influx may be caused both by spontaneous arrivals in the Union and by evacuation programmes.[90] In this respect, the Directive is broader in scope than the Commission's proposal, which did not embrace mass influxes caused by evacuation programmes, 'imminent mass influxes' and those which did not pose a difficulty for the processing of claims.

Thus temporary protection regimes are of exceptional character. However, it has been suggested that there is nonetheless a danger that temporary protection might be used in situations where the granting of Convention status would be possible.[91]

The Directive provides that the mechanism of temporary protection should be put into place by a decision of the Council (by QMV), on the basis of a Commission proposal.[92] The decision will then have one year's validity, with the possibility of extension for two further periods of six months.[93] Where the reasons for temporary protection persist, the Council may then decide (again, by qualified majority and on a proposal by the Commission) to extend the regime for another year.[94] Thus the maximum duration of temporary protection is three years. This

---

[88] Council Directive 2001/55/EC of 20 July 2001 on minimum standards for giving temporary protection in the event of a mass influx of displaced persons and on measures promoting a balance of efforts between member states in receiving such persons and bearing the consequences thereof [2001] OJ L212/12.

[89] Article 2a.

[90] Article 2c and 2d.

[91] ECRE Information Note on the council Directive 2001/55/EC of 20 July 2001 on minimum standards for giving temporary protection in the event of a mass influx of displaced persons and on measures promoting a balance of efforts between member states in receiving such persons and bearing the consequences thereof, available at <www.ecre.org/statements/tpsumm.shtml>.

[92] Article 5.

[93] Article 4(1).

[94] Article 4(2).

feature of the Directive reflects the need to ensure that the inherent uncertainty which attaches to temporary protection status does not prevail for too long. The European Parliament had advocated no longer than two years, but the final solution of three years was adopted.

One of the most important, and indeed welcome, features of the Directive is that it does not prejudice the right to claim asylum. In particular, the granting of temporary protection does not prejudge recognition of refugee status under the Geneva Convention,[95] and the Directive stipulates that beneficiaries of temporary protection 'must be able to lodge an application for asylum at any time'[96] and that 'the examination of any asylum application not processed before the end of the period of temporary protection shall be completed after the end of that period'.[97] However, under Article 19, member states 'may provide that temporary protection may not be enjoyed concurrently with the status of asylum seeker while applications are under consideration', and, under Article 18, 'the criteria and mechanisms for deciding which member state is responsible for considering an asylum application shall apply'.

The rights accorded are wide-ranging, but restrictive. They include residence permit and appropriate documentation;[98] suitable accommodation;[99] necessary assistance in terms of social welfare, means of subsistence and emergency medical care and essential treatment of illness;[100] family reunification;[101] special provisions for vulnerable groups[102] and unaccompanied minors.[103] However, several rights are ultimately subject to a policy choice by the member states. Thus, for example, the right to work is to be accorded both to employed and self-employed persons, 'subject to prevailing rights of other EU nationals or third country residents at the discretion of member states'.[104] The educational rights are also variable. For minors, education is to be roughly on the same terms as for nationals[105] while for adults its provision is at discretion of member states. One NGO has described the standard of rights as reasonable, with the exception of the low standard of medical care provided for.[106]

A burden-sharing mechanism is also contained in the Directive, based upon a 'spirit of Community solidarity'.[107] Member states are

---

[95] Article 3(1).
[96] Article 17(1)
[97] Article 17(2).
[98] Article 8.
[99] Article 13(1).
[100] Article 13(2).
[101] Article 15.
[102] Article 13(4).
[103] Article 16.
[104] Article 12.
[105] Article 14(1).
[106] ECRE Information Note, *supra* note 91.
[107] Article 25(1).

obliged to indicate their reception capacity before the Council takes its decision and may indicate additional capacity afterward. If demand is higher than reception capacity, the Council may recommend additional support for the member state(s) affected.[108] One notable lacuna is that the procedural aspects of temporary protection are not dealt with.

3 Uniform system

The final dimension of the post-Amsterdam development of asylum policy is the uniform asylum system. The emphasis here is on establishing a common system including substantive provisions, procedural measures and material entitlements. This contrasts with many other areas of EU law, where typically procedural measures are left to the member states to be defined in accordance with the national legal context. In the asylum context, where policy is informed by assumptions of generous asylum systems working as 'pull' factors for asylum seekers, this policy of harmonisation is also seen as a necessary part of the burden-sharing effort.

i) Toward a harmonised interpretation of the Refugee Convention and complementary protection

The definition of a refugee is laid down in the Refugee Convention. The correct interpretation of the Refugee Convention is reflected in UNHCR guidelines.[109] However, significant divergences exist between member states as regards their interpretation of the Refugee Convention. A key point of divergence is that of non-state persecution. Certain member states disregard such persecution, in a mis-interpretation of the Refugee Convention.[110] Previous attempts to harmonise the interpretation of the refugee definition reflected compromise at the lowest common denominator. This was a point of particular criticism levelled against the Joint Position of March 1996.[111]

Subsidiary or complementary protection, on the other hand, is designed for people who, for whatever reason, do not meet with the strict definition of a refugee as outlined in the Refugee Convention yet are nonetheless in need of protection. This is not to be confused with temporary protection which is designed to meet the increased demand for protection in the EU in a crisis situation. It should also be noted that while complementary protection may not be based on the Refugee Convention, it has legal foundations in other international legal

---

[108] Article 25(3).
[109] *UNHCR Handbook on Procedures and Criteria for Determining Refugee Status* (January 1992).
[110] See paragraphs 65 and 98 of the *UNHCR Handbook* on non-state agent persecution.
[111] Council, *Joint Position on Harmonised Application of the Term 'Refugee' in Article 1 of the 1951 Geneva Convention*, OJ L 63, 13 (March 1996), at 2-7.

instruments, in particular the ECHR. As such, it is not the subject to domestic discretion (as appears from the Irish statutory context). It is based on a state's obligations, rather than on a state's largesse.

On 12 September 2001, the Commission proposed a new measure on the common definition of a refugee and complementary protection.[112] The stated aim of the proposal is to create a 'level playing field' on asylum, thereby ending 'asylum shopping'. Ireland has decided to participate in the adoption of this measure.[113]

Article 9 on sources of harm and protection deals with the agent of persecution issue, and acknowledges that persecution can originate from non-state agents in circumstances where a state is unable or unwilling to provide effective protection. However, on the negative side, the proposal also accepts (in Article 10 on the internal protection alternative) that when part of the state from where the applicant comes is deemed safe, he or she has no claim for international protection.

Article 15 sets out the grounds of subsidiary protection as a well-founded fear of

(a) torture or inhuman or degrading treatment or punishment, or
(b) violation of a human right, sufficiently severe to engage a member state's international obligations or
(c) a threat to his or her life, safety or freedom as a result of indiscriminate violence arising in situations of armed conflict, or as a result of systematic or generalised violations of their human rights.

The proposal also contains specific rules on assessing claims for international protection and obliges member states to provide appropriate medical or other assistance to persons who have undergone torture, rape or other serious forms of psychological, physical or sexual violence.

There are also minimum rights and benefits to be enjoyed by the beneficiaries of both refugee and subsidiary protection status. In the main, the rights and benefits attached to both international protection statuses are the same. However, in recognition of the primacy of the Refugee Convention and of the fact that the need for subsidiary protection may in some cases be more temporary, entitlement to some important rights and benefits (such as access to work and to integration programmes) is incremental for beneficiaries of subsidiary protection.

The November 2002 JHA Council agreed on many (but not all) of the provisions concerning the definition of refugee status and subsidiary protection. Discussions on the *content* of the status began in December 2002 and the issue was before the JHA Council in February 2003, which failed to reach an agreement on the text.

---

[112] See Document 6733/03, 28 Feb 2003 (outcome of the Feb 2003 JHA Council). For the initial proposal, see COM (2001) 510.

[113] Response to parliamentary question posed by Conor Lenihan TD to the Minister for Justice, Equality and Law Reform, 12 February 2003. The UK has also opted in.

There are many outstanding issues relating to the content of the status, but the indication is that the Commission's proposals have been significantly watered down. In particular, the Commission's objective of providing equal status with nationals on a range of issues has been scaled back, with the Directive likely to provide instead only for equal status with other third-country nationals. For refugees, this is in accordance with the minimum standards in the Geneva Convention, but at least it will be easier to enforce those standards if they appear in the form of a Directive. For persons with subsidiary protection, any binding text would be an improvement on the current position at international or EU level. However, the Directive is vague about the permissible extent of access to employment and the status of family members and seems likely to set low standards as regards residence permits for all persons and as regards international movement and long-term residence status for beneficiaries of subsidiary protection status.

ii) Harmonisation of asylum procedures

In September 2000, the Commission proposed a Directive harmonising asylum procedures.[114] In chronological terms, this was the first Commission proposal in the post-Amsterdam era, though it failed to attain any degree of approval in Council. In June 2002, the Commission tabled a revised proposal, and this is the subject of on-going negotiations. The Council's working party began discussion of the revised proposal in late January 2003,[115] along with a parallel Austrian proposal for a Regulation designating all EU member states, applicant countries due to join in 2004 and Norway, Iceland and Switzerland as 'safe third countries'.[116] Ireland has opted into these deliberations and is taking an active role.[117]

iii) Harmonisation of reception conditions

The Commission proposed a harmonising Directive setting out minimum standards of reception for asylum seekers.[118] The proposal comprises five sets of rules dealing with

- the objective and scope of the proposal
- the reception conditions that should be granted, in principle, at all stages and in all kinds of asylum procedures

---

[114] Commission Proposal for a Council Directive on minimum standards on procedures in member states for granting and withdrawing refugee status, COM(2000)578, [2001] OJ C62 E/231.

[115] For the text of the proposal, see COM (2002) 326, June 2002.

[116] OJ 2003 C 17.

[117] Response to parliamentary question posed by Conor Lenihan TD to the Minister for Justice, Equality and Law Reform, 12 February 2003.

[118] COM(2001)181, [2001] OJ C213/286, 31 July 2001.

- the requirements (or minimum standards) of some reception conditions (material reception conditions and health care) which member states are required to ensure
- provisions for reducing or withdrawing access to some or all reception conditions as well as the possibility of review before a court of a decision on reduction or withdrawal of reception conditions
- several rules to ensure its complete implementation as well as the improvement of national reception systems.

This Directive was adopted formally in January 2003, following tortuous negotiations in the Council.[119] Member states have to implement the Directive by February 2005. However, Ireland has not opted into this provision.[120] The Directive applies to asylum applications proper, and not in the case of temporary protection for mass influx.[121] It enshrines only minimum standards.[122] It contains provisions on information exchange[123] and documentation.[124]

Although the Directive only once mentions the detention of asylum seekers,[125] Article 7 is tantamount to a legitimation of this practice, and its provisions require careful scrutiny. In particular, it permits member states to 'confine applicants to a particular place of residence in accordance with their national law'.[126] It also makes reference to free movement only within an 'assigned area'[127] with a procedure to grant 'temporary permission' to leave such place or residence.[128] Family unity is to be pre-served only 'as far as possible'[129] and medical screening is permissible.[130] As regards social rights, the provisions of the Directive reflect a consid-erable dilution of the Commission's proposal.[131] In particular, applicants may be required to pay for their maintenance and medical treatment and sanctions may be imposed for failure to disclose assets.[132]

---

[119] Council Directive 9/2003 of 27 January 2003 laying down minimum standards for the reception of asylum seekers [2003] OJ L31/18.

[120] Response to parliamentary question posed by Conor Lenihan TD to the Minister for Justice, Equality and Law Reform, 12 February 2003.

[121] Article 3(3).

[122] Article 4.

[123] Article 5.

[124] Article 6.

[125] Article 13(2) on 'General rules on material reception conditions and health care' refers to 'persons who are in detention'.

[126] Article 7(3).

[127] Article 7(1).

[128] Article 7(5).

[129] Article 8.

[130] Article 9.

[131] The educational rights of minors are set out in Article 10. The healthcare provisions in Article 15 relate to a minimum requirement of 'emergency care and essential treat-ment of illness' as well as a 'special needs' provision. The special needs provisions apply to persons referred to in Article 17, a non-exhaustive list including minors, unaccompanied minors, disabled people, elderly people, pregnant women and victims of violence, subject to individual needs assessment.

[132] Article 16(1)(b).

As regards the most controversial issue of the right to work for asylum seekers, Article 11 gives broad discretion to member states. They are required merely to specify a period of time after the asylum application during which the asylum applicant does *not* have access to the labour market.[133] If the first instance decision is not made within one year, and the delay is not attributable to the applicant, member states must 'decide the conditions for granting access to the labour market.[134] It would appear contrary to a purposive reading of this provision if member states were permitted to establish unnecessarily restrictive conditions to this access. However, its drafting may well preclude the provision's direct effect. In addition, member states may employ labour market policies based on a 'European preference'.[135] Other provisions grant even more leeway to member states, such as that on vocational training.[136]

Removal

i) Mutual recognition of expulsion decisions

An initiative of the French government has led to the adoption of a Directive on the mutual recognition of expulsion decisions.[137] The United Kingdom exercised its opt-in to the adoption and application of this measure on 18 October 2000. However, the Irish government did not do so. The Directive aims to ensure that member states recognise and enforce expulsion decisions of other states. The definition of 'expulsion decision' is widely drafted. Article 4 appears to require that there be a route to legally challenge such expulsion decisions (as is the case under Directive 64/221 in relation to Community nationals) but on careful reading this may be an illusory guarantee. It states that member states must ensure that the third country national be able to bring proceedings for a remedy against any expulsion decision, 'in accordance with the enforcing member state's legislation'. This reference to a right as guaranteed in national law may render the right dependent on national law, rather than based on the Directive itself.

The Council is currently considering a German proposal for a Directive on transit for expulsion, and a Commission proposal for a Decision on allocating the costs of expulsion.[138]

---

[133] Article 11(1).
[134] Article 11(3).
[135] Article 11(4).
[136] Article 12.
[137] Council Directive 2001/40/EC of 28 May 2001 on the mutual recognition of decisions on the expulsion of third country nationals [2001] OJ L149/34.
[138] OJ 2003 L 4/4; COM (2003) 49, Feb 2003.

iv) Readmission agreements

Refer to Section II*1*(b)(ii) *above*

SECTION III: Asylum Policy and the
Draft Constitutional Treaty for the European Union

A draft Constitutional Treaty for the European Union[139] was recently issued by the Convention on the Future of Europe. The latter is a drafting body established by the member states of the European Union, comprising representatives of national governments (of member states and candidate countries), national parliaments (of member states and candidate countries), the European Parliament and the European Commission, chaired by former French President, Valery Giscard d'Estaing.[140] The Convention's mandate derives from the Declaration on the Future of Europe attached to the Treaty of Nice, and the Laeken Declaration of the European Council. After over a year of deliberations, the draft Constitutional Treaty was issued but its status remains uncertain. The Convention on the Future of Europe is in the final stages of its deliberations. Thereafter, an intergovernmental conference will be convened in 2004, in order to finalise the drafting, and approve the Constitutional Treaty. A national ratification must take place in Ireland, entailing the inevitable popular referendum.

Notwithstanding the uncertain status of the draft Constitution, it warrants scrutiny here. In particular, the incorporation of the EU Charter of Fundamental Rights and the increase in judicial control provided may hold the potential to develop a more human rights based EU asylum policy. Other aspects of the draft Constitution will also impact on asylum policy, in particular the changes to lawmaking procedures. However, as these are of particularly uncertain status, they are not considered in detail here. One proposed institutional change that should however be noted is that the lawmaking procedures in the asylum field are to entail co-decision between the Council and the European Parliament, with the Council acting unanimously. This development would finally break the legacy of intergovernmentalism, as detailed in Section I*1* above.

1 The EU Charter of Fundamental Rights (EUCFR)

i) Paradoxical nature

The Charter is currently non-binding – it was jointly solemnly declared at Nice in December 2000 by the Commission, Council and Parliament.

---

[139] *Draft Treaty Establishing a Constitution for Europe*, CONV 820/1/03 REV 1, Brussels, 27 June 2003.

[140] For details, see <european-convention.eu.int/>.

However, it has now been incorporated into the draft Constitutional Treaty for the European Union, as Part II thereof.

To understand the Charter, a number of preliminary points on the Charter's peculiar nature must be made. The Cologne European Council created a mandate for the drafting of a Charter to make existing protection of fundamental rights at EU level 'more visible' – a limited ambition. In contrast, the drafting method was such as to guarantee innovative outcomes. A Convention of national government representatives and parliamentarians (European and national) was established and both its composition and method of deliberation were novel. In some respects, it reflected a politicisation of Europe's constitutionalisation, previously dominated by judicial influence. In addition, for the first time, the task of drafting an EU foundational text was relinquished from the hands of member state governments – the masters of the treaties – thereby relinquishing some of their constitutive function. Although this was very much a partial relinquishing, in that the remit of the Convention was defined by member states with the final decision as to the status of the Charter remaining in governmental hands, the alteration of the notion of constitutive function had resonance. The result reflects this initial paradox.

Frequently, justiciable bills of rights are 'short and dark', characterised by indeterminate language granting wide interpretative scope to the judges concerned. While the Charter shares these features in some respects, certain provisions seek to render the Charter's provisions dense and embedded. These provisions include in particular the Charter's General Provisions (and the proposed amendments thereto), which purport to clarify the scope and effects of the instrument.[141] The provisions aim to clarify the scope of the Charter,[142] its links with existing instruments[143] and its preservation of the status quo as regards the extent of EU competences.[144] These preliminary points reveal the paradoxical

---

[141] It should be noted that these final provisions were amended by the Convention on the Future of Europe in light of the Report to the Convention on the Future of Europe of the Working Group *Incorporation of the Charter/ accession to the ECHR*, CONV 354/02 WG II 16, Brussels, 22 October 2002, available at <http://register.consilium.eu.int/pdf/en/02/cv00/00354en2.pdf>.

[142] Article 51 of the Charter clarifies that it is addressed to the Union, and to member states 'only when they are implementing Union law'.

[143] Article 52(2) of the Charter provides that rights in the Charter that are covered by other parts of the [Treaties/draft Constitutional Treaty] 'shall be exercised under the conditions and within the limits defined by these relevant parts'. Article 52(3) of the Charter provides that where Charter rights 'correspond to' ECHR rights, 'the meaning and scope of those rights shall be the same as those laid down by the [ECHR]'. Article 52(4) provides that where rights are derived from the 'constitutional traditions common to the member states, those rights shall be interpreted in harmony with those traditions'.

[144] Artcile 51(2) of the Charter provides that 'This Charter does not extend the field of application of Union law beyond the powers of the Union or establish any new power or task for the Union, or modify powers and tasks defined in other parts of the Constitution'.

nature of the Charter. It is at once the embodiment of existing protections and yet replete with all the promise of innovative development.

ii) Asylum-related provisions

Article 18 of the Charter is entitled 'The Right to Asylum' and provides:

> The right to asylum shall be guaranteed with due respect for the rules of the Geneva Convention of 28 July 1951 and the Protocol of 31 January 1967 relating to the status of refugees and in accordance with the Treaty establishing the European Community.

The interpretative note[145] to the Article states, 'this Article is in line with the Protocol on Asylum attached to the Treaty' (ie the Spanish Protocol). The interpretative notes to the Charter were originally without legal status, and were described as without 'legal value and ... simply intended to clarify the provisions'.[146] However, in this respect, the draft Constitutional Treaty[147] contains a highly significant change. Although the Convention on the Future of Europe chose not to alter the drafting of the substantive provisions of the Charter, it did alter the final provisions (Articles 51–54 of the Charter) and the preambular language. Concerning the latter, the new version of the Charter (contained in Part II of the draft Constitutional Treaty) provides:

> [T]he Charter will be interpreted by the courts of the Union and the member states with due regard to the explanations prepared at the instigation of the Praesidium of the Convention which drafted the Convention.

This seems to preclude a fundamental rights argument based on Article 18 of the Charter, in order to overcome the restrictive effects of the Spanish Protocol.

Also relevant to the area of asylum is Article 19 of the Charter, which provides the following.

1) Collective expulsions are prohibited.
2) No one may be removed, expelled or extradited to a State where there is a serious risk that he or she would be subjected to the death penalty, torture or other inhuman or degrading treatment or punishment.

---

[145] It should be noted that the original explanations were also updated by the Convention on the Future of Europe. *Updated Explanations relating to the text of the Charter of Fundamental Rights.* CONV 828/03 Brussels, 9 July 2003.

[146] This is noted on the contents page of the version of the Charter: *Charter of Fundamental Rights of the European Union: Explanations relating to the complete text of the Charter* (Office for Official Publications of the European Communities, Luxembourg, 2001).

[147] *Draft Treaty establishing a Constitution for Europe*, CONV 820/1/03 REV 1, Brussels, 27 June 2003.

Paragraph (1) reflects Article 4 of Protocol 4 to the ECHR. Paragraph 2 is said to incorporate ECHR caselaw, in particular *Ahmed v. Austria*[148] and *Soering*.[149] However, it appears to go further than the European Court of Human Rights' position in that it prohibits removal to face the death penalty *per se*, rather than the death row phenomenon as 'inhuman and degrading treatment.' Article 19 of the Charter is however consonant with Article 2(2) EUCFR which provides that 'No one shall be condemned to the death penalty or executed'. These provisions effectively give 'complementary protection' a constitutionally protected status in the EU, a welcome development. Thus it is apparent that at least the core of the rights to asylum and complementary protection are protected.

Many other provisions of the Charter have implications for the Community's legislative programme under Title IV. Traditional fair procedure guarantees are included,[150] which must guide the EU in adopting measures on asylum procedures. Of greater potential significance are the socio-economic rights enshrined in the Charter.[151] For example, Article 15(1) of the Charter provides that 'Everyone has the right to engage in work and to pursue a freely chosen or accepted occupation'. How is the restriction on the right to work in the Reception Standards Directive to be reconciled with this guarantee? There is at least an arguable constitutional challenge to be brought to those restrictions. Similarly, Article 35 EUCFR provides 'Everyone has the right to preventive health care and the right to benefit from medical treatment under the conditions established by national laws and practices'.[152] Again, this guarantee could be the source of a legal challenge to the validity of the Reception Conditions Directive's provisions on health care. Naturally, there is much detail to be worked out in relation to such challenges,[153] but my argument at this stage is that the Charter may provide a useful baseline for a human rights based asylum policy,

---

[148] (1997) 24 E.H.R.R 278.

[149] (1989 11 E.H.R.R 439.

[150] Articles 47-50 of the Charter.

[151] For a general discussion see Costello, C. (ed), *Fundamental Social Rights – Current European Legal Protection and the Challenge of the EU Charter of Fundamental Rights* (ICEL No. 28, 2001) and Hervey, T. and Kenner, J. (eds), *Economic and Social Rights under the Charter of Fundamental Rights of the European Union* (Hart Publishing, Oxford, 2003).

[152] The reference to 'national laws and practices' may be problematic, in that it may be read as suggesting that the right depends entirely on the discretion of national authorities for its realisation. However, a more 'constitutional' reading would be that the right is primarily to be realised through national policy choices, simply reiterating the current division of competences in the area of public health between the EU and the member states.

[153] One of the most intriguing legal questions is how the Court should review the Directives in light of the fact that these enshrine only minimum requirements. The best response would seem to be that even though the Directive enshrines only minimum requirements, they must still comply with the Charter's fundamental rights provisions.

where the need to reach political compromise may not lead to the dilution of fundamental rights guarantees.

2 Judicial Control

From an asylum policy standpoint, the other significant change to be introduced is that the jurisdiction of the Court of Justice will be extended by the draft Constitutional Treaty. This change comes about due to the effective abolition of the 'pillar' structure that emerged with the Treaty on European Union. Instead, the activities of the Union as a whole are dealt with under the same basic framework. As a result, in general, the jurisdiction of the Court is the same throughout the Union's activities.[154] In the asylum context, this means that the current restrictions on the Court's jurisdiction enshrined in Article 68 EC are no longer applicable, a very welcome development from the point of view of the rule of law and fundamental rights protection.

It was also anticipated that the Charter and the draft Constitution would provoke a re-thinking of the restrictive *locus standi* rules to bring direct challenges to EU measures, under Article 230(4) EC. At present, if an individual wants to challenge the validity of an EU measure, for example a measure in the asylum policy field, arguing that it infringes her fundamental rights, she must demonstrate 'direct and individual' concern. This standing requirement in effect precludes challenges to generally applicable measures and, in effect, depends on a closed defined category of affected individuals. Thus, for example, if the EU legislated to deny asylum seekers freedom of expression, this could not be challenged directly, because the category of affected individuals is open and ill-defined. The answer to this apparent lacuna in legal protection is that an individual can bring an *indirect* challenge via a national court. If the national judge can be convinced that the validity of the EU measure is dubious, then she is obliged to refer the matter to the ECJ for adjudication. However, this indirect route is precarious, because it depends on the accessibility and receptiveness of the national judge and legal system to the challenge. Despite many persuasive critiques of this jurisdictional system, most notably by Advocate General Jacobs in the *UPA* case, the Court of Justice has refused to countenance a fundamental re-think of the standing requirements. At the Convention on the Future of Europe, the current system was also, lamentably, left intact. The only significant change is that the draft Constitution emphasises that the national judicial system must facilitate the bringing of indirect challenges to the validity of Union measures. Article I-28 of the draft Constitutional Treaty thus provides, 'member states shall provide rights of appeal sufficient to ensure effective legal protection in the field of Union law'.

---

[154] With the notable remaining exception of the Foreign and Security Policy domain.

CHAPTER 4

Sanctuary in Strasbourg: the Implications of the European Convention on Human Rights on Irish Asylum Law and Policy

Suzanne Egan

Introduction

Domestic refugee law and policy is derived from and shaped by the state's international obligations in this arena.[1] The influence of international obligations is perhaps most obviously manifested in the Refugee Act 1996, several provisions of which are clearly based on key obligations contained in the Convention Relating to the Status of Refugees 1951.[2] While that Convention is properly regarded as the 'Magna Carta' of refugees,[3] ironically many of the more subtle elements of international refugee protection may be derived from an international instrument which does not even mention the term 'refugee' or 'asylum seeker', that is the European Convention on Human Rights 1950 (ECHR). Contracting states to that Convention are obliged to guarantee a broad range of civil and political rights to all persons in their jurisdiction[4] – including refugees and asylum seekers.[5] Unlike the Refugee Convention, however, the advantage of the ECHR is that the substantive catalogue of rights contained therein is reinforced by a very well-developed supervisory machinery involving the European

---

[1] The long title to the Refugee Act 1996 proclaims it as an Act to give effect to *inter alia* the Convention Relating to the Status of Refugees 1951 [hereinafter Refugee Convention] and its 1967 Protocol (1996, No. 17).

[2] See, for example, section 2 which substantially replicates the definition of refugee status in Article 1 A (2) of the Refugee Convention and section 5 which does the same as regards Article 33(1) of the Convention.

[3] J. Read, *Magna Carta for Refugees* (New York, 1953).

[4] Article 1 of the Convention provide that: 'The High Contracting Parties shall secure to *everyone within their jurisdiction* the rights and freedoms defined in Section 1'.

[5] Article 1 of the Convention does not contain any limitation as to nationality: *Austria v. Italy* (Application 788/60) (1961) Y.B.E.C.H.R. vol. 4 at 16.

Court of Human Rights in Strasbourg. Established by the Convention, the Court has jurisdiction to issue legally binding judgments in individual cases as regards the implementation by the contracting states of the Convention guarantees.[6] Failure to abide by the terms of the Convention may result in a contracting state being found in breach of international law with tangible political consequences.[7]

Ireland is one of the 45 contracting states to the Convention and was in fact the first state to recognise the compulsory jurisdiction of the European Court of Human Rights in 1953. Domestic implementation has until now, however, been limited to ensuring that domestic law conforms to the requirements of the guaranteed rights without enabling individuals to rely on those rights directly in domestic proceedings. However, in July 2003, the Oireachtas passed into law the European Convention on Human Rights Act 2003 which is professed to be aimed at enabling 'further effect to be given', subject to the Constitution, to certain provisions of the Convention in Irish law. It will further incorporate the ECHR into Irish law.[8] The legal and practical implications are discussed at the end of this chapter.

The purpose of this chapter is two-fold: first to present an overview of the jurisprudence of the European Court of Human Rights in regard to five discrete areas of asylum law and policy – protection against *refoulement*, detention, family unity, reception practices and remedies. This analysis also serves to highlight aspects of domestic law or policy that might be contentious under the Convention based on the jurisprudence of the Court. The second section of the chapter attempts to predict the immediate impact which the 2003 Act may have in terms of domestic asylum law and policy.

1 Protection from *refoulement*

Probably the most notorious example of innovative treaty interpretation in the human rights field is the jurisprudence of the European Court of Human Rights[9] in relation to Article 3 of the Convention, particularly as regards the rights of asylum seekers. That Article provides that: 'No one shall be subject to torture, or to inhuman or degrading treatment or punishment'.

---

[6]   Article 34 of the Convention provides for the right of individual petition to the Court. An inter-state complaint may also be initiated by the terms of Article 33.

[7]   The Committee of Ministers is charged with the task of enforcing judgments of the European Court of Human Rights under Article 46 of the Convention. In this respect, the most powerful weapon in the arsenal of the Committee of Ministers resides in Article 8 of the Statute of the Council of Europe. Article 8 provides that the Committee of Ministers may expel any member state from the Council of Europe for violation of Article 3 of that Statute which in turn requires respect for the rule of law and the protection of human rights and fundamental freedoms.

[8]   European Convention on Human Rights Act 2003, No. 20 of 2003.

[9]   Hereinafter, 'the Court'.

This is an absolute right in the sense that no derogation can be made from it under the terms of Article 15 of the Convention in times of war or public emergency.[10] In other words, there can never be any excuse for treatment in violation of Article 3. In the seminal case of *Soering v. United Kingdom*,[11] the European Court of Human Rights held that the extradition of a fugitive by a contracting state 'may give rise to a violation by that state of Article 3 where there are *substantial grounds* for believing that the person, if extradited, faces a real risk of being subjected to torture or inhuman or degrading treatment or punishment'.[12] The case involved a German national who was being detained in Britain, pending extradition to the US where he faced capital murder charges in the State of Virginia. The essence of his claim, which was accepted by the Court, was that if the UK were to extradite him to the US, it would be acting in violation of Article 3 by exposing him to inhuman or degrading treatment within the meaning of Article 3. The 'inhuman or degrading treatment' at issue in this case was the 'death row phenomenon' in operation in the State of Virginia in which he might have been detained for some 6-8 years.

The significance of the judgment lay in the Court's teleological or purposive interpretation of the Article 3 guarantee. The UK government tried to argue that it should not be held responsible for treatment which may occur outside its jurisdiction. In response, the Court held that Article 3 must be interpreted in such a way that its safeguards would be 'practical and effective'.[13] This interpretation emphasises the absolute nature of the Article 3 guarantee because it involves assigning responsibility for a breach of the Convention to a state for taking action which might, *as a direct consequence,* expose a person to the treatment proscribed by the Article. While an obvious implication of the judgment in *Soering* was that state parties to the ECHR would now have to bear Article 3 in mind when considering extradition requests, it also raised the question of whether the same principle could be applied in other contexts, most notably in the context of asylum and refugee claims.[14]

This is in fact what happened in the subsequent judgment of the Court in the case of *Cruz Varas v. Sweden*.[15] In that case, the Court

---

[10] Article 15(2).

[11] (1989) 11 E.H.R.R. 439.

[12] *Ibid.* paragraph 91 of the Court's judgment.

[13] *Ibid.* para. 88.

[14] For further analysis of the decision in *Soering*, see generally: M. O'Boyle, 'Extradition and Expulsion Under the European Convention on Human Rights: Reflections on the Soering Case' in J.O'Reilly (ed.), *Human Rights and Constitutional Law* (Dublin: The Roundhall Press, 1992), p. 93; Lillich, 'The Soering Case' 85 *A.J.I.L.* 128; and S. Egan, 'Human Rights Considerations in Extradition and Expulsion Cases: The European Convention on Human Rights Revisited', (1998) 2 *Contemporary Issues in Irish Law and Politics* 188.

[15] (1992) 14 E.H.R.R. 1.

held that the substantive test for breach of the Convention which it had laid down in *Soering's* case applied to expulsion decisions and *a fortiori* in cases of actual expulsion.[16] In other words, a contracting state would be liable for a breach of Article 3 if it expelled an alien to a country where there are substantial grounds for believing that the person faces a real risk of torture, inhuman or degrading treatment or punishment.[17] This result was reaffirmed in the case of *Vilvarajah v. United Kingdom*[18] and is at this stage a well-established principle of Article 3 jurisprudence.[19] In the later case of *Chahal v. UK*[20] the Court further clarified that the guarantee articulated in *Cruz Varas* and *Vilvarajah* is not circumscribed in any way by the activities of the

---

[16] It should be noted that in cases of this kind, where the applicant claims a threatened breach of Article 3 on the basis of an expulsion or deportation that is imminent, on receipt of an application, the Court will normally request the respondent state under Rule 39 of its Rules of Procedure not to expel or extradite the applicant until it has had an opportunity to examine the application. In the *Cruz Varas* case, the Court held by a narrow majority of ten votes to nine that the Convention did not provide for the power of the former Commission of Human Rights to order binding interim measures of this nature. In the recent case of *Mamatkulov and Abdurasulovic v. Turkey* (Court Judgment 6 February 2003), however, a Chamber of the Court held that the failure by a state to abide by a Rule 39 indication issued by the European Court of Human Rights would give rise to a violation of the right of individual petition in Article 34 of the Convention. The Court in this case distinguished the decision in *Cruz Varas* on the basis that the Court had not considered its own power to order interim measures in that case but rather had confined itself to examining the Commission's power.

[17] *Supra* note 15 at paras. 69-70.

[18] (1992) 14 E.H.R.R. 248.

[19] A similar principle may be read into the terms of Article 2 of the Convention, which guarantees the right to life, insofar as expulsion to a state where the applicant runs a real risk of unlawful killing would doubtless violate that provision. The Court has also indicated that removal to a state in which a person would be at risk of an unfair trial might violate Article 6 of the Convention which guarantees that right: 'The Court does not exclude that an issue might exceptionally be raised under Article 6 by an extradition decision in circumstances where the fugitive has suffered or risks suffering a flagrant denial of fair trial in the requesting country': *Soering v. United Kingdom, supra* note 15 at para.113.

[20] (1997) 23 E.H.R.R. 413. The applicant was a Sikh separatist leader who was detained in the UK on grounds of national security pending deportation to India. The government alleged that he had been involved in terrorist activities in India and elsewhere. He denied these allegations. His application for asylum was refused in the UK and he remained in detention for some four and a half years while various challenges were being mounted against the decision by the UK to deport him to India. He claimed, amongst other things, that deportation to India would expose him to ill-treatment in violation of Article 3. The Court held that Article 3 was applicable to the facts. What is significant about this judgment is that the Court rejected the government's claim that the perceived threat which the applicant posed to national security in the UK was a factor to be taken into consideration in considering the application of Article 3. The Court held that the prohibition in Article 3 was absolute. The activities of the person in question, however undesirable or dangerous, cannot be a material consideration. Therefore, in the Court's view, it was not necessary for it even to consider the government's allegations about the applicant's activities or the perceived threat to national security.

person in question. Activities that are undesirable or dangerous cannot be a material consideration.[21]

As the Court itself recognised in the judgments, its interpretation of Article 3 in these cases yields a broader basis for protection than that which exists under the 1951 Convention Relating to the Status of Refugees.[22] Article 33(1) of the latter Convention, to which Ireland is also a party, provides that:

> No Contracting State shall expel or return (refouler) a refugee in any manner whatsoever to the frontiers of territories where his life or freedom would be threatened on account of his race, religion, nationality, membership of a particular social group or political opinion.

Article 33(2) creates an exception to that obligation in respect of someone whom the state has 'reasonable grounds for regarding as a danger to the security of the country in which he is residing'. The Court's interpretation of Article 3 of the ECHR is, in principle at least, broader than the guarantee of *non-refoulement* in Article 33 of the Refugee Convention because it can be triggered whether or not the applicant's freedom would be threatened on grounds of race, religion, nationality, membership of a particular social group or political opinion. Moreover, Article 3 does not contain an implicit proviso such as the one made explicit in Article 33(2) of the Refugee Convention.

Further clarification of the parameters of Article 3 protection was provided in the case of *Ahmed v. Austria*[23] and *HLR v. France*[24] in which the Court indicated that the failure or absence of state protection from serious harm threatened by non-state agents of persecution can give rise to a violation of Article 3. In other words, an applicant does not have to show that the threat of ill-treatment emanates from the government.[25]

While the development of these principles is no doubt encouraging, on the other hand it must be noted that asylum seekers who claim the benefit of the Article 3 principle face a very high standard of proof. As

---

[21] '…[t]he activities of the individual in question, however undesirable or dangerous, cannot be a material consideration': *Ibid.* para. 80.

[22] 'The protection afforded by Article 3 is thus wider than that provided by Articles 32 and 33 of the United Nations 1951 Convention Relating to the Status of Refugees': *Ibid.*

[23] (1997) 24 E.H.R.R. 278.

[24] (1998) 26 E.H.R.R. 29.

[25] The applicant in *HLR* challenged his deportation by France to Colombia on the basis that he would be exposed to a real risk of vengeance by drug traffickers in Colombia over whom the Colombian government had no control. The Court held that in order to establish a claim in these circumstances, the applicant would have to show that there was a real risk, and that the authorities of the receiving state are not able to obviate that risk by providing appropriate protection: *Ibid.* para. 40. On the facts, however, unfortunately for the applicant, the Court was not convinced that the alleged risk was real in his case.

the Court made clear from the outset in *Soering* and *Cruz Varas*, the standard of proof required of the applicant is that of showing 'substantial grounds' that there is a real risk of ill-treatment contrary to Article 3 in the receiving state. This evidential test is probably higher than the standard normally demanded by national tribunals implementing the refugee definition and Article 33 of the Refugee Convention in national law.[26] Normally, in order to satisfy the refugee definition and claim the protection of Article 33, an applicant will be required to show that there is a 'reasonable risk' or a 'serious possibility' of harm in the receiving country. But here, the standard demanded by the European court appears to be pitched very high. Indeed, it is almost a 'balance of probabilities' type standard.[27]

How has the Court applied this test in practice? In the *Cruz Varas* case, the Court found that the applicant had not satisfied the substantive test on the facts. He had already been expelled from Sweden to Chile where he claimed he would be persecuted on account of his political opinion. The Court found that he had failed to show substantial grounds of a real risk of treatment in violation of Article 3. Essentially, the Court disbelieved the substance of his story and, in any case, was satisfied that the political climate in Chile had changed. In the later case of *Vilvarajah v. United Kingdom*[28] the Court held that the expulsion of a group of young, Tamil, male Sri Lankans back to Sri Lanka did not violate Article 3. The Court did not believe that, in light of all the circumstances known to the government at the time of the expulsion, the risk of ill treatment had been substantiated. It looked at improvements in the situation in the country at the time. It also took the view that the applicants' position was no worse than that of other male Tamils. Here, the Court reiterated that there must be a real risk, as opposed to a 'mere possibility'.

This latter decision is open to criticism because of the Court's apparent willingness to defer to findings of the national authorities – especially the finding that the applicants' position was no worse than that of other male Tamils. This point is repeated by the Court in the later case of *HLR v. France,*[29] in the case of the Colombian applicant who feared expulsion by France to Colombia. In deciding that there was no violation of Article 3 on the facts, the Court noted that the applicant's situation was no worse than that of other Colombians

---

[26] '... claimants must produce 'concrete evidence' of a 'real risk' of torture and so forth. Concrete evidence has not been defined, but a 'real risk' is clearly more than a 'reasonable risk' or a 'serious possibility', such as is accepted by many national tribunals and appears to require that the likelihood of relevant prejudicial treatment be established as more likely than not, that is, on a balance of probabilities or more': G. Goodwin-Gill, *The Refugee in International Law*, at 320.

[27] *Ibid.*

[28] *Supra* note 18.

[29] *Supra* note 24.

generally. Again, the Court seems to be demanding a particularly high standard of proof from individuals – ie a completely individualised set of facts. Thus, while the Court has indeed been creative in reading this right into the Convention, it appears that it has set a very high threshold for individual applicants to satisfy in practice.[30]

Humanitarian considerations

In the case of *D v. United Kingdom*,[31] the Court once again appeared to stretch the application of Article 3 beyond established parameters. The case concerned the proposed removal by the United Kingdom of a convicted drug courier to his country of origin, St Kitts. The applicant was dying of AIDS and claimed that Article 3 would be violated if he were returned to St Kitts on account of the fact that he had no accommodation, family, moral or medical support in that country and no access to medical treatment. The Court had to decide whether there was a real risk that his removal would be contrary to the standards in Article 3 in view of his present medical condition. In its decision on the merits, the Court noted that the applicant was now entirely reliant on the medical and palliative care which the United Kingdom had been providing to him since 1994. It also noted that he had entered the final stages of the illness and it was not disputed that his removal to St Kitts would hasten his death. With this context in mind, the Court held that although the conditions awaiting him in St Kitts did not in themselves breach Article 3 standards, his removal at this stage would hasten his death and expose him to a risk of dying under most distressing circumstances and thus to inhuman treatment in violation of Article 3.

The Court was clearly keen to stress, however, that its judgment should not be read in a wider context and that it was clearly confined to the very particular facts of the case. In a passage which seems to have been calculated at warding off prospective opportunistic applications, the Court stated that:

> ...[a]liens who have served their prison sentences and are subject to expulsion cannot in principle claim any entitlement to remain on the territory of a Contracting State in order to benefit from medical, social or other forms of assistance provided by the expelling State during their stay. But in the exceptional circumstances, and in view of the humanitarian considerations at stake, the implementation of the decision to remove would violate Article 3.[32]

---

[30] Note the positive decision made by the Court on the facts of the case in *Hilal v. United Kingdom*, 6 March 2001(2001) 33 E.H.R.R. 2.
[31] (1997) 24 E.H.R.R 423.
[32] *Ibid.* para. 54.

The subsequent judgment of the Court in the case of *Bensaid v. United Kingdom*[33] confirms that the threshold to be satisfied in cases of this kind is a very high one indeed. In that case, the applicant alleged that his proposed expulsion from the United Kingdom to Algeria placed him at risk, *inter alia*, of inhuman and degrading treatment contrary to Article 3. The applicant was a schizophrenic suffering from a psychotic illness. He had been living in the United Kingdom for some six years before difficulties with his immigration status resulted in a decision by the United Kingdom to remove him to Algeria. At the time of the Court's consideration of his case, he had been living in the United Kingdom for some eleven years. For almost the entire duration of this time, the applicant had been receiving free medication which had enabled him to manage his symptoms. His complaint was that if he were returned to Algeria, he would no longer be able to obtain the relevant medication free as an outpatient. His only option would be to be admitted as an in-patient in a hospital some 75-80km from his family home. Thereafter, there would be a possibility of the drug being made available to him as an outpatient on payment, although the cost on such basis would likely be prohibitive.[34] The applicant's physician had stated her opinion in the domestic proceedings that if returned to Algeria, there was a substantial likelihood of significant and lasting adverse effects on his mental well-being and even that there was a potential risk that he would either take his own life or that of another person.[35]

The Court found that the implementation of the decision to remove the applicant to Algeria would not violate Article 3 of the Convention. In its view, the risk that the applicant would suffer a deterioration in his condition if returned to Algeria, and the risk that he would not receive adequate support or care in that country, was 'to a large extent speculative'.[36] Likewise, the evidence provided as regards difficulties in travelling to the hospital where he might receive treatment and the effects on his health of such factors was also held to be speculative.[37] Accordingly, while the Court accepted the seriousness of the

---

[33] (2001) 33 E.H.R.R. 10.

[34] The Court also found as a fact that other medication, used in the management of mental illness, was likely to be available: *Ibid.* para. 36.

[35] In the words of the physician, it was '...[h]ighly likely that stressful life events such as deportation together with the more stressful environment he would be likely to encounter in Algeria would trigger exacerbation of his symptoms...If he were unable to obtain appropriate help, if he began to relapse I think that there would be a great risk that his deterioration would be very great and he would be at risk of acting in obedience to the hallucination telling him to harm himself or others...Thus I do think that there is a substantial likelihood that forcible repatriation would result in significant and lasting adverse effect': *Ibid.* para. 21.

[36] *Ibid.* para. 39.

[37] *Ibid.*

applicant's medical condition, it did not believe that there was a sufficiently real risk of ill-treatment, given the high threshold set by Article 3 in such cases. To wit, the applicant's situation was distinguishable from the 'exceptional circumstances' of the *D* case.[38]

Given the medical evidence in the case that there was a high likelihood of deterioration in the applicant's mental condition if deported, and the uncertainty as regards the possibility of appropriate treatment for the applicant in Algeria, this decision is clearly open to criticism. Arguably, the judgment is an obvious attempt to confine the application of the principle in the *D* case to the horrendous type of circumstances contemplated there.[39] A more benign analysis of the decision, however, is that the judgment 'provides helpful guidance on where the Court is likely to draw the line in Article 3 cases'.[40]

Threats to 'physical or moral integrity'

Before leaving this issue, it is worth noting a more recent development in the Court's jurisprudence under Article 8 of the Convention that may be of benefit to asylum seekers who fail to reach the threshold required by Article 3. Article 8 of the Convention guarantees, amongst other things, the 'right to respect for private and family life'. In *X and Y v. The Netherlands*[41] and in *Costello-Roberts v. U.K*[42] the Court has recognised that interferences with the moral and physical integrity of an individual may give rise to an interference with the right to respect for private life. The *Costello-Roberts* judgment indicates that it is a difficult test to satisfy. In that case the Court rejected that the slippering of an eight year old boy with a rubber soled gym-shoe was an 'interference with physical or moral integrity'. Nonetheless, this principle may be of relevance to asylum seekers in that an asylum seeker who fails to show a substantial risk of 'degrading' treatment, may nonetheless be able to show that expulsion would give rise to a substantial risk of an interference with his or her physical or moral integrity.

This argument was considered by the Court with disappointing

---

[38] *Ibid.* paragraph 40.
[39] The somewhat anguished reasoning of Judges Bratza, Costa and Greve in their separate opinion (in which they also found no violation of Article 3) would seem to support this critique. Even though they rule out a violation of Article 3 on the basis that the case does not disclose the same exceptional circumstances of the *D* case, the trio held that there existed '...powerful and compelling humanitarian considerations in the present case which would justify and merit reconsideration by the national authorities of the decision to remove the applicant to Algeria': *Ibid.* para. 16 of the separate opinion.
[40] Case Comment [2001] E.H.R.L.R 584-587 at 587.
[41] (1985) 8 E.H.R.R. 235.
[42] (1995) 19 E.H.R.R. 112.

results in the *Bensaid* case.[43] While the Court in that case explicitly
stated that the preservation of mental stability is an 'indispensable
precondition to the effective enjoyment of the right to respect for
private life',[44] the Court, quite incomprehensibly, refused to accept that
deportation would substantially have affected the applicant's moral
integrity. Moreover, it held that any interference with private life in
the United Kingdom resulting from the dislocation associated with
deportation was justified as being necessary in a democratic society for
the aims of protecting the economic well-being of the country and the
prevention of disorder or crime.[45] In the words of one commentator,
the judgment '...provides legal advisers with no guidance as to when
such an interference will have occurred'.[46]

Procedural irregularity and Article 3

The Court has indicated that Article 3 requires substantive examination
of an applicant's asylum claim and that resort to technical or procedural devices that put a person at risk of *refoulement* will breach
Article 3. In *Jabari v. Turkey*[47] an Iranian national claimed a violation of
Article 3 in respect of Turkey's decision to deport her from its territory
back to Iran where she claimed she would be prosecuted for adultery
and subjected to inhuman punishment. Her asylum application in
Turkey had been rejected for being 'out of time'. Turkish law required
that asylum claims must be lodged within five days of arrival in
Turkey.[48] Having regard to the evidence submitted with respect to the
treatment of women found guilty of adultery in Iran, the Court held
that the deportation, if executed, would be in breach of Article 3. In
reaching this decision, it held that the automatic and mechanical application of such a short time-limit for submitting an asylum application
was at variance with the fundamental values in Article 3.[49] This position
had been exacerbated by the fact that judicial review of her claim had

---

[43] *Supra* note 33. The Court also declared admissible a complaint which raised this
argument in *Hilal v. United Kingdom*, Application no. 45276/99, 8 February 2000:
http://www.dhcour.coe.fr. However, in its judgment on the merits, the Court held
that it was not necessary to examine the substance of the complaint on Article 8
grounds since a positive violation on the facts was found to exist on the basis of
Article 3: (2001) 33 E.H.R.R. 2.

[44] *Supra* note 33 at para. 14.

[45] *Ibid.* para. 15. Compare the reasoning of this decision with the Court's judgment in
Berrehab v. Netherlands, infra note 77.

[46] *Supra* note 40 at 587.

[47] Judgment of the European Court of Human Rights, Application No. 40035/98 (11 July
2000) (2001) INLR 136.

[48] The UNHCR in Turkey had recognised her to be 'refugee'. This determination had
the effect that Turkey would normally grant such a person a residence permit until
she or he was resettled in a third country, but since she had not claimed asylum on
time, this meant that she was liable for deportation: *Ibid.* para. 29.

[49] *Ibid.* para. 40.

been limited to considering the formal legality of the deportation rather than the substance of the applicant's fears.

This judgment might well be a cause for concern amongst Irish policy makers in the light of recent proposals to amend the Refugee Act 1996. Section 7 of the Immigration Act 2003,[50] which amends the Refugee Act 1996, provides for very severe consequences where an asylum seeker fails to inform the Refugee Applications Commissioner of his or her address within five working days of the making of an asylum application. It provides that the applicant's application will be deemed to be 'withdrawn'; and further, that a determination of *refusal* to grant refugee status may be made in respect of applications deemed to be 'withdrawn'.[51] A refusal of refugee status in those circumstances will not be subject to appeal.[52] Similar provisions apply in the context of persons who fail to present for a first-instance interview or appeal hearing.[53] Applying the logic of the Court's decision in *Jabari* to these new provisions of the Refugee Act 1996, inserted by the Immigration Act 2003, similar concerns may be raised about the possibility of reject-ing an asylum claim simply on the basis of a failure by an applicant to fulfil procedural requirements.

The Dublin Convention

The Court has also had occasion to consider the responsibility of the contracting states under Article 3 in implementing the provisions of the Dublin Convention 1990.[54] That Convention forms part of the European Union's strategy for the achievement of the internal market as regards free movement of persons. It is aimed at avoiding multiple applications for asylum being lodged in the territory of the member states. To this end, the Convention provides, *inter alia*, that an asylum request will be examined by one of the member states and sets forth criteria for determining which state shall be responsible for determining the asylum request.[55]

Implementation of the Convention may be problematic in situations where the contracting states to that Convention apply different substantive rules in determining asylum requests. What are the state's obligations under Article 3 of the ECHR in implementing the Dublin Convention? This issue was faced by the Court in the recent case of

---

[50] No. 26 of 2003.
[51] Section 9(4A) Refugee Act, as amended.
[52] Section 13(2)(c) Refugee Act, as amended.
[53] Sections 11(10) and 16(2A) Refugee Act, as amended.
[54] *Convention Determining the State responsible for Examining Applications for Asylum Lodged in One of the Members States of the European Communities* (Dublin 15 June 1990).
[55] Section 22 of the Refugee Act 1996 implements the provisions of the Convention in Irish law.

T.I. v. United Kingdom,[56] in which a Sri Lankan applicant complained to the Court about his threatened removal by the United Kingdom to Germany under the provisions of the Dublin Convention. The applicant argued, *inter alia*, that if the UK removed him to Germany, this would violate Article 3 of the Convention on the basis that German law did not provide equivalent protection against *refoulement* for persons who fear persecution at the hands of non-state agents of persecution.

In these circumstances, the Court held that the indirect removal of an applicant to an intermediary country (in this case Germany) does not affect the contracting state's responsibility to ensure that the applicant is not, as a result of its decision to expel, exposed to treatment contrary to Article 3 of the Convention. In other words, contracting states to the ECHR cannot hide behind their obligations under the Dublin Convention in fulfilling their obligations under Article 3 of the ECHR. By implication, in implementing their obligations under the Dublin Convention, contracting states are clearly obliged to consider whether removal to the other contracting state may place an applicant at risk of torture and ill-treatment contrary to Article 3. This will involve an assessment by the contracting state of whether there are effective procedural safeguards in the other state protecting the applicant from removal to the country of origin.

While this interpretation of ECHR obligations as regards implementation of Dublin Convention obligations is encouraging, the Court's substantive assessment of the risk at issue in this case is not. The Court seemed willing to accept that the risk of removal in this case was neutralised in part because of the possible application of a particular statutory provision which was discretionary in nature and which had never before been applied to an individual in the applicant's circumstances.

2 Detention of asylum seekers

One of the most contentious issues in regard to the legal regulation of asylum seekers in European states has been the practice in some countries of detaining (or, as it may sometimes be euphemistically referred to, 'retaining') asylum seekers pending consideration of their claim.[57] A glance at Article 5 of the European Convention on Human Rights might appear to indicate that the Convention authorises the detention of asylum-seekers and that it is therefore of little practical value to them in this regard.

Article 5(1) provides that

---

[56] Admissibility Decision, Application No. 43844/98, 7 March 2000: http://www.dhcour. coe.fr.

[57] See the survey of the various measures taken in this respect by European States in S. Egan and K. Costello, *Refugee Law Comparative Study* (Irish Government Publications, March 1999), chapter 4.

No one shall be deprived of his liberty save in the following cases and *in accordance with a procedure prescribed by law*....(f) the lawful arrest or detention of a person to prevent his effecting an unauthorised entry into the country or of a person against whom action is being taken with a view to deportation or extradition.

In fact, the Court's case law in relation to this provision is both positive and negative. In the case of *Amuur v. France*[58] the Court held Article 5 of the Convention to be applicable in circumstances where asylum seekers were being confined in the international zone of an airport under constant surveillance and without access to a telephone. In the course of its judgment, the Court indicated the differentiation that may be made between 'restrictions of liberty' in this context that will not fall foul of Article 5 and 'detention' within the meaning of Article 5. It held that holding aliens in an international zone does involve a restriction on liberty, but one that is in every respect the same as confinement in detention centres pending deportation. Confinement in an international zone, accompanied by suitable safeguards, is acceptable only to enable states to prevent unlawful immigration while at the same time complying with their international obligations, for example those arising under the Refugee Convention and the ECHR. However, holding asylum seekers for excessive periods of time could turn what would otherwise be a restriction on liberty into a deprivation of it. When holding asylum seekers, account should be taken of that fact that they are not criminals and of their need to have speedy access to a refugee determination procedure. In this case, confinement of the applicants for some twenty days, fifteen of which had been without access to a lawyer, constituted a deprivation of liberty. The fact that they were theoretically 'free' to leave the country to return to a third state which they claimed might deport them back to their country of origin, did not alter the character of the confinement as 'detention' within the meaning of Article 5(1). That detention would only be justifiable under the terms of Article 5(1) if it were 'in accordance with a procedure prescribed by law' and if it conformed with the requirements of Article 5(1)(f). The Court held that the detention at issue was not 'in accordance with a procedure prescribed by law'. This was because the national rules authorising the detention were not sufficiently 'accessible and precise' within the meaning of Article 5(1) to be lawful under the Convention.

More recently, in *Conka v. Belgium*,[59] the Court held that any form of deception in the manner of detaining asylum seekers for the purposes of deportation may render the detention itself invalid on Convention grounds. In that case, the Belgian authorities had sent a notice to the

---

[58] (1996) 22 E.H.R.R. 533.
[59] (2002) 34 E.H.R.R. 54.

applicants requiring them to attend at a police station 'to enable the files concerning their applications for asylum to be completed'. When they arrived at the station they were served with an order to leave the state, accompanied by a decision for their removal from the state and their detention for that purpose. In assessing the lawfulness of the detention under Article 5(1), the Court stated that '…[a]cts whereby the authorities sought to gain the trust of asylum seekers with a view to arresting and subsequently deporting them may be found to contravene the general principles stated or implicit in the Convention'.[60] Moreover, it followed that

> …[e]ven as regards overstayers, a conscious decision by the authorities to facilitate or improve the effectiveness of a planned operation for the expulsion of aliens by misleading them about the purpose of a notice so as to make it easier to deprive them of their liberty is not compatible with Article 5.[61]

While the judgments in *Amuur* and in *Conka* may be of benefit to asylum seekers who are deprived of their liberty on ill-defined, inaccessible or arbitrary grounds, the Court's judgment in the case of *Chahal v. United Kingdom* is not so sanguine.[62] In that case, the applicant claimed a violation of Article 5 of the Convention because of his detention for some four and a half years in total on national security grounds pending deportation from the UK to India. He had applied for political asylum, claiming that he would be persecuted if returned to India. He remained in detention throughout his applications for judicial review against the negative determination on his asylum request. In its opinion on the merits of his case, the former Commission of Human Rights had found that there was a violation of Article 5(1) of the Convention on account of the excessive length of the detention. In its view, the domestic proceedings in his case were not carried out with 'due diligence'. Although the applicant had benefited from the delay in the way that anyone facing extradition or deportation would, his complaint was not that he was not sent back more quickly but that he had been kept in detention pending the making of a decision in his case.[63] In its judgment in the case, the Court confirmed the principle that deportation proceedings must be conducted with due diligence, otherwise a detention would cease to be permissible under the Convention. However, it disagreed with the Commission's view that the detention in this case had violated Article 5(1) on the ground of

---

[60] *Ibid.* para. 14.

[61] *Ibid.* para. 15. The Court also found a violation of Article 4 of Protocol 4 which forbids the collective expulsion of aliens, as well as a violation of Article 13 in conjunction with that provision.

[62] (1997) 23 E.H.R.R. 413.

[63] *Ibid.* Opinion on the Merits, pp. 437–454, paras. 116-122.

the exceptional circumstances of the case. Although Mr Chahal had been detained for a long time in totality, none of the individual periods of his detention could be regarded as excessive taken alone or in combination. Neither was the detention arbitrary and hence not 'lawful' within the meaning of Article 5(1)(f).[64] There had been a violation of Article 5(4) of the Convention, however, by reason of the applicant's inability to challenge the lawfulness of his detention in a meaningful way before a court.[65]

While the applicant in *Chahal* failed to persuade the Court of a violation of Article 5(1)(f) on the facts of his case, it is important to reiterate that the Court did endorse the principle enunciated by the Commission that where a person is detained pending deportation, those proceedings must be prosecuted with due diligence.[66] This would suggest, therefore, that, detention pending deportation or extradition would be unlawful where a difficulty emerges with the implementation of the removal in circumstances where it is impossible to obtain travel documents[67] for an individual or where no other state accepts responsibility for receiving that individual – circumstances which are by no means unheard of in the asylum context.

3 Family Unity

The European Convention on Human Rights is also of relevance to a person who has been recognised as a refugee in a receiving state, but who has been denied the right to bring family members to the state to join him or her there. In this respect, the guarantee in Article 8 of the Convention to a right to *respect* for 'family life' is the pertinent provision. Just as the guarantee in Article 3 of the Convention has been raised in connection with extradition and expulsion, Article 8 has been similarly raised in connection with admission and expulsion.

Article 8(1) of the Convention provides as follows:

> Everyone has the right to respect for his private and family life, his home and his correspondence.

This right is qualified by a second paragraph which provides for justifiable restrictions by states on the guarantee in paragraph 1, as follows.

> There shall be no interference by a public authority with the exercise of this right except such as is in accordance with the law and is necessary in a democratic society in the interests of national security, public safety or

---

[64] *Ibid.* Court Judgment, paras. 108-123.

[65] In this respect, the Court noted that the national court reviewing the lawfulness of the detention did not have access to the evidence relating to the alleged security threat posed by the applicant. See also *Conka v. Belgium, supra* note 59.

[66] See also *Ali v. Switzerland*, 28 E.H.R.R. 304, Commission Opinion, paragraph 41.

[67] See Anna Austin's paper on 'The Right to Liberty and Security', (unpublished paper) Irish Centre for European Law, Trinity College, Lecture Series (2001), p. 15.

the economic well-being of the country, for the prevention of disorder or crime, for the protection of health or morals, or for the protection of the rights and freedoms of others.

The European Court of Human Rights has held that there are two types of obligations in Article 8 – positive and negative. Negative obligations imply that the state must refrain from arbitrarily interfering in a person's private or family life. A violation of a negative obligation arises where it is established that the state has interfered in the private or family sphere protected by paragraph (1), in circumstances where there is no justification for that interference under the conditions set out in paragraph 2.[68] Positive obligations arise in circumstances where the state is required to be pro-active in protecting a person's private and family life.[69]

Although not involving refugees or asylum seekers, the judgment of the Court in *Abdulaziz, Cabales and Balkandali v. United Kingdom*[70]

---

[68] The methodology of the Court in analysing state justification for interference with the rights set forth in paragraph 1 is well rehearsed elsewhere. It is sufficient to note here that a dominant factor in the Court's reasoning is usually whether the respondent state can show successfully that the interference is 'necessary' in a democratic society for one of the stated aims. Necessity implies that there must be some 'pressing social need' for the interference, that the interference is 'proportionate to the aim being pursued', and that the reasons put forward for the interference were 'relevant' and 'sufficient'. In examining the question of necessity, the Court has stated that the Convention leaves to the state a 'margin of appreciation' or area of discretion. Ultimately, it is up to the Court to decide whether the government has exceeded its discretion in a particular case. The scope of the margin of appreciation granted to the state varies depending on the variety of considerations at work in a given case. In general terms, the scope of the discretion may be influenced by, amongst other things, the right in question, the nature of the interference complained of, and very often the aim sought to be achieved by the interference. Moreover, the existence or not of a European consensus on a particular issue will often influence the Court's decision whether to grant a wide or narrow margin of appreciation to the state as regards the actions taken by it at the domestic level. In many cases, the scope of the margin of appreciation granted in a particular case will prove crucial to the ultimate decision of the Court on the facts. An excellent analysis of the foregoing is set forth in P. Van Dijk and G.J.H. Van Hoof, *Theory and Practice of the European Convention on Human Rights*, 3rd edn. (The Hague: Kluwer, 1998) at Chapter 8, pp. 761-773; and Chapter 2, sections 2.5 and 3.2.

[69] In fulfilling their positive obligations under Article 8 of the Convention, contracting states are also afforded a margin of appreciation by the Convention. As with cases of negative interference, the scope of this margin of appreciation may also be influenced by the existence or not of a European consensus in respect of the obligation alleged to exist by the applicant. Moreover, where positive obligations are concerned, the Court has acknowledged that in determining the steps to be taken to ensure compliance with the Convention, a fair balance must be struck between the needs and resources of the community and of individuals. Even though paragraph 2, strictly speaking, only applies to cases of negative interference, the Court has stated that in striking the required balance, the aims mentioned in the second paragraph 'may be of a certain relevance'. The difficulty, therefore, for an applicant who seeks to argue that the state has failed in its positive obligations under Article 8 is that he or she will first have to convince the Court of the existence of an interest which the state has failed to respect: See generally, C. Warbrick, 'The Structure of Article 8' [1998] 1 *E.H.R.L.R.* 32 at 35.

[70] (1985) 7 E.H.R.R. 471.

is of importance in this context, because of the Court's recognition in that case that immigration measures may infringe upon the right to respect for family life. The applicants in that case were settled immigrants in the UK who claimed a violation of Article 8 because of the state's refusal to allow their foreign husbands to come and join them there. The Court held that there was no breach of the state's positive obligation to respect family life in this case on the basis that the duty imposed by Article 8 cannot extend to a general obligation on the part of contracting states to respect the choice of married couples of the country of matrimonial residence and to accept non-national spouses for settlement. There was no violation of Article 8 on its own,[71] in circumstances where the applicants had not shown that there were any obstacles to establishing family life in their own or their husband's home countries *or that there were any special reasons as to why that could not be expected of them.*

This latter clause may indicate that a more favourable outcome is surely to be expected in the case of a recognised refugee who is denied family reunion on the receiving state's territory.[72] Such an optimistic prediction is not necessarily certain on the basis of subsequent case law. The case of *Gül v. Switzerland*[73] demonstrates the difficulty of establishing such a claim. The applicant was a Turkish national who had been living in Switzerland since 1983. He had gone there originally to seek refugee status, leaving his wife and two children in Turkey. His wife later joined him in Switzerland to receive medical treatment which was unavailable in Turkey. She subsequently gave birth to a child in Switzerland who was placed in a state-run institution because the mother was unable to care for her. A specialist doctor certified that it would be fatal for the applicant's wife to return to Turkey. The applicant was denied refugee status in Switzerland but was granted permanent residence status to remain there on humanitarian grounds. The couple's request to the Swiss authorities to allow their seven-year-old child who had remained in Turkey to come and join them in Switzerland was rejected on the grounds that the right to family reunion did not attach to resident permits based on humanitarian grounds. They claimed that this refusal constituted a violation of Article 8 of the Convention. The Court failed to find a violation in their case, holding that there had not been any failure on the part of the state to

---

[71] It should be noted that the Court did find that there had been a violation of Article 8 of the Convention in conjunction with the principle of non-discrimination in Article 14 by reason of the State's discriminatory application of the Immigration Rules.

[72] Hugo Storey points out that other facts might surely succeed in such a claim: 'Presumably, however, the same conclusion might not be drawn had the applicants been long-settled or lacked foreknowledge of the immigration pitfalls that might ensure after marrying': 'The Right to Family Life and Immigration Case Law at Strasbourg' (1990) 39 *I.C.L.Q* 328 at 335.

[73] (1996) 22 E.H.R.R. 93.

respect family life. The state has the right to control the entry of non-nationals. The extent to which it is obliged to admit the relatives of settled immigrants will vary according to the circumstances of the persons involved and the general interest. As it had previously held in *Abdulaziz*, the Court reiterated the point that Article 8 does not impose a general obligation on contracting states to authorise family reunion on their territory. On the facts, the Court was not satisfied that there were obstacles to preventing family life developing in Turkey, noting, in particular, that the son in question had grown up in the cultural and linguistic environment of that country. A similar decision was made by the Court in the case of *Ahmut v. The Netherlands*.[74]

This *Gül* decision is open to criticism, not only because the Court appears to have misconstrued the factual circumstances of the case,[75] but also because it reveals an almost transparent motivation to defer to the contracting states' strong interest in maintaining sovereign discretion in immigration matters. [76] Had the applicant been a recognised refugee, it is to be hoped that his or her inability to return to the country of origin might have tilted the balance of interests in favour of finding a violation. Even so, the decision does not augur well for refugees where adult or even semi-adult children are concerned, if the Court takes the view that they are capable of leading their own independent lives without the company of their parents in the country of origin.

Recently, the Court appears to have taken a more measured approach to the balancing of interests raised by these cases. In *Sen v. Netherlands*[77] it was again confronted by a very similar factual scenario to that arising in *Gül*. The case concerned the refusal of the Dutch authorities to grant a residence permit to the applicant's eldest child (then aged twelve years) to live with her family in the Netherlands. The parents had been legally resident in that state for several years and two more children had been born to the couple during that period. They had left their eldest child with a close relative in Turkey initially because of marital difficulties which had since been resolved. The

---

[74] (1997) 24 E.H.R.R. 62.

[75] See the commentary by Nuala Mole on this case in her monograph entitled *Problems Raised by Certain Aspects of the Present Situation of Refugees from the Standpoint of the European Convention on Human Rights*, Human Rights Files, No. 9 rev. (Council of Europe Publishing, 1997), pp. 22-23. The Commission of Human Rights, in its opinion on the merits, had found a violation of Article 8 in this case. It seemed to take a closer look at the facts of the case, noting that the son's position in Turkey was not satisfactory, noting in particular his irregular attendance at school: 22 E.H.R.R. 104, paragraph 62.

[76] See the dissenting judgments of Judges Martens and Russo who held that a refusal to admit the child was disproportionate in the circumstances. They held that the real motivation of the state was a fear of opening the floodgates in the immigration context. State interests, however, in their view, should not crush the interests of individuals: *Supra* note 70 at pp. 115-122.

[77] (2003) 36 E.H.R.R. 7

Dutch authorities refused to grant the permit on public interest grounds, citing as a relevant factor the view that the child no longer belonged to the parents' family unit, having lived most of her life in Turkey without financial assistance from her parents.

While the Court purported to apply the exact same principles as it had in the *Gül* decision, the application of those same principles to the facts produced very different results. The Court in *Sen* refused to treat negatively the applicants' deliberate decision originally to leave their child behind them in Turkey.[78] Rather, the Court placed particular emphasis on the most realistic opportunity for the family of develop-ing family life together in the present day. Taking into account the fact that the parents and the other children born to the couple had been living as a family for several years in the Netherlands, the Court took the view that the 'best way of developing a family life with the family as it existed' would be for their eldest child to come and join them there.[79] This more balanced approach in assessing the positive obligations of the state is to be preferred to the overt emphasis on state interests in the previous decisions of *Gül* and *Ahmut*.

Article 8 could also be of relevance in the case of a failed asylum seeker where deportation would risk breaking up family life in exis-tence in the contracting state. In this connection, the European Court of Human Rights has held that expulsion and deportation of a non-national may raise issues under Article 8, specifically as regards the right to respect for family life. See, for example, the case of *Berrehab v. The Netherlands*[80] in which the Court held that the deportation from the state of a non-national, who had recently been divorced from his Dutch wife, would violate Article 8. Having regard to the fact that the deportation would break up existing family ties between the applicant and his daughter, who was a Dutch national, the Court held that the expulsion would be disproportionate to the legitimate aim of protecting the economic well-being of the country. In a trail of subsequent cases, the Court has had to examine the compatibility with the Convention of the proposed deportation of adult, second-generation immigrants to their state of nationality on account of their conviction for serious crimes. The Court has acknowledged that while states have to take appropriate measures to ensure the maintenance of public order, where decisions are taken which might affect family life, they are not

---

[78] 'This event, which occurred during Sinem's early childhood, cannot however be regarded as constituting an irrevocable decision to establish their place of residence in that country forever and to maintain with their child only an occasional and strained relationship, definitively renouncing her company and thereby abandoning any idea of reuniting their family. The same goes for the fact that the applicants were unable to show that they had participated financially in bringing up their child': *ibid*. para. 40.

[79] *Ibid* para. 40.

[80] (1989) 11 E.H.R.R. 322.

to be taken lightly. The Court appears to take into account the applicant's connections with the Convention state, as well as the extent, if any, of his or her ties with the state of nationality.[81] In *Boultif v. Switzerland*[82] it elaborated on the guiding principles which it would take into account in relation to cases where the main obstacle to expulsion is the difficulties which would arise for the family in living in the applicant's country of origin.[83] The trail of cases[84] decided by the Court in this area illustrate that the failure by a contracting state to take into account family circumstances both in the contracting state itself and in the state of nationality may ground a claim to a violation of Article 8 of the European Convention on Human Rights in Strasbourg.[85]

Article 8 jurisprudence on the subject of deportation as it affects family unity was referred to recently in the controversial decision of the Supreme Court in *D.L. v. Minister for Justice, Equality and Law Reform*.[86] In that case, the Court had to consider whether the deportation of the

---

[81] See, for example, the case of *Moustaquim v. Belgium* (1991) 13 E.H.R.R. 802. See also the case of *Beljoudi v. France* (1992) 14 E.H.R.R. 801 in which the deportation of the non-national who had been convicted of serious crime was held to violate the right to respect for family life. The Court held that the applicant's criminal record had to be weighed against other factors, including the real existence of family ties between him and his French wife, his persistent and unsuccessful attempts to get French nationality and the fact that he had had no contact with his own state of nationality. Deportation in these circumstances would imperil the unity of the marriage and would be disproportionate to the legitimate aim of prevention of crime. See also *Nasri v. France* (1996) 21 E.H.R.R. 458. By contrast, the applicant in the case of *Boughanemi v. France* (1996) 22 E.H.R.R. 229 failed to convince the Court of any violation in similar circumstances to the previous cases. It would seem that the seriousness of the offences for which he had been convicted was the controlling factor for the Court in finding that deportation would not be disproportionate in the circumstances.

[82] (2001) 33 E.H.R.R. 50.

[83] These criteria are as follows: the nature and seriousness of the offence; the length of the applicant's stay in the expelling country; the time elapsed since the crime was committed; the applicant's conduct during the intervening period; the nationalities of the persons concerned; the applicant's family situation, such as the length of the marriage and other factors expressing the effectiveness of the couple's family life; whether the spouse of the applicant knew of the offence when they entered into the relationship; whether the couple have any children and if so, the ages of those children; and the seriousness of the difficulties which the spouse is likely to encounter in the country of origin.

[84] The above survey is by no means comprehensive. More recent jurisprudence includes the cases of *Yildiz v. Austria* (2003) 36 E.H.R.R. 32 and *Al-Nashif v. Bulgaria* (2003) 36 E.H.R.R. 37. In the latter judgment, the Court emphasised the importance of procedural fairness in deportation proceedings. A violation of Article 8 was found to exist in that case because the interference in the applicant's family life generated by the deportation order made against him was not based on a legal regime which met the requirements of lawfulness set forth in Article 8(2) of the Convention.

[85] See generally, N. Rogers 'Immigration and the European Convention on Human Rights: Are New Principles Emerging?' (2003) E.H.R.L.R. 53.

[86] 23 January 2003 [2003] IESC 1.

non-national parents of an Irish born citizen would infringe the constitutional rights of the child to the society, care and company of his
or her parents. In a lengthy judgment, the Court concluded by a 5/2
majority[87] that the Minister for Justice, Equality and Law Reform may
deport the parents and siblings of an Irish born child if he or she is
satisfied that for good and sufficient reason the common good requires
that the residence of the parents or siblings within the state should be
terminated. Such a decision may be made by the minister even if, as a
necessary consequence, the child who is an Irish citizen must leave the
state in order to remain in the family unit. Such a decision does not
contravene the constitutional rights of the child to the society, care and
company of his or her parents, since the Constitution does not require
that those rights be exercised *within* the state.[88] In reaching a decision
as to whether the common good requires the deportation of the family
members of an Irish born child, the minister must, having regard to the
constitutional rights of the child, take into account all of the relevant
factual circumstances of the case. Relevant factors that may be taken
into consideration include the length of time the family has been in the
state; the application of the Dublin Convention to which Ireland is a
party; and the need to preserve respect for and the integrity of the
asylum and immigration system.

Article 8 case law, in the view of a number of judges in the majority, served to bear out their particular interpretation of the Irish
constitutional position.[89] Fennelly J. who dissented, however, took the
view that the case law of the European Court of Human Rights in this
area was still in a state of evolution and, more particularly, that none
of the decided cases involved deportation of the parents of a citizen
child. Most interestingly, he concluded that he would not go further
than stating that it seems probable '...that the ECHR would not accept
as a reason for expulsion, which had disruptive effect on family life,

---

[87] McGuinness and Fennelly JJ. dissented.

[88] The majority of the Court distinguished the previous decision of the Supreme Court
in the case of *Fajujonu v. Minister for Justice* [1990] 2 IR 151. In its view, the latter
judgment was not an authority in law for the propositions advanced by the applicants
in the instant cases. Rather, it was an authority for the more general proposition –
finessed in the current judgment – that in the particular circumstances that arose in
that case and which might occur in similar cases in the future, the minister was obliged
to consider whether there were grave and substantial reasons associated with the
common good which required the deportation of the non-national members of the
family in that case. Since there was no evidence that the minister had taken those factors into consideration in that case, the plaintiffs were given liberty to apply to the
High Court in the event of his deciding to proceed with their deportation.

[89] See the judgments of Hardiman J., *supra* note 83 at para. 329 (with whom Geoghegan
J. agrees) and Denham J. It is interesting to note that Murray J. took the view that the
issues and circumstances arising in the ECHR cases were so removed from the facts
and issues in the case before him that they had no meaningful bearing on it, while
Keane C.J. expressed no opinion on the matter.

an abstract argument, unrelated to some concrete need of the state, but based simply on the general need to maintain the integrity of the immigration system'.[90] Given the importance of this judgment for failed asylum seekers who have given birth to children in Ireland while awaiting determination by the state of their asylum claims, it will be interesting to see how the European Court of Human Rights would rule on this matter if it were ever to be confronted by similar facts.[91]

4 Reception of asylum seekers

The conditions and circumstances in which asylum seekers are required to live whilst awaiting a decision on their applications for refugee status may also raise issues under the Convention. In Ireland, the most contentious issues arising in this respect include the policies of dispersal, direct provision and the refusal of the state to allow asylum seekers generally to work pending determination of their claims to refugee status.[92] None of these issues has been addressed squarely by the Convention institutions. Nonetheless, it is worth considering whether any of them might be raised effectively under Article 3 of the Convention as constituting 'degrading' treatment, or under Article 8 as a possible violation of the right to respect for private life. In a separate opinion in the case of *HLR v. France*, one member of the former European Commission of Human Rights argued that the refusal to accord the means of subsistence to a person whose expulsion had been ruled to be in violation of Article 8 fails to meet the requirements of that Article.[93] As Nuala Mole has commented, '...[T]he same must apply to those who cannot be expelled whilst their applications to remain are being determined'.[94]

The policy of dispersal could conceivably raise an issue under Article 2 of the Fourth Protocol to the Convention, to which Ireland is party. It provides for the right of everyone lawfully within the territory to 'liberty of movement and freedom to choose his residence'. The fact that this right may be legitimately curtailed by restrictions imposed 'in accordance with law and justified by the public interest in a democratic

---

[90] *Ibid.* Fennelly J. at para. 517.
[91] The applicants in *D.L. v. Minister for Justice, Equality and Law Reform* have made an application to the European Court of Human Rights in Strasbourg based on Article 8 of the Convention.
[92] See the survey of the position of other European states in regard to the right to work during the asylum determination procedure in S. Egan and K. Costello, *Refugee Law Comparative Study* (Irish Government Publications, March 1999), pp. 421-427. The authors recommend that the state should recognise this right after a certain length of time has expired.
[93] Dissenting Opinion of Mr Barreto (1998) 26 E.H.R.R. 29 at 42.
[94] N. Mole, *supra* note 75 at 39.

society' may be of relevance.[95] It is certainly arguable, however, whether a 'policy' of dispersal would qualify as being 'in accordance with the law' having regard to the manner in which that phrase has been interpreted elsewhere in the Convention.[96]

Article 14 of the Convention provides for a limited basis upon which discrimination arguments can be raised before the Court. It provides for a general duty of non-discrimination by contracting states in securing the enjoyment of Convention rights. In this respect, Article 14 is not a free-standing equality norm, but rather a subordinate equality norm. In order to claim that a law or administrative practice is discriminatory, an applicant must first show that the law or practice falls within the ambit of a Convention right. Once that condition is satisfied, the Court may proceed to analyse whether the state has discriminated against the applicant in guaranteeing the right in question.[97] Because many of the issues raised as regards discrimination against asylum seekers during the procedure relate to economic rights, it is difficult to pin-point particular rights in the Convention to which Article 14 can be anchored.[98] This deficiency may be remedied in the near future in view of the recent adoption by the contracting states of Protocol No. 12 to the Convention. Under the terms of this Protocol, the contracting states may each opt to adhere to an open-ended equality norm which guarantees equality before the law in relation to the enjoyment of *any* right set forth by law. At the time of writing, the Protocol has not entered into force for any of the contracting states.[99] When it does, and provided of course that Ireland ratifies it, the Protocol may provide an enhanced

---

[95] See paragraph (4) of Article 2, Protocol No. 4 to the Convention. Paragraph 3 of the same Article also provides for restrictions that are 'in accordance with law and are necessary in a democratic society in the interests of national security or public safety, for the maintenance of *ordre public*, for the prevention of crime, for the protection of health or morals, or for the protection of the rights and freedoms of others'.

[96] The interpretation by the Court of the same phrase as it occurs in Article 8(2) of the Convention is a useful point of comparison. According to settled case law, the phrase 'in accordance with law' requires that the interference with the guaranteed right must have some *basis* in domestic law; the law must be adequately accessible; and it must be foreseeable, ie the law must be formulated with sufficient precision so as to enable persons to regulate their conduct: *Silver v. United Kingdom* (1983) 5 E.H.R.R. 347.

[97] That enquiry takes the form of a two-pronged assessment: first, whether there is a difference in treatment between the applicant and another similarly situated group; and if so, whether there is a reasonable and objective justification for the difference in treatment. The Court is prepared to accept that a difference in treatment has a 'reasonable and objective justification' if it is satisfied that the difference is based on a legitimate aim and if the means used to achieve that aim are proportionate to the aim pursued: *Belgian Linguistics Case (No. 2)* (1970) 1 E.H.R.R. 252.

[98] Discrimination in relation to the right to freedom of movement could conceivably be raised by reference to Article 14 in conjunction with Article 2 of Protocol No. 4.

[99] See the paper presented by Grainne Mullan, 'Article 14 of the European Convention on Human Rights – Discrimination Against Equality?', (unpublished paper) Irish Centre for European Law Lecture Series, Trinity College, 19 February 2001.

means of challenging the various policies applied to asylum seekers during the determination procedure.

5 Remedies

Article 13 of the Convention provides that

> Everyone whose rights and freedoms as set forth in this Convention are violated shall have an effective remedy before a national authority notwithstanding that the violation has been committed by a person acting in an official capacity.

This right imposes an obligation on the contracting states to provide a pre-emptive remedy for any of the rights provided for in the Convention.[100] A person need only show that they have an 'arguable' claim regarding a breach of one of the substantive rights in the Convention in order to raise a claim about a breach of Article 13.

Is this Article of any practical value to an asylum claimant who challenges the quality of the appeal mechanisms available under national law to challenge a negative decision on his or her claim? In other words, could she or he argue that there was no effective remedy in domestic law in respect of an arguable claim under Article 3, 2 or possibly even Article 8? In this respect, the Court has considered whether the remedy of judicial review is an effective remedy within the meaning of Article 13 in respect of Article 3 complaints. In *Vilvarajah v. United Kingdom*[101] the Court held that the remedy of judicial review, as applied by the English courts, was an 'effective' remedy within the meaning of Article 13 for controlling the exercise of ministerial discretion in asylum cases, even where the facts of the particular case are in dispute. The standard of judicial review examined in that case was the remedy as interpreted by the House of Lords in *Bugdaycay v. Secretary of State for the Home Department*[102] in which that Court had held that the basis for administrative decisions in asylum claims demands 'most anxious scrutiny'. [103]

As noted above, an applicant might also contend that his or her deportation from the state violates Article 8 of the Convention because it would have the effect of splitting up family life. In this context, it has been argued that the remedy of judicial review is unlikely to be regarded as an effective remedy in expulsion cases concerning family and private life issues, where matters of factual appreciation arise.[104]

---

[100] 'The effect of Article 13 is thus to require the provision of a domestic remedy allowing the competent 'national authority' both to deal with the substance of the relevant Convention complaint and to grant appropriate relief': *Soering v. United Kingdom*, *supra* note 11. at paragraph 120.

[101] *Supra* note 18.

[102] [1987] 1 ALL E.R. 940.

[103] See text *infra* as regards the implications of incorporation of the Convention into Irish domestic law on the remedy of judicial review based on this case law.

[104] K. Reid, *A Practitioner's Guide to the European Convention on Human Rights* (Sweet and Maxwell, 1998) p. 282.

This is because the remedy of judicial review in such cases does not necessarily involve the Court in assessing the proportionality of the decision not to allow the person to remain on humanitarian or family life grounds.

The ECHR and domestic refugee law: impact of incorporation?

The core of domestic refugee law is contained in the Refugee Act 1996, as amended by the Immigration Act 1999 and the Immigration Act 2003. Section 2 of the Refugee Act 1996 incorporates the refugee definition,[105] while section 5 of the Act implements the principle of *non-refoulement* in Article 33(1) of the Refugee Convention,[106] making it explicit that this guarantee applies to asylum seekers. Section 3 guarantees the rights set forth in the Refugee Convention to persons who are recognised as refugees under the Act. Much of the rest of the Act is devoted to delineating the procedure[107] for determining refugee status, involving the Refugee Applications Commissioner[108] and the Refugee Appeal Tribunal.[109] Section 11 of the Immigration Act 1999 and Section 7 of the Immigration Act 2003 amend this procedure in certain key respects. This procedure includes an accelerated component whereby claims to refugee status may be subject to speedier procedures whereby the applicant is not entitled to an oral hearing of his or her case on appeal to the Appeal Tribunal.

The Immigration Act 1999 is also important because it sets out the deportation process which will apply where a person fails to satisfy the refugee definition. Section 3(6) of that Act gives the Minister for Justice, Equality and Law Reform discretion to grant permission to a person to remain in the state on various other grounds, including humanitarian grounds or family reasons.

---

[105] Section 2 thus replicates exactly the terms of Article 1 (A) (2) of that Convention, as amended by the 1967 Protocol, which essentially defines a refugee as a person: *'who owing to a well founded fear of being persecuted for reasons of race, religion, nationality, membership of a particular social group or political opinion, is outside the country of his or her nationality and is unable or, owing to such fear, is unwilling to avail himself or herself of the protection of that country; or who, not having a nationality and being outside the country of his or her former habitual residence, is unable or, owing to such fear, is unwilling to return to it...'.* The Irish Law is unique in Europe, however, by specifically providing in section 1 that the term 'membership of a particular social group' shall include membership of a trade union and membership of a group of persons whose defining characteristic is their belonging to the female or the male sex or having a particular sexual orientation.

[106] See *supra* text following note 22.

[107] Sections 8, 9, 11, 12, 13, 16 and 17.

[108] Section 6 of the Refuge Act 1996 and First Schedule.

[109] Section 15 of the Refugee Act 1996, as amended by section 11(1)(j) of the Immigration Act 1999 and Second Schedule.

The Illegal Immigrants (Trafficking) Act 2000 is also relevant to refugees and asylum seekers because it provides that certain negative decisions in the asylum and deportation process may *only* be challenged by means of judicial review. It restricts the time period for seeking leave to apply for judicial review in those cases to a fourteen-day time period, and also requires that persons who wish to challenge negative decisions in the asylum/deportation process must show 'substantial grounds' as to why leave to appeal by way of judicial review should be granted. Section 10 of that Act is also somewhat controversial in that it amends the provisions of the Immigration Act 1999 concerning the detention of prospective deportees from the state. The combined effect of both Acts is that a deportee can be detained pending deportation for up to eight weeks, on various grounds, including a reasonable suspicion on the part of a member of the Garda Síochána that the person 'intends to avoid removal from the State'.[110]

The relevance of incorporation of the European Convention on Human Rights to the statutory scheme relating to asylum seekers and refugees was dependent on the method of incorporation adopted by the Oireachtas.[111] The two main options were direct incorporation or indirect (or interpretative) incorporation. The latter was chosen in the European Convention on Human Rights Bill 2003. The direct method would have involved reproducing the text of the Convention as part of Irish domestic law either in the Constitution or in a statute. This method would allow an individual to rely directly on Convention provisions to challenge domestic law or an administrative act as being inconsistent with the Convention. Accordingly, any of the substantive arguments outlined above could be raised directly before an Irish court, by direct reliance on the substantive provision. Direct incorporation would thus open up avenues for refugees and asylum seekers that are currently closed under the existing statutory framework. For example, section 2 of the Refugee Act 1996 requires that a person must show a fear of being persecuted on grounds of race, religion, nationality etc. Direct incorporation would allow an applicant to rely on the open-ended principles articulated by the Court in *Soering* and *Cruz Varas* where no such nexus to civil or political status can be established.[112] Certain elements of the asylum procedure could also be vulnerable to challenge directly in the courts on the basis of Article 13 of the

---

[110] Section 5 of the Immigration Act 1999 as amended by section 10(b) of the Illegal Immigrants (Trafficking) Act 2000.

[111] See the paper presented by Dr Gerard Hogan on 'The Incorporation of the ECHR into Irish Domestic Law', ICEL Lecture Series, 15 January 2001.

[112] Of course, in *Finucane v. McMahon* [1990] I.R. 165 and *Russell v. Fanning* [1988] I.R. 505, the same basic principle that was articulated by the European Court of Human Rights in *Soering* was located by the Supreme Court in the Irish Constitution, although the relevance of these decisions to refugee claims has not yet been explored by that Court.

Convention in conjunction with Article 3. For example, the denial of an oral hearing to persons whose claims are subjected to an accelerated procedure under section 13 of the Refugee Act 1996, as amended, might raise issues under Article 13, as may the failure of the Refugee Applications Commissioner to provide detailed reasons at first instance in terms of the ability of the applicant to bring an effective appeal before the Appeals Tribunal.[113]

However, the method of incorporation chosen was by indirect means, otherwise known as the 'interpretative' method. The core provisions of the European Convention on Human Rights Act 2003 provide essentially that any statutory provision or rule of law shall be interpreted, in so far as possible, in a manner that is compatible with the Convention.[114] Where an existing statute is found to be incompatible with the Convention, the Irish courts may issue a declaration that the law is incompatible.[115] However, this declaration of incompatibility 'shall not affect the validity, continuing operation or enforcement of the statutory provision or rule of law in respect of which it is made'.[116] Thus, under this approach, the courts would not be empowered to strike out domestic legislation or administrative acts as being invalid according to Convention guarantees. Rather, the incorporation Act simply gives the courts jurisdiction to make a declaration that the law is incompatible with the Convention. The Taoiseach shall then cause a copy of the order containing a declaration of incompatibility to be laid before both Houses of Parliament within twenty-one days. The only 'remedy' open to a litigant affected by any such incompatibility will be to apply to the Attorney General for compensation. However, the Act makes it clear that the government is under no obligation to pay compensation.[117]

---

[113] See A. Austin, 'Ireland to Strasbourg: Form and Substance of the Convention System', unpublished paper delivered at the Law Society of Ireland Conference, The Incorporation of the European Convention on Human Rights Into Irish Law (Saturday, 14 October 2000).

[114] *Ibid,* section 2.

[115] *Ibid*, section 5.

[116] *Ibid*.

[117] Section 5(4) of the European Convention on Human Rights Act 2003 states: 'Where (a) a declaration of incompatibility is made, (b) a party to the proceedings concerned makes an application in writing to the Attorney General for compensation in respect of an injury or loss or damage suffered by him or her as a result of the incompatibility concerned and, (c) the Government, in their discretion, consider that it may be appropriate to make an *ex gratia* payment of compensation to that party ("a payment") the Government may request an adviser appointed by them as to the amount of such compensation (if any) and may, in their discretion, make a payment of the amount aforesaid or of such other amount as they consider appropriate in the circumstances.' See the critique of the provisions of the Act made by the Human Rights Commission in its Submission on the Bill to the Joint Oireachtas Committee on Justice, Equality, Defence and Women's Rights (June 2002).

Placing that method of incorporation into the context of refugee law implies that the incorporation statute simply requires the courts to interpret the Refugee Act 1996, the Immigration Act 1999 (as amended by the Illegal Immigrants (Trafficking) Act 2000) and the Immigration Act 2003 in a way that is compatible with Convention rights.[118] Section 3 of the Act also places an obligation on 'State bodies' to act in conformity with the Convention. This means that the Refugee Applications Commissioner and the Appeals Tribunal will be placed under an obligation to interpret the Refugee Act 1996 as well as the Immigration Act 1999 and the Immigration Act 2003 in a manner that conforms with the state's obligations under the Convention.

As regards the Refugee Act 1996, an obligation to interpret its provisions in a manner that conforms to the ECHR cannot change the clear statutory language in Section 2 which provides that refugee status can only be granted to persons on specified grounds. Indirect incorporation of ECHR obligations will not widen those grounds. As regards the interpretation of Section 2 of the 1996 Act in the context of claims arising from circumstances in which the agent of persecution is not the government of the state of origin, Irish practice already conforms to European Court jurisprudence as espoused in the *Ahmed* and *HLR v. France* decisions noted above.[119] However, if an attempt was ever made to change the prevailing interpretation of the refugee definition, it is conceivable that ECHR jurisprudence, as mentioned above, could be cited as persuasive authority as to why the state should not return a person to a country where he or she fears persecution at the hands of non-state agents of persecution. The European Convention on Human Rights Act 2003 may also influence the operation of the Dublin Convention by immigration officers, the Refugee Applications Commissioner and the Appeal Tribunal insofar as Article 3 implications will have to be taken into account in implementing that Convention.

In my view, a key area in which ECHR incorporation may make a difference is in relation to the exercise of the minister's discretion under section 3(6) of the Immigration Act 1999. Post-incorporation, the minister will be placed under an obligation to exercise his discretion in considering whether to allow a person to stay on 'humanitarian grounds' in a manner that conforms with the Convention, i.e. to take Convention obligations under Article 8 into account in exercising his discretion to grant permission to remain in the state.

As regards prospective challenges to any such decision by the

---

[118] Section 2(1) of the European Convention on Human Rights Act 2003 states 'In interpreting and applying any statutory provision or rule of law, a court shall, in so far as is possible, subject to the rules of law relating to such interpretation and application, do so in a manner compatible with the State's obligations under the Convention provisions'.

[119] *Supra* notes 23 and 24.

minister, it must be remembered that section 5 of the Illegal Immigrants (Trafficking) Act 2000 prescribes that certain key decisions and actions taken in the asylum and immigration context can *only* be challenged by means of judicial review. It also sets out different requirements for the processing of judicial review applications in this area than those which apply to judicial review proceedings generally. The European Convention on Human Rights Act 2003 will not change these hurdles. Its effect will be to add an extra plank to the practitioner's arguments in challenging the minister's decision that he failed to exercise his discretion in a manner that conforms with the Convention.

It is arguable that indirect incorporation of the ECHR by the 2003 Act will affect the *scope* of judicial review in such cases, i.e. from an 'irrationality standard' to a 'proportionality' type standard. Unfortunately, in *Vilvarajah v. United Kingdom*[120] the European Court of Human Rights held that judicial review is an effective remedy under the Convention for controlling the exercise of ministerial discretion, even in cases where the facts of the particular case are in dispute. The standard of judicial review examined in the *Vilvarajah* case was interpreted by the House of Lords in the *Bugdaycay* case in which that Court held that the basis for administrative decisions in asylum cases demands 'most anxious scrutiny'.[121] This is also the type of standard which might be demanded of an Irish court in asylum cases.

In the case of *Sekou Camara v. The Minister for Justice, Equality and Law Reform & Others*,[122] Kelly J. applied the concept of 'curial deference' to decisions of the former asylum Appeals Authority. By classifying the Appeals Authority as an 'expert administrative tribunal' and applying this concept to it, the effect of this judgment is that the courts should exercise even greater judicial restraint in relation to decisions of the Appeals Authority (and presumably, by extension the Refugee Appeals Tribunal). It might be argued that this interpretation of the role of the court in these cases runs counter to the standard applied by the House of Lords in *Bugdaycay,* which in turn was endorsed by the European Court of Human Rights in the *Vilvarajah* case.[123] Hence, it may be argued post-incorporation that European Court jurisprudence demands closer scrutiny of administrative decisions in asylum and deportation cases than Kelly J. was prepared to recognise in *Camara*. Of course, the necessity to resort to Convention arguments may be diverted if the

---

[120] *Supra* note 18.

[121] *Supra* note 103.

[122] Unreported, High Court, 26 July 2000.

[123] See the judgment in *Vilvarajah* where the Court upheld the remedy of judicial review in the UK in the context of asylum appeals, noting that the courts in the UK ' ...have stressed their special responsibility to subject administrative decisions in this area to the most anxious scrutiny where an applicant's life or liberty may be at risk': *supra* note 18 at para.125.

Supreme Court is ever given the opportunity of reversing[124] Kelly J.'s ruling in that case.[125]

Conclusion

The above analysis demonstrates the capacity of the European Convention on Human Rights to penetrate and mould particular aspects of asylum law and policy in this jurisdiction. Despite the fact that no mention of refugee protection or asylum is made in the body of the Convention itself, the European Court of Human Rights has generally interpreted the Convention in a creative manner so as to make the rights 'practical and effective' for asylum seekers and refugees. By focusing on the principles already articulated by the Court, it has been possible to identify particular areas of domestic law and policy which deserve further attention. In particular, the emphasis placed by the Court on procedural fairness and regularity leaves open to question current legislative proposals for amendment of the refugee determination procedure as well as the state's reception policies for asylum seekers. Incorporation of the Convention may produce limited, though important, results, particularly in the area of judicial review.

---

[124] Kelly J.'s decision is clearly vulnerable to challenge on administrative law principles: G. Hogan, 'Judicial Review, The Doctrine of Reasonableness and the Immigration Process', paper presented at the Bar Council Conference on Refugee Law, January 26, 2001.

[125] It is of course arguable that section 5 of the Illegal Immigrants (Trafficking) Act 2000 itself breaches the Convention for not being an 'effective remedy' within the meaning of Article 13. In *Soering* and *Vilvarajah*, the Court of Human Rights rejected the applicants' complaints that the remedy of judicial review as interpreted by the English courts was not an effective remedy in such circumstances. The Court was satisfied that the remedy was 'effective' since the English courts could review the 'reasonableness' of an extradition or expulsion decision in the light of the factors relied on by the applicants in those cases to establish the risk of inhuman or degrading treatment. A different view might be taken by the Court as regards the effectiveness of the remedy of judicial review in respect of similar cases in the Irish context, given the provisions of section 5 of the Illegal Immigrants (Trafficking) Act 2000. In particular, the fact that the applicant must first show 'substantial grounds' for contending that the decisions in their cases should be quashed might be a relevant consideration. If Kelly J.'s decision in *Camara* as regards the role of the courts in judicial review proceedings in asylum appeals is endorsed by the Supreme Court, this would arguably buttress an argument before the European Court of Human Rights that the remedy of judicial review as applied by the Irish courts, in the context of section 5, is not an effective remedy for the purposes of Article 13 of the Convention. Given that the constitutionality of section 5 has already been upheld, arguments of this nature would have to be made before the European Court of Human Rights itself in an individual application.

CHAPTER 5

The Asylum Procedure

Ursula Fraser

Introduction

Ireland became a member of the United Nations in 1956 and acceded to the 1951 Convention relating to the Status of Refugees (hereafter 'Refugee Convention') in the same year.[1] The Refugee Convention contained a limitation whereby it expressly covered events only occurring before 1 January 1951. This dateline accorded with the wishes of governments at the time of drafting to limit their obligations to refugee situations that had occurred, or might occur, based on events already known at that time. In 1967 a Protocol was annexed to the Refugee Convention which abolished this temporal limitation.[2] Ireland signed this Protocol in 1968. It is still open to states to limit their protection obligations geographically to events occurring in Europe but Ireland has not made a reservation to this effect.

The Refugee Act 1996 gives statutory effect to Ireland's obligations under the Refugee Convention. Until the Refugee Act became law in November 2000, these obligations were met by administrative procedures.[3] These procedures were formalised in a letter sent by the then Minister for Justice to the office of the United Nations High Commissioner for Refugees (UNHCR) in London in 1985. The courts subsequently declared the so-called 'Von Arnim' letter[4] legally binding.[5]

Irish asylum procedures were put on a statutory footing when the Refugee Act was signed into law in June 1996. However, due to the exponential growth in the number of asylum seekers coming to

---

[1] 1951 Geneva Convention relating to the Status of Refugees, signed 28 July 1951 and entered into force on 21 April 1954.

[2] 1967 New York Protocol relating to the Status of Refugees, signed 31 January 1967 and entered into force on 4 October 1967.

[3] For a full analysis of the drafting of the Refugee Act and amendments thereto, see Ingoldsby, B., 'The Refugee Act 1996 and its Amendments', paper delivered at the Bar Council Seminar: *Refugee and Asylum Law in Ireland*, Kings Inns, Dublin, 26 January 2001.

[4] Named after the UNHCR addressee.

[5] *Fakih v. Minister for Justice* [1993] 2 IR 406; *Gutrani v. Minister for Justice* [1993] 2 IR 427.

Ireland, it soon became apparent that substantial changes needed to be made to the Refugee Act in order to make it workable. The Act had been drafted against a background of less than 500 asylum seekers per annum and, in particular, the powers of the Refugee Applications Commissioner and the structure of the Refugee Appeals Board[6] needed to be revised to take account of the increasing number of asylum applications.

As an interim measure, a second letter was sent to UNHCR on 10 December 1997 – the 'Hope Hanlan' letter.[7] This letter set out Irish asylum procedures in much greater detail, following in many procedural respects the provisions of the (uncommenced) Refugee Act.[8] In practical terms, the responsibility for assessment of asylum claims shifted from UNHCR to the Asylum Division of the Department of Justice, Equality and Law Reform at this time. The 'Hope Hanlan' letter provided the basis for dealing with asylum applications until 20 November 2000, when the Refugee Act finally came into force.

The drafting of the Immigration Act 1999 and, to a lesser extent, the Illegal Immigrants (Trafficking) Act 2000 provided opportunities for the government to make the necessary changes to the Refugee Act. The Immigration Act 1999 contained the first tranche of amendments to the Refugee Act.[9] These amendments were mainly concerned with the structures of the independent bodies for refugee assessment under the Refugee Act, but also included a new provision for permitting the fingerprinting of asylum applicants with a view to reducing the scope for multiple asylum applications.[10] The Illegal Immigrants (Trafficking) Act 2000, the primary purpose of which was to create an offence of trafficking in illegal immigrants, made further, mainly technical, amendments to the Refugee Act.[11]

Since the coming into effect of the Refugee Act on 20 November 2000, its operation has been kept under constant review. That review process has culminated in an extensive series of amendments, con-

---

[6] As it was then proposed. Before it commenced operations the Refugee Appeals Board changed its title to the 'Refugee Appeals Tribunal'.

[7] Named after the UNHCR addressee.

[8] The Minister for Justice, Equality and Law Reform commenced five sections of the Refugee Act that did not need amendments: section 1 (interpretation), section 2 (definition of a refugee), section 5 (prohibition on *refoulement*), section 22 (Dublin Convention) and section 25 (saving for extradition).

[9] The principal objective of the Immigration Act 1999 was to restore the statutory basis for deportation after the old deportation power, contained in the Aliens Act 1935, was deemed inconsistent with the Constitution, *Laurentiu v. Minister for Justice, Equality and Law Reform* [2000] 1 ILRM 1. Section 11(1) of the Immigration Act 1999 contains the amendments to the Refugee Act.

[10] Section 9A of the Refugee Act, as amended.

[11] Section 9 of the Illegal Immigrants Trafficking Act 2000. The Act also altered the time limits in relation to judicial review applications for most aspects of the asylum and immigration procedures (section 5) and increased the powers of the Gardaí to enforce deportation orders (section 10).

tained in the Immigration Act 2003. This Act is designed principally to improve the efficiency with which asylum applications are determined (in particular those which are likely to be ill-founded or the processing of which is the responsibility of another country) and to encourage greater levels of co-operation by asylum applicants in the investigative process.[12] These amendments were brought into effect in September 2003.[13]

The Irish asylum process is conducted under the Refugee Act, as amended, by the Refugee Applications Commissioner ('the Commissioner'), an independent office established under that Act to carry out investigations of all asylum applications made in the state.[14] The Commissioner also makes recommendations at first instance to the Minister for Justice, Equality and Law Reform ('the minister') as to whether the applicant should be declared to be a refugee.[15] Negative recommendations can be appealed to the Refugee Appeals Tribunal ('the Tribunal'), another independent body consisting of lawyers of five or more years' experience.[16] The Tribunal exercises a quasi-judicial function and consists of a chairperson and a number of members (currently thirty-one, with Department of Finance sanction

---

[12] The Immigration Act 2003 also introduces the concept of carrier liability (sanctions imposed on transporters who do not ensure that passengers travelling to Ireland possess the necessary documentation or undergo the requisite immigration checks) into Irish law and updates various other aspects of immigration law. See Immigration Act 2003 (Carrier Liability) Regulations 2003, SI No. 447 of 2003.

[13] See press release 'McDowell announces the commencement of extensive amendments to Refugee Act 1996 with effect from 15 September 2003' (www.justice.ie).

[14] The Commissioner is also responsible for investigating applications for family reunification by recognised refugees. Once an asylum applicant is recognised as a refugee, he or she is entitled to apply for family reunification (section 18 of the Refugee Act, as amended). Approximately 300 people staff the Commissioner's office. In general, the Commissioner's staff do not have formal legal training but UNHCR provides regular training on refugee-related issues. An in-house training unit was set up in 2002 with which the Commissioner intends to replace the need for external training (annual report of the Refugee Applications Commissioner 2002, p. 17).

[15] For the statutory responsibilities of the Refugee Applications Commissioner see the Refugee Act as amended, Immigration Act 1999, Illegal Immigrants (Trafficking) Act 2000, S.I. No. 342 of 2000 – Refugee Act 1996 (Appeals) Regulations 2000, S.I. No. 343 of 2000 – Dublin Convention (Implementation) Order 2000, S.I. No. 344 of 2000 – Refugee Act 1996 (Places and Conditions of Detention) Regulations 2000, S.I. No. 345 of 2000 – Refugee Act 1996 (Application Form) Regulations 2000, S.I. 346 of 2000 – Refugee Act 1996 (Temporary Residence Certificate) Regulations 2000, S.I. 426 of 2002 – Refugee Act (Temporary Residence Certificate) Regulations 2002 and S.I. 571 of 2002 – Refugee Act 1996 (Appeals) Regulations 2002 and the Immigration Act 2003.

[16] This experience does not have to be in refugee or human rights law. However, the Tribunal carries out regular training of its members in conjunction with UNHCR and international refugee law experts. Tribunal members are appointed on a part-time basis for three years and most members also run private legal practices.

for thirty-two) who are appointed by the Minster for Justice, Equality and Law Reform.[17] While the chairperson has power to determine appeals, in practice his main role is to manage work flows and develop standards. Members of the Tribunal are independent and sit alone to hear appeals to decide whether the first-instance recommendation should be upheld or reversed. The minister makes his decision based on the recommendations emerging from the independent process.

This chapter traces the asylum procedure set out in the Refugee Act 1996, as amended in 1999, 2000 and 2003. It is divided into four parts: admissibility, substantive investigation, appeals and final stages.

1 Admissibility

a) First safe country

Not all asylum applicants who arrive in Ireland are entitled to have their applications heard in the state. Another country, where an asylum applicant transited or lodged (or had an opportunity to lodge) an asylum application, may be vested with the legal responsibility to deal with the application.

In 1990, EU member states signed the Dublin Convention, which came into force in September 1997.[18] The Dublin Convention codifies the 'first safe country' principle whereby an asylum seeker is technically obliged to seek refuge in the first safe country in which he or she arrives. However, the reality, accepted by states globally, is that it may not be safe to claim asylum in the first country of arrival. The conflicts in west and central Africa and the Middle East have shown how one country's violation of human rights can affect a whole region, rendering the search for nearby safety sometimes impossible. It is recognised that asylum seekers travel to particular destinations that they consider safe and this may entail a transit, or sojourn, in another country *en route*.

The United Nations High Commissioner for Refugees (UNHCR) has

---

[17] The Refugee Appeals Tribunal was initially described as the 'Refugee Appeals Board' in the Refugee Act. On 5 October 2000, asylum appeals were deferred until new statutory procedures were put in place to enable the Tribunal to commence its work on 20 February 2001. For the statutory responsibilities of the tribunal see the Refugee Act, as amended by the Immigration Act 1999, the Illegal Immigrants (Trafficking) Act 2000 and the Immigration Act 2003; Refugee Act 1996 (Section 14 and 15 and Second Schedule)(Commencement) (No. 2) Order 2000, S.I. No. 308 of 2000; Refugee Act 1996 (Appeals) Regulations 2002, S.I. No. 571 of 2002; Dublin Convention (Implementation) Order 2000, S.I. No. 343 of 2000; Refugee Act 1996 (Transitional) Regulations 2000, S.I. No. 348 of 2000; Refugee Act 1996 (Commencement) Order 2000, S.I. No. 365 of 2000 and Refugee Act 1996 (Appeals) Regulations 2003, SI No. 424 of 2003.

[18] *Convention determining the State responsible for examining applications for asylum lodged in one of the member states of the European Communities* signed in Dublin on 15 June 1990, OJC 254, 18.08.1997, p. 1.

developed the principle of first safe country in line with international law and standards. In 1979, the UNHCR Executive Committee (EXCOM) adopted Conclusion No. 15, 'Refugees without an asylum country',[19] which states that

> [r]egard should be had to the concept that asylum should not be refused solely on the ground that it could be sought from another State. Where, however, it appears that the person, before requesting asylum, already has a connection or close links with another State, he may if it appears fair and reasonable be called upon first to request asylum from that State;[20]

> Agreements providing for the return by States of persons who have entered their territory from another contracting State in an unlawful manner should be applied in respect of asylum seekers with due regard to their special situation.[21]

Although not legally binding, UNHCR EXCOM Conclusions are politically binding due to the obligation to co-operate with UNHCR that states assume upon ratifying the Refugee Convention.[22] In a subsequent EXCOM Conclusion in 1989 ('Problems of refugees and asylum-seekers who move in an irregular manner from a country in which they had already found protection'), UNHCR, although discouraging irregular migration from a country where a durable solution is available, sets out a number of criteria that need to be satisfied before an asylum seeker can be returned to a country considered safe for the purposes of seeking asylum. The criteria are as follows.

1) That he or she will be permitted to enter and remain safely until a durable solution is found.
2) That he or she will be treated in accordance with basic human standards.
3) That he or she will be protected from *refoulement*.
4) That he or she will not be subject to persecution.[23]

These UNHCR EXCOM Conclusions set the minimum standards to be applied when states employ the first safe country principle (which is also, more commonly, known as the 'safe third country' principle).

b) Allocating responsibility under the Dublin Convention

The Dublin Convention sets out fixed criteria for determining which EU member state is to assess and accept a particular asylum application. In this respect the Dublin Convention seeks to prevent the 'refugees in

---

[19] UNHCR EXCOM Conclusion No. 15 (XXX) of 1979 (see www.unhcr.ch).
[20] *Ibid.* para (iv).
[21] *Ibid.* para. (vi).
[22] Article 35 of the Refugee Convention.
[23] UNHCR EXCOM Conclusion No. 58 (XL) of 1989 (www.unhcr.ch).

orbit' phenomenon whereby member states, due to asylum applicants' irregular migratory patterns and consequential jurisdictional disputes, were not accepting responsibility for the adjudication of asylum claims.[24]

The Dublin Convention was superseded, from 1 September 2003, by the so-called Dublin Regulation.[25] The adoption of the Dublin Regulation places the matter of allocating member state responsibility on a Community law footing rather than on the international law basis of the Dublin Convention and is intended to simplify the procedures as between states for applying the allocation criteria. The following paragraphs set out a description of the criteria for allocating responsibility for the determination of asylum claims among member states, as set out in the Dublin Convention. The basic features of the Dublin Convention are retained in the Dublin Regulation and any significant changes are noted.

The hierarchy of criteria in the Dublin Convention is, in summary and in descending order of applicability, as follows.

1   **Family connection:** Where an applicant for asylum has a member of his family[26] who has been recognised as a refugee by a member state, that state is responsible for examining the application – subject to the agreement of the asylum applicant and the family member (Article 4 of the Dublin Convention).[27]

2   **Valid visa or residence permit:** If a member state has issued the asylum applicant with a visa or a residence permit, that state is responsible[28] (Article 5 of the Dublin Convention).

---

[24] In addition, the Dublin Convention purports to assist the EU's objective of sharing the burden of asylum applications more equitably throughout the EU.

[25] *Council Regulation establishing the criteria and mechanisms for determining the member state responsible for examining an asylum application lodged in one of the member states by a third-country national* (EC Regulation No. 343/2003 of 18 February 2003, O.J No. L50 of 25 February 2003).

[26] Article 4 states that the 'family member in question may not be other than the spouse of the applicant for asylum or his or her unmarried child who is a minor of under eighteen years, or his or her father or mother where the applicant for asylum is himself or herself an unmarried child who is a minor of under eighteen years'. Under the Dublin Regulation, it is open to member states to extend the definition of a 'family member' to include unmarried partners in a stable relationship (where the national legislation treats unmarried couples in the same manner as it treats married couples under its aliens law). The definition of minor children is further clarified under the Dublin Regulation – they may be born in or out of wedlock, or adopted, and they must be dependent on their parents (Article 2(i) Dublin Regulation).

[27] This is replicated in Article 7 of the Dublin Regulation. Article 8 of the Dublin Regulation provides that if the asylum applicant has a family member whose application has not yet been determined at first instance, that member state bears the responsibility of examining the application for asylum, if the person concerned consents.

[28] Article 5 of the Dublin Convention and Article 9 of the Dublin Regulation address the awkward situation whereby an asylum applicant has more than one valid visa or residence permit issued by different member states. This is worked out through a complicated hierarchy which, in summary, establishes responsibility based on the longest period of validity, or the latest expiry date, of the residence permits or visas.

3   **First member state entered irregularly:** the member state whose
    territory was first entered irregularly by the asylum applicant from a
    non-EU state has responsibility (Article 6 Dublin Convention).[29]

4   **member state that permitted regular entry:** If the asylum applicant
    was admitted to a member state in compliance with its normal immi-
    gration rules, that member state is responsible. There is an exception
    to this rule: if the applicant was first admitted to a member state which
    does not require him or her to have a visa, and he or she moves on
    to another member state which also does not require him or her to
    have a visa, and applies for asylum in the second member state then
    the second state has responsibility for dealing with the application.
    Simple movement through a transit area without leaving it does not
    count as regular entry into the first member state but if an application
    for asylum is made while in a transit zone, the member state where
    the transit zone is bears responsibility (Article 7 Dublin Convention).[30]

5   **None of the above:** If a responsible member state cannot be desig-
    nated on the basis of Articles 4 to 7, the first member state with which
    the application for asylum is lodged is responsible for examining it
    (Article 8 Dublin Convention).[31]

A member state in which an application has been made always has the
option to deal with the application itself rather than invoking the above
criteria to transfer responsibility.[32] Also, by virtue of Article 9 of the Dublin
Convention, a member state may volunteer to accept and assess an asylum application 'for humanitarian reasons, based in particular on family
or cultural grounds' even if another member state has responsibility.[33]

---

[29] Article 10 of the Dublin Regulation also designates responsibility on the basis of irreg-
    ular entry of an asylum seeker but this responsibility ceases after twelve months
    (Article 10(1)). According to Article 6 of the Dublin Convention, if an applicant has
    been living in the member state where he or she applies for asylum for more than six
    months beforehand, the member state where the application was made is responsible
    regardless of the means of entry to the EU. The Dublin Regulation reduces this period
    of six months to five months (Article (10(2)). The Dublin Regulation also stipulates
    that if an asylum applicant has been living for periods of time of at least five months
    in several member states, the member state where this has been most recently the
    case is responsible (Article 10(2)).
[30] Articles 11 and 12 of the Dublin Regulation replicate these provisions.
[31] Article 13 of the Dublin Regulation replicates this provision.
[32] Known as the 'opt-out' clause, Article 3(4) of the Dublin Convention allows member
    states to examine an application for asylum even if such examination is not its
    responsibility under the criteria defined in the Dublin Convention and Article 3(2) of
    the Dublin Regulation restates this provision.
[33] The Dublin Regulation adds one final criterion to the hierarchy of responsibility
    which facilitates greater family unity where the technical application of the criteria
    would otherwise lead to family separation (Article 14). The Dublin Regulation also
    elaborates the 'humanitarian' clause to encourage family unity, making particular
    mention of the need to unite dependent relatives on account of pregnancy, a new-
    born child, a serious illness or handicap or old age (Article 15(2)). Member states are
    further encouraged to bear in mind the need to keep unaccompanied minors close
    to their family (Article 15(3)).

Once the responsibility of one member state has been established, the Dublin Convention ensures that an asylum seeker can pursue his or her claim in the designated member state only.[34] An asylum applicant can be readmitted to the member state responsible at various stages

(a) where his or her claim was under examination before he or she moved to another member state without permission[35]

(b) where he or she had withdrawn his or her application from the responsible member state and lodged a subsequent application in another member state[36]

(c) where his or her application for asylum had been rejected prior to his or her illegal arrival in another member state[37]

(d) where he or she withdraws the asylum application at the admissibility stage of the asylum procedure (ie when the Dublin Convention or safe third country criteria are being considered).[38]

c) Safe countries and divergent state practice

Underpinning the Dublin Convention is an assumption that all member states are safe countries of asylum and that transferring asylum applicants from one to another can take place without question. But this ignores the persistence of divergent member state laws, policies and practices. The Dublin Convention also allows for the removal of asylum applicants to countries outside the EU for the purposes of examination of their asylum claim.[39] Article 3(5) of the Dublin Convention (which is reflected in Article 3(3) of the Dublin Regulation) states:

> Any member state shall retain the right, pursuant to its national laws, to send an applicant for asylum to a third State, in compliance with the provisions of the Geneva Convention, as amended by the New York Protocol.

There is no right for an applicant to appeal a transfer decision on substantive protection grounds in the Dublin Convention process; an asylum applicant may only appeal the technical decision to transfer. The UK House of Lords considered this restriction in 1999 when cases brought by two asylum seekers, one of Somali and one of Algerian

---

[34] Article 10 of the Dublin Convention. Article 16 of the Dublin Regulation follows this provision.

[35] Article 10(1)(c) of the Dublin Convention.

[36] Article 10(1)(d) of the Dublin Convention.

[37] Article 10(1)(e) of the Dublin Convention.

[38] Article 3(7) of the Dublin Convention. This provision is replicated in Article 4(4) of the Dublin Regulation.

[39] Transfers to non-EU countries under the Dublin Convention do not frequently arise in the Irish context due to the fact that asylum applicants normally travel to Ireland via another member state. This may change with the growth in air travel and an increase in direct flights to Dublin from turbulent countries.

origin, were heard.[40] Both asylum applicants challenged a decision to transfer them to other EU member states. Both feared what is known as 'non-state agent persecution' in their countries of origin. The Somali national had sought asylum in Germany and her application was refused by the German authorities on the basis that the persecution she alleged did not emanate from governmental sources (there was a breakdown of central authority in Somalia so proving state persecution would have been almost impossible). Under the terms of the Dublin Convention, Germany had accepted responsibility for her return. The Algerian national feared persecution from the Groupe Islamique Armé (GIA) and contended that the Algerian government was not in a position to offer him protection. The French authorities demanded at least tacit state support for persecution to give rise to a successful claim for refugee status. Concluding that the German and French authorities interpreted the definition of persecution in Article 1(A) of the Refugee Convention in a narrower manner than the UK asylum authorities, the House of Lords decided that the removal of the applicants to France and Germany was likely to result in their deportation to Somalia and Algeria respectively.[41] The House of Lords stated that the correct interpretation of Article 1(A) of the Refugee Convention included non-state agent persecution and, therefore, the UK Secretary of State had erred in authorising the transfer of the asylum seekers.

The UK legislation was subsequently amended by the UK Immigration and Asylum Act 1999. This Act provides that a state with which there exist arrangements for determining responsibility for considering asylum applications (such as the Dublin Convention) must be a place from which a person will not be sent to another country 'otherwise than in accordance with the Refugee Convention'.[42]

The fact that these cases involving non-state agent persecution came to prominence should not deflect from the reality that diverging protection practices among member states are more widespread. The differing interpretations of asylum applications based on persecution because of gender or sexual orientation are two examples.[43] In order

---

[40] *R v. Secretary of State for the Home Department, Ex Parte Adan* [2001] 2 AC 477.

[41] Germany has since changed its legal position to conform fully with the Refugee Convention. Also, as part of the EU's harmonisation process, the *Commission Proposal for a Council Directive on minimum standards for the qualification and status of third country nationals and stateless persons as refugees or as persons who otherwise need international protection* ('Qualifications Directive') states that for a person to qualify as a refugee under the 1951 Convention, it is immaterial whether the persecution feared stems from the state or from non-state actors provided that, in the latter case, the state is unable or unwilling to offer effective protection ((COM (2001) 510 final, Brussels 21 September 2001, Articles 9(1) and 11(2)(a)).

[42] Sections 11(1)(b) and 12(7)(c) of the UK Immigration and Asylum Act 1999.

[43] Irish legislation includes both gender and sexual orientation as specific grounds of persecution for the purposes of an asylum application (See Sections 1 and 2 of the Refugee Act, as amended).

for the 'Dublin' procedures to operate efficiently and in accordance with international human rights law and standards, harmonisation of the asylum procedures throughout the EU is crucial. This is a point frequently acknowledged by the EU and national institutions. The move towards harmonisation of, *inter alia*, asylum procedures, criteria and standards for granting refugee status and reception conditions is well under way. The need for harmonised criteria for granting refugee status (or other forms of protection) that accord with applicable international law and standards, is particularly important in the context of shifting responsibility for dealing with asylum applications.

d) Irish procedure

In Ireland, Section 22 of the Refugee Act empowers the minister to make Orders to give effect to the Dublin Convention. The current Order sets out the procedure whereby the Dublin Convention issue is determined at first instance by the Commissioner and may be appealed to the Tribunal.[44] The process is as follows.

- If it appears at any stage when or after the asylum application is made[45] that another member state may be responsible under the Dublin Convention for dealing with that application, the applicant is put on notice of this and invited to make representations to the Commissioner on the matter within five working days.[46]
- In the meantime, the Commissioner consults with the member state likely to be responsible and seeks the acceptance of responsibility by that state. Since 1 January 2003 these enquiries are supported by fingerprint checks on the EURODAC database, maintained by all member states, of the fingerprints taken from each asylum applicant when an application is made.[47]
- If the Commissioner determines that another member state is responsible, the asylum applicant is notified of that decision and of the right to appeal (within five working days) to the Tribunal.
- The Tribunal determines the appeal on papers only; there is no oral hearing.

---

[44] Dublin Convention (Implementation) Order 2000 S.I No. 343 of 2000; see also Refugee Act 1996 (Section 22) Order 2003, SI No. 423 of 2003. Before the Dublin Convention became operable in 1997 in Ireland the Department of Justice, Equality and Law Reform was applying, within the context of its administrative asylum procedure, the safe third-country rule, a practice endorsed by the courts (*Anisimova v. Minister for Justice, Equality and Law Reform*, High Court 18 February 1997, Supreme Court 28 November 1997).

[45] Though not later than six months after the asylum application is made (Article 11(1) Dublin Convention).

[46] The burden of proof is on the asylum applicant to show that his or her application should be examined in Ireland. Section 11A(2) Refugee Act, as amended in 2003.

[47] Council Regulation No. 2725/2000 concerning the establishment of 'Eurodac' for the comparison of fingerprints for the effective application of the Dublin Convention (Official Journal L 316, 15.12.2000), which came into effect on 15 February 2003.

- If there is no appeal, or the appeal is unsuccessful, the matter is referred to the minister to make a deportation order. There is no opportunity to make representations to the minister prior to deportation for Dublin Convention cases.
- The deportation order requires that the applicant leave the state. If the applicant does not comply voluntarily (a criminal offence), compliance may be enforced and the person may be detained for that purpose.
- If the applicant is unable to produce a valid travel document the minister issues a *laissez-passer*.

The Dublin Convention contains time limits for responses to queries and acknowledgement of responsibility. In default of a response within the various time limits set out in the Dublin Convention, the member state in default is fixed with responsibility for the application. Uniquely, Irish law governing the Dublin Convention required that in default of acceptance of responsibility, Ireland must deal with the application but this has effectively been repealed by the Immigration Act 2003.[48] In a bid to increase efficiency, the Dublin Regulation shortens the time limits for transfer and acceptance of responsibility. A requested member state must give a decision on the request to take charge of an applicant within two months from the date of receipt of the request.[49] A requesting member state may plead urgency and, in such circumstances, a response must be delivered as soon as possible but no later than one month.[50] Failure to act in the two-month or one-month period is tantamount to acceding to a request.[51] Transfer of an asylum applicant to the member state deemed responsible must take place within six months or else responsibility falls back on the member state where the asylum application was lodged.[52]

e) Effect of the Immigration Act 2003 on 'Dublin' procedures

The replacement Section 22 of the Refugee Act (provided at Section 7(1) of the Immigration Act 2003) contains a number of significant developments in the minister's powers to make subsidiary legislation in respect of 'Dublin' procedures. The power is expanded to enable full effect to be given to the Dublin Regulation and to the Agreement extending the operation of the Dublin Convention to Norway and Iceland. The minister is also enabled to make other changes to the

---

[48] See replacement Section 22 of the Refugee Act, provided at Section 7(1) of the Immigration Act 2003.

[49] Article 18(1) of the Dublin Regulation.

[50] Article 18(6) of the Dublin Regulation.

[51] Article 18(7) of the Dublin Regulation.

[52] Article 19(3) of the Dublin Regulation. Article 19(4) of the Dublin Regulation allows for extension of this time limit to one year if the transfer cannot be carried out due to imprisonment of the asylum applicant or up to a maximum of eighteen months if the asylum applicant absconds.

'Dublin' procedures regardless of whether they are rooted in the Convention or the Regulation. Orders for the purposes of giving effect to any agreements made with safe third countries to return asylum applicants are also permitted.[53]

The Immigration Act 2003 has put on a statutory footing, for the first time, the concept of safe third country in Irish law. This envisages a situation where Ireland can transfer asylum applicants to countries outside the EU in order for their asylum applications to be processed. In order to designate a third country 'safe', the Minister for Justice, Equality and Law Reform must (with the concurrence of the Minister for Foreign Affairs) have regard to the following:

> (i)   whether the country is party to and complies generally with its obligations under the Geneva Convention, the Convention against Torture … and the International Covenant on Civil and Political Rights …
> (ii) whether the country has a democratic political system and an independent judiciary
> (iii) whether the country is governed by the rule of law.[54]

In order to transfer asylum applicants to a safe third country there must be a formal agreement between Ireland and the other country,[55] which must include provision for prompt response times.[56]

Also included in the replacement Section 22 of the Refugee Act is the possibility that transfer decisions may be made by appointed officials of the minister or by an immigration officer. Until the changes made by the Immigration Act 2003, the Commissioner retained sole responsibility for Dublin Convention procedures. The assignment of extra personnel for the implementation of 'Dublin' procedures is, according to the government, in the interests of efficiency:

> [f]or instance, if such decisions are to be made at ports of entry based on quick response times to requests to other convention countries or safe third countries to take back an application, it is convenient to assign that duty to immigration officers.[57]

Reflecting the possible new role of immigration officials, the minister may by Order change the current procedure to require that an application for asylum cannot be investigated at first instance by the

---

[53] Section 22(1) of the Refugee Act, as amended.

[54] Section 22(5)(a) of the Refugee Act, as amended in 2003. The Minister for Foreign Affairs has a further power to amend or revoke a designation (Section 22(6)(b) of the Refugee Act as amended). The Minister for Justice, Equality and Law Reform has the same power to revoke (Section 22(7) of the Refugee Act as amended).

[55] Section 22(5)(b) of the Refugee Act, as amended in 2003.

[56] Section 22(5)(b) (I) and (II) of the Refugee Act, as amended in 2003.

[57] Immigration Bill 2002, Explanatory Memorandum (Dáil Éireann) Government amendments, footnote 131, p. 38.

Commissioner until it has been determined by an immigration official or person authorised by the minister that another country does not have responsibility.[58] This clearly envisages a situation whereby asylum applicants will, upon arrival to Ireland, immediately undergo the 'Dublin' (or admissibility) procedure. Admission to the regular asylum procedure might not be permitted until this initial hurdle has been crossed.

At present, enquiries under the Dublin Convention can take weeks or months. Clearly the new 'Dublin' regime envisages a very short procedure based on rapid response arrangements with other countries. New powers of detention may be introduced to facilitate these foreshortened procedures. An asylum applicant may be detained for up to forty-eight hours pending a transfer decision.[59] It is intended that such detention will take place at the border and that it may only occur when special agreements are in place between Ireland and other countries whereby swift exchanges of information and responses to requests for transfer are formally provided for. Detention is unlikely to be imposed unless such arrangements exist because it would serve no useful purpose.[60] The minister's explanation for these changes, when he introduced them at committee stage in the Dáil, points to the possibility[61] that if such arrangements are in place between, say, Ireland and the UK or Ireland and France, people who claim asylum on arrival to the state having come from one of these countries could be detained briefly and, if the other state accepted responsibility within a short time, the immigration officer could make an on-the-spot decision to return the asylum applicant without delay.

The Immigration Act 2003 does not alter the Tribunal's responsibility to hear appeals against decisions to transfer under the 'Dublin' procedures. Under these procedures, an asylum applicant is given five working days to make written representations to the Tribunal stating why he or she should not be transferred. If the appeal is successful, the Commissioner is sent the application for a substantive investigation. If unsuccessful, or if an asylum seeker fails to respond to the notification that he or she may be transferred under the Dublin Convention, the file is sent to the minister to set proceedings in train for the transfer. In line with the option under the Dublin Regulation, the replacement

---

[58] Section 22 (2)(d) Refugee Act, as amended in 2003.
[59] Section 22(2)(j) Refugee Act, as amended in 2003.
[60] Immigration Bill 2002, Explanatory Memorandum (Dáil Éireann) Government amendments, footnote 137, p. 39. See Immigration Act 2003 (Removal Places of Detention) Regulations, SI No 444 of 2003; Immigration Act 2003 (Approved Ports) Regulations 2003, SI No. 445 of 2003 and Immigration Act 2003 (Removal Direction) Regulations 2003 SI No. 446 of 2003.
[61] Arising out of the provision at Article 23 of the Dublin Regulation for bilateral administrative arrangements between member states for simpler administrative arrangements and shorter time-limits for dealing with requests.

Section 22 provides that an appeal from a decision to transfer an asylum applicant to an EU member state or safe third country will not have suspensive effect.[62] In other words, transfer of an asylum applicant will have immediate effect even if an appeal is lodged. In the event that an appeal against a transfer is successful, the asylum seeker will be permitted to re-enter the state for the purposes of having his or her application examined.

In 2002, a total of 6,380 enquiries were made by the Commissioner to other member states to ascertain if an asylum applicant should be transferred from Ireland under the terms of the Dublin Convention. The actual number of transfers made to other member states under the Dublin Convention during 2002 was sixty-four. Ireland received thirty-eight asylum seekers from other Convention countries during the same period. These statistics are surprising given that there are few direct flights to Ireland from countries that are known for producing asylum seekers. This indicates a high level of non-compliance by responsible member states and it also reflects the difficulties with the means of proof required to confirm responsibility.[63] It remains to be seen how the Dublin Regulation and the new procedures under the Refugee Act, as amended, will affect this trend. It is unclear how these provisions will apply in the context of asylum seekers who apply within the state as distinct from the point of entry (see below).

2 First-instance investigation

a) Making an asylum application at the border

Most applications for refugee status are made within the state at the office of the Commissioner, with approximately 17 per cent of applications made at points of entry to the state, such as ports or airports. If an asylum application is made at a point of entry, it is generally during routine immigration checks that it emerges that a person wishes to claim asylum.[64] In such instances, refusal, or intended refusal, of leave to land is not pursued once it becomes apparent that a person is unwilling to leave the state for fear of persecution.[65] If this is the case, the person is briefly interviewed by an immigration officer and fingerprinted. Section 8(1)(a) of the Refugee Act states that

---

[62] Article 19(2) of the Dublin Regulation.

[63] Article 18(5) of the Dublin Regulation seeks to assist in this regard: 'If there is no formal proof, the requested member state shall acknowledge its responsibility if the circumstantial evidence is coherent, verifiable and sufficiently detailed to establish responsibility'.

[64] Immigration controls are carried out pursuant to the Aliens Act 1935 and the Aliens Order 1946, as amended by the subsequent Orders under the Aliens Act 1935.

[65] Section 9(1) of the Refugee Act, as amended, requires that the applicant be given leave to enter the state.

[a] person who arrives at the frontiers of the State seeking asylum in the State or seeking the protection of the State against persecution or requesting not to be returned or removed to a particular country or otherwise indicating an unwillingness to leave the State for fear of persecution –

(i)   shall be interviewed by an immigration officer as soon as practicable after such arrival …

The interview takes place (with the assistance of an interpreter, where necessary and possible) and is, in effect, a continuation of the normal enquiries that an immigration officer might make of any intending entrant to the state. The purpose of the interview is to

- verify that the person wishes to seek asylum
- the grounds upon which the claim is based
- the identity of the person
- the nationality and country of origin of the person
- the mode of transport used and route travelled to the state
- the reason why the person came to Ireland and the legal basis for his or her entry.[66]

The immigration officer is obliged to inform the asylum applicant, where possible in a language that he or she understands, that a formal application for a declaration of refugee status (ie an asylum application) may be made. In such circumstances, immigration officers also inform asylum applicants that they may consult a solicitor and UNHCR for this purpose.[67] The immigration officer subsequently sends a copy of the interview to the Commissioner.

The state does not have a policy of systematically detaining asylum seekers. Nonetheless, provision for the detention of asylum seekers is made in the Refugee Act, as amended. An asylum seeker may be detained where an immigration officer or a member of the Garda Síochána, with reasonable cause, suspects that an applicant

- poses a threat to national security or public order in the state
- has committed a serious non-political crime outside the state
- has not made reasonable efforts to establish his or her true identity
- intends to avoid removal from the state in the event of his or her application being transferred to a Dublin Convention country or a safe third country
- intends to leave the state and enter another state without lawful authority
- without reasonable cause has destroyed his or her identity or travel documents or is in possession of forged identity documents.[68]

---

[66] Section 8(2) (a) to (f) of the Refugee Act, as amended.
[67] Section 8(1)(c) of the Refugee Act, as amended.
[68] Section 9(8) of the Refugee Act, as amended.

The detained asylum applicant must be brought before a District Court judge as soon as practicable and if the judge decides that one of the above grounds for detention correctly applies detention for a period of twenty-one days may be imposed.[69] Thereafter, a District Court judge must review detention every twenty-one days. It is open to the judge to impose residency or reporting requirements on an asylum applicant instead of detention.[70]

b) Lodging an asylum application at the office of the Refugee Applications Commissioner

Whether an asylum application is made at the border or within the state, the asylum applicant must present himself or herself to the office of the Commissioner to initiate investigation of the asylum application. If an asylum application has not been made at the border, the asylum applicant, upon lodging his or her application at the Commissioner's office, is given a brief interview with the same objective as the one described above (to establish identity, means of travel to Ireland etc). UNHCR is notified of all asylum applications made in the state. Officers from the Commissioner's office, immigration officers and members of the Garda Síochána are authorised to fingerprint asylum seekers.[71] The reason for fingerprinting is to detect multiple asylum applications and to help in the process of determining if another country might be responsible for examining an asylum application. Fingerprints are stored at Garda headquarters where they are kept solely for the purposes of comparison with other asylum seekers' fingerprints. Fingerprints are also sent to the central database in Luxembourg. The data protection rules that apply to fingerprinting of asylum seekers are set out in the Refugee Act:

---

[69] Section 9(10) of the Refugee Act, as amended in 2003. The twenty-one-day period is an extension of the nine day period that existed in the Refugee Act prior to amendment by the Immigration Act 2003. The UNHCR Representation in Ireland, in its comments to the proposed draft amendments to the Immigration Bill 2002 (as it was then) of June 2003 urged that the ten-day period be maintained.

[70] Section 9(10)(b)(ii) of the Refugee Act, as amended. The UNHCR Representation in Ireland, in its comments to the proposed draft amendments to the Immigration Bill 2002 (as it was then) of June 2003, expressed its hope that the state's policy of not detaining asylum seekers continues. Stating its general policy on detention, UNHCR commented that 'detention of asylum applicants is inherently undesirable and should only be used as a last resort, when alternatives to detention have been exhausted'. If detention must be imposed, UNHCR maintains that it should be limited to the need to (1) verify identity, (2) determine the elements on which the claim to refugee status or asylum is based, (3) deal with cases where refugees or asylum seekers have destroyed their travel and/or identity documents in order to mislead the authorities of the state in which they intend to claim asylum or (4) protect national security or public order. UNHCR also asserts that asylum applicants should not be detained in prisons and if special facilities are not available, asylum applicants should at least be separated from convicted criminals.

[71] Section 9(A)(1) of the Refugee Act, as amended.

[E]very fingerprint of an applicant taken [...] and every copy thereof shall, if not previously destroyed, be destroyed –

(a) in the case the applicant becomes a citizen of the State, before the expiration of one month after the granting of the certificate of natural-isation or of Irish citizenship to him or her or the acknowledgement by the Minister of the validity of his or her declaration accepting Irish citizenship, as the case may be;

(b) in any other case, before the expiration of 10 years after the taking of such fingerprints.[72]

Once fingerprints are taken, the Commissioner provides each asylum applicant with a temporary residence certificate. This document, with-out prejudice to any other permission granted to remain, certifies that the asylum applicant will not be removed from the state until a final determination has been made on his or her asylum application. This may be at the end of a Dublin Convention procedure, when an asylum application is withdrawn or deemed withdrawn or when refugee status is refused.[73] An asylum applicant may not leave the state unless the consent of the minister is obtained.[74]

c) Investigation by the Commissioner

i) Substantive interview and legal aid

Asylum applicants are generally given fourteen days from the day they lodge their asylum application with the Commissioner's office to complete and return a lengthy questionnaire about their asylum application. The Commissioner informs asylum applicants of their entitlement to consult a solicitor and the local UNHCR office.[75] An interview is subsequently scheduled which is conducted by a caseworker, with the aid of an interpreter where necessary, and a legal representative if the applicant so wishes. In the case of an unaccom-panied minor, a social worker may also attend. Most applicants are interviewed within three months of arrival. Sometimes a second inter-view takes place if further examination is necessary.[76]

The answers supplied by the asylum applicant in the questionnaire create the basis for the interview. This is why it is very important for asylum seekers to access legal assistance at the earliest possible oppor-tunity and particularly when filling out the questionnaire. The Refugee Legal Service (established under the aegis of the Legal Aid Board, the state-funded body that provides legal aid in non-criminal matters to

---

[72] Section 9A(7) of the Refugee Act.
[73] Section 9(1), (2) and (3) of the Refugee Act, as amended in 2003.
[74] Section 9(4)(a) of the Refugee Act, as amended.
[75] Section 11(8) of the Refugee Act, as amended.
[76] Section 11 of the Refugee Act, as amended, sets out the legal details of a first-instance investigation.

persons on low income) has a section in the reception area of the Commissioner's office to accept requests for legal aid. There are also three branches nation-wide. The Refugee Legal Service offers confidential and independent legal services to all asylum applicants in Ireland. It offers a range of services including advice prior to submitting the asylum questionnaire, written submissions to the Commissioner, representation before the Tribunal, assistance at the end of the asylum process for applications for leave to remain in the state, deportation proceedings and judicial review. The Refugee Documentation Centre, which also operates under the aegis of the Legal Aid Board, assists the Refugee Legal Service and other agencies dealing with asylum issues by retaining extensive country of origin and legal information in its library.[77]

The issues raised in the asylum questionnaire, such as the political and human rights situation described by an asylum applicant, are researched by a caseworker from the Commissioner's office prior to the interview. The purpose of the interview is to elicit the asylum applicant's story. Legal representatives rarely attend first-instance interviews and, if they do, their role is limited to making comments at the end of the interview. After the interview, asylum applicants are enabled to review the contents of the interviewer's notes by being asked to sign each page. The Commissioner has discretion to take account of representations made after the interview. Alternatively, clarifications that need to be made can be addressed at the appeal stage.[78]

ii) Proving a claim for asylum

Following an asylum seeker's substantive interview (or interviews), the Commissioner prepares a report in writing of the results of the investigation. The Commissioner's task is to make a recommendation as to whether an applicant is entitled to refugee status by reference to section 2 of the Refugee Act:

> [I]n this Act 'a refugee' means a person who, owing to a well-founded fear of being persecuted for reasons of race, religion, nationality, membership

---

[77] A query and research service is available at the documentation centre to all bodies involved in the asylum process. Although this service is not strictly available to members of the public they can make an appointment to use the centre to carry out individual research.

[78] Section 11(3)(a) of the Refugee Act, as amended in 2003. Prior to the passing of the Immigration Act 2003, it was open to asylum applicants to clarify inconsistencies in their statements within seven working days after the interview. The Commissioner is no longer *obliged* to take account of any representations made by the asylum applicant, UNHCR, or any other person concerned after the interview has taken place. Thus, the Commissioner no longer has to wait seven working days from the date of the interview before a recommendation on the application can be made (Immigration Bill 2002, Explanatory Memorandum (Dáil Éireann) Government amendments, footnote 32, p. 14).

of a particular social group or political opinion, is outside the country of his or her nationality and is unable or, owing to such fear, is unwilling to avail himself or herself of the protection of that country; or who, not having a nationality and being outside the country of his or her former habitual residence, is unable or, owing to such fear, is unwilling to return to it...

The fear of persecution maintained by an asylum seeker must be well-founded and connected to one of the grounds in the refugee definition, ie race, religion, nationality, membership of a particular social group or political opinion.[79] Given the difficulties related to proving an asylum claim, unsubstantiated subjective fears may also be taken into account. For objective information, decision-makers consult international and domestic case law, country of origin information from organisations such as Amnesty International, UNHCR, the US Department of State, the UK Home Office, internet news, and general reference books. Approximately 13 per cent of asylum applicants gain refugee status in Ireland at first instance.

Proving the veracity of an asylum application poses difficulties for asylum applicants and their legal representatives, as well as for decision-makers. Most asylum seekers do not have documentary evidence to prove that they have been, or might be, persecuted. The Refugee Act 1996, as originally drafted, was silent on the burden of proof for both the asylum seeker and the decision-maker. Amendments made to the Refugee Act by the Immigration Act 2003 attempt to address this uncertainty by prescribing the burden of proof for a number of aspects of the asylum procedure. By new section 11A of the Refugee Act, the burden of proving an asylum application shifts to the asylum applicant where he or she is a national of (or has a right of residence in) a country that is designated safe.[80] The burden of proof also shifts to the applicant if he or she has lodged a prior application for asylum in a country that is a party to the Refugee Convention. In either of these cases, an asylum applicant will be presumed not to be a refugee unless he or she shows reasonable grounds for the contention that he or she is a refugee.[81] Thus, asylum applicants who emanate from countries that do not normally produce refugees or from where they have already submitted a claim for asylum face higher evidential obstacles.

The shifting of the burden to asylum applicants, if strictly applied, may cause excessive problems to those who are genuinely in need of protection but who cannot prove their case with documentation or

---

[79] The definition of 'social group' in Irish asylum law extends to 'membership of a trade union and also includes membership of a group of persons whose defining characteristic is their belonging to the female or the male sex or having a particular sexual orientation' (section 1 of Refugee Act, as amended).

[80] According to section 12(4) of the Refugee Act, as amended in 2003.

[81] Section 11A(1) Refugee Act, as amended in 2003.

other forms of evidence. Shifting the burden in this manner is contrary to guidelines in the UNHCR *Handbook on Procedures and Criteria for Determining Refugee Status*. According to the handbook (which is not a legally binding document but is generally considered of persuasive value) the duty to ascertain and evaluate all relevant facts in an asylum application is shared between the applicant and the examiner.

Linked to the burden of proof is the standard of proof. Irish asylum legislation does not address the standard of proof to be applied in asylum cases. In civil law cases the standard of proof is the 'balance of probabilities' and in criminal law the level of proof required must reach the higher standard of 'beyond reasonable doubt' to convict an accused. Neither standard is appropriate for asylum cases.

> This is because the nature of the evidence available in connection with most asylum claims is, inescapably in the circumstances, third-hand, anecdotal or otherwise of dubious reliability and verifiability. A reasonable stab at describing the standard to be applied might be whether it is possible, and not improbable, that the applicant is a refugee.[82]

It is difficult to be scientific about the standard of proof but UNHCR guidelines state that the benefit of the doubt should be afforded in circumstances where the asylum seeker has made a genuine effort to substantiate his or her claim and all possible evidence has been obtained and checked or the applicant has fully explained the lack of evidence. When the Immigration Bill (as it was then) was being discussed at Committee Stage in June 2003, UNHCR recommended to the government that an extra provision be inserted in the Refugee Act to the effect that the benefit of the doubt be afforded when

(a) the applicant has made a genuine effort to substantiate his or her claim
(b) all available evidence has been obtained and, where possible, checked and
(c) the examiner is satisfied that the applicant's statements are coherent and plausible and do not run counter to generally known facts relevant to his or her case ...[83]

This approximates to the standard applied by the Commissioner[84] but the Oireachtas chose not to insert such a provision in the Immigration Act 2003.

Central to the assessment of asylum claims is the issue of credibility. Section 11B of the Refugee Act (as inserted by the Immigration Act 2003) requires the Commissioner or, on appeal, the Tribunal, to have regard to thirteen specific factors when conducting a credibility assessment of an asylum applicant:

---

[82] Ingoldsby, B., *supra* note 3, p. 7
[83] UNHCR Representation to Ireland's Comments on the proposed amendments to the Immigration Bill 2002 (June 2003 in relation to Section 11A of the Refugee Act).
[84] Annual report of the Refugee Applications Commissioner 2002, p. 34.

(a) whether the applicant possesses identity documents, and, if not, whether he or she has provided a reasonable explanation for the absence of such documents;

(b) whether the applicant has provided a reasonable explanation to substantiate his or her claim that the State is the first safe country in which he or she has arrived since departing from his or her country of origin or habitual residence;

(c) whether the applicant has provided a full and true explanation of how he or she travelled to and arrived in the State

(d) where the application was made other than at the frontiers of the State, whether the applicant has provided a reasonable explanation to show why he or she did not claim asylum immediately on arriving at the frontiers of the State unless the application is grounded on events which have taken place since his or her arrival in the State;

(e) where the applicant has forged, destroyed or disposed of any identity or other documents relevant to his or her application, whether he or she has a reasonable explanation for so doing;

(f) whether the applicant has adduced manifestly false evidence in support of his or her application, or has otherwise made false representations either orally or in writing;

(g) whether the applicant, without reasonable cause, having withdrawn his or her application and not having been refused a declaration [for refugee status] has made a subsequent application [for refugee status];

(h) whether the applicant, without reasonable cause, has made an application following the notification of a proposal [to deport];

(i) whether the applicant has complied with [the duty to co-operate in the investigation of his or her application and determination of appeal];

(j) whether the applicant has, without reasonable cause, [left or attempted to leave the State without the consent of the Minister];

(k) whether the applicant has, without reasonable cause [failed in his or her duty to keep the Commissioner informed of his or her address];

(l) whether the applicant has, without reasonable cause [failed to fulfil his or her duty to comply with residence or periodic reporting requirements imposed by an immigration officer];

(m) whether [during the determination of an appeal] the applicant has furnished information in relation to the application which he or she could reasonably have furnished during the investigation of the application by the Commissioner but did not so furnish.[85]

This section seeks to put a legal framework on factors that decision-makers can take into account when assessing the (often subjective) matter of credibility. As well as acting as a checklist for decision-makers, this provision limits the scope for judicial review based on

---

[85] Section 11B Refugee Act, as amended in 2003.

assertions that inappropriate matter was taken into account in assessing credibility. Although there are no prescribed consequences for an asylum applicant whose credibility is called into question under this section, most of the considerations are linked with a failure to co-operate with the asylum process which does have serious consequences.

iii) Duty to co-operate

In the past, one of the main criticisms levelled at the Department of Justice, Equality and Law Reform and, later, the Commissioner's office when it took over asylum processing at first instance, was the delay in decision-making. During the mid-1990s, as applicant numbers grew significantly, delays in the assignment of matching resources to deal with the applications meant that it was not uncommon for asylum applicants to wait for a number of years for a decision on their applications. The situation has improved significantly since 1999. Now, an asylum seeker who is in compliance with the process is likely to receive a first instance decision within four months.[86] One of the more common reasons for delays in particular cases is more likely to be lack of active participation with the process on the part of asylum applicants. The Immigration Act 2003 addresses this issue by imposing a stronger duty to co-operate.

The Commissioner informs asylum applicants of the statutory duty to co-operate with the asylum process (at section 11C of the Refugee Act, as amended in 2003) and the consequences for failure to comply.[87] Among the statutory obligations on asylum applicants is the duty to keep the Commissioner informed of an up-to-date address. Section 9(4A) of the Refugee Act, as amended, states that

(a) [a]n applicant shall inform the Commissioner of his or her address and of any change of address as soon as possible.
(b) Where 5 working days have elapsed since the making of an application for a declaration and the applicant has not informed the Commissioner of his or her address, the application shall be deemed to be withdrawn.

Thus, the Commissioner may dispose of cases where the asylum applicant does not give an address for correspondence and nothing further is heard.[88] To further ensure co-operation with the asylum process, immigration officers and authorised officers of the Department of

---

[86] Annual report of the Office of the Refugee Applications Commissioner 2002. The Office of the Refugee Applications Commissioner has made commendable achievements in reducing the backlog of asylum applications. For example, at the end of 2002, there were practically no applications pending from before July 2002.

[87] Section 11(8) (e) to (g) Refugee Act, as amended in 2003.

[88] Immigration Bill 2002, Explanatory Memorandum (Dáil Éireann) Government amendments, footnote 17, p. 9.

Justice, Equality and Law Reform are empowered to require that an asylum applicant reside or remain in a particular place and/or to report periodically to immigration or departmental officials or to the Garda Síochána.[89] If an asylum applicant fails to comply with these requirements or leaves the state without the permission of the minister or takes up employment, he or she may be found guilty of an offence and be liable to a fine and/or imprisonment.[90] Failure to comply in such cases may also result in an asylum application being deemed withdrawn.[91]

The Immigration Act 2003 also creates consequences for asylum seekers who do not attend interviews. According to its 2002 annual report the Commissioner's office scheduled 12,681 interviews during 2002 and approximately 4,500 asylum applicants did not show up. Under the Refugee Act, as amended, an asylum application can be deemed withdrawn if an asylum seeker fails to attend for interview without good reason.

> Where an applicant does not attend for interview with an authorised officer under this section on the date and at the time fixed for the interview then, unless the applicant, not later than 3 working days from that date, furnishes the Commissioner with an explanation for the non-attendance which in the opinion of the Commissioner is reasonable in the circumstances, his or her application shall be deemed to be withdrawn.[92]

An asylum application may also be deemed to be withdrawn if an asylum seeker does not generally co-operate with the Commissioner or if he or she does not furnish information relevant to his or her application.[93] In such cases, an opportunity is given to the asylum applicant to explain.[94]

> The Commissioner shall send to the applicant a notice in writing inviting the applicant to indicate in writing (within 15 working days of sending of the notice) whether he or she wishes to continue with his or her application and, if an applicant does not furnish an indication within the time specified in the notice, his or her application for a declaration shall be deemed to be withdrawn.[95]

---

[89] Section 9(5)(a) and (b) Refugee Act, as amended in 2003.

[90] On summary conviction to a fine not exceeding £500 (635) or to imprisonment for one month, or both (Section 9(7) Refugee Act, as amended in 2003).

[91] Section 11(8)(f) Refugee Act, as amended in 2003.

[92] Section 11(10) of the Refugee Act, as amended in 2003.

[93] Section 11C of the Refugee Act, as amended in 2003, imposes a general duty to co-operate during first-instance investigation and upon appeal.

[94] This also applies in cases where the Commissioner is notified by an official from the Department of Justice, Equality and Law Reform that an asylum seeker has attempted to leave the state (or has left the state), or where the asylum applicant has not informed the Commissioner of a change of address or has not fulfilled requirements to reside in a particular place or report periodically.

[95] Section 11(11) Refugee Act, as amended in 2003.

An application that is deemed withdrawn due to non-compliance results in the termination of the investigation of an application and a recommendation that the applicant not be declared to be a refugee. The minister makes a negative recommendation in each case where there is such a recommendation.[96] There is no appeal from a recommendation in these circumstances[97] although it may be open to an applicant to apply to make a renewed application for refugee status.[98]

UNHCR considers these penalties for procedural non-compliance to be contrary to the spirit and object of the Refugee Convention. While appreciating the need to tackle the problem of asylum applicants who do not fulfil certain procedural requirements, UNHCR's position is that

> [a] person can be found to be or not to be a refugee only after a substantive interview has been conducted, in light of the refugee definition. Therefore, rejecting an applicant who has not been interviewed is not in keeping with the object and purpose of the 1951 Convention and the 1967 Protocol. UNHCR recommends that such applications be considered abandoned and closed. This is a technical matter and will have no impact on the initiative to remove withdrawn cases from the procedure.[99]

It is worth re-emphasising that the Commissioner is statutorily obliged to inform the asylum applicant at the earliest possible opportunity of all of the duties that he or she must fulfil and the possible consequences for failure to comply. The asylum applicant is therefore on notice of his or her duties. This is crucial given the severity of the consequences.

d) Recommendations of the Commissioner

The report drawn up based on the first-instance investigation refers to the matters raised by the asylum applicant during the interview and to other matters considered appropriate by the Commissioner. The Commissioner's report must set out the findings and include a recommendation as to whether an applicant should or should not be declared to be a refugee.[100] The Commissioner must send a copy of the report to the asylum applicant, to his or her solicitor (if known) and to UNHCR, if it requests a copy.

If the Commissioner recommends that an asylum applicant be granted

---

[96] Section 17(1A) Refugee Act, as amended in 2003.

[97] Section 13 (2) Refugee Act, as amended in 2003.

[98] Section 17(7) of the Refugee Act, as amended. In such circumstances a request to the minister for special permission is necessary.

[99] UNHCR Representation to Ireland's Comments on the Irish Immigration Bill 2002, June 2003. For similar commentary, see *Submission to the Dáil Joint Committee on Justice, Equality, Defence and Women's Rights on Immigration Bill 2002* by Amnesty International, Irish Refugee Council, Irish Council for Civil Liberties and Irish Commission for Justice and Peace, 13 May 2003.

[100] Section 13(1) Refugee Act, as amended in 2003.

refugee status, he or she is notified and a positive recommendation is sent to the minister for a formal declaration of refugee status. The minister is normally obliged to follow a positive recommendation of the Commissioner and issue a declaration of refugee status.[101] However, where an asylum application (or appeal) has been withdrawn, or deemed withdrawn, a declaration is refused.[102]

An asylum applicant, who receives a recommendation from the Commissioner that he or she should not be declared to be a refugee is notified of the right to appeal to the Tribunal. If there is no appeal lodged by the applicant within the allotted timeframe, the negative recommendation is sent to the minister[103] whereupon arrangements are put in train for the removal of the person from the state in accordance with Section 3 of the Immigration Act 1999.

e) Accelerated procedures and prioritisation

Accelerated procedures are a common feature of asylum systems in many countries and have frequently proved controversial with refugee advocates because of the accompanying reduction of procedural rights. Under the Refugee Act, as originally drafted in 1996, so-called 'manifestly unfounded' applications were subjected to an accelerated procedure.[104] In contrast to the regular procedure, as described above, asylum applicants whose cases were deemed manifestly unfounded were given a shorter time period within which to appeal (ie ten working days instead of fifteen) and there was no right to an oral hearing. The manifestly unfounded procedure implied a foreshortened first-instance procedure insofar as the Tribunal, if it disagreed with the finding of the Commissioner that a case be deemed manifestly unfounded, had a power to remit asylum applications to the Commissioner for re-investigation. The Immigration Act 2003 has repealed the provision of the Refugee Act relating to manifestly unfounded claims and has replaced it with a new system for prioritisation and acceleration of certain classes of cases.[105] Under the new system, all asylum applications are given a substantive first-instance investigation.[106]

If the Commissioner concludes, at the end of a substantive investigation, that an asylum applicant should not be declared to be a refugee and included in the report is a finding under Section 13(6) of the Refugee Act, as amended, an appeal is dealt with by an accelerated procedure. This means that there is no oral hearing and the appeal

---

[101] Section 17(1)(a) of the Refugee Act, as amended.

[102] Section 17(1A) of the Refugee Act, as amended in 2003.

[103] Section 13(4) Refugee Act, as amended in 2003.

[104] Section 12 of the Refugee Act, as originally passed.

[105] Sections 12 and 13 of the Refugee Act, as amended in 2003.

[106] Whereas a critique of accelerated procedures is offered below in Chapter 8, this section simply explains how the new accelerated procedures are expected to apply.

period is reduced to ten days. The findings that may be made by the Commissioner that channel an asylum applicant into an accelerated procedure are as follows:

   (a) that the applicant showed either no basis or a minimal basis for the contention that the applicant is a refugee;

   (b) that the applicant made statements or provided information in support of the application of such a false, contradictory, misleading or incomplete nature as to lead to the conclusion that the application is manifestly unfounded;

   (c) that the applicant, without reasonable cause, failed to make an application as soon as reasonably practicable after arrival in the State;

   (d) the applicant had lodged a prior application for asylum in another state party to the Geneva Convention (whether or not that application had been determined, granted or rejected);[107] or

   (e) the applicant is a national of, or has a right of residence in, a safe country of origin for the time being so designated under section 12(4).[108]

Technically, even if one or more of the scenarios listed in (a) to (e) apply in a particular case, the Commissioner may still make a recommendation that an applicant be *granted* refugee status. So, for example, if an applicant did not make an asylum application upon arrival to the State and instead waited a number of months, this would not be relevant if the Commissioner's investigation led to a conclusion that an applicant should be declared to be a refugee. According to the government's Explanatory Memorandum:

> Findings of the type listed in the subsection are a basis for accelerating the hearing of an appeal where a negative recommendation has been made by the Commissioner, but are not necessarily a basis for the negative recommendation itself.[109]

The Immigration Act 2003 also introduces a second, even speedier, accelerated procedure. The minister may direct the Commissioner to investigate certain classes of asylum applications to which this 'special procedure' applies.[110] The special procedure reduces the time period within which an asylum applicant may appeal against a negative recommendation from the Commissioner to *four* working days. For the

---

[107] Section 17(4) of the Refugee Act, as amended, states that 'the Minister shall not give a declaration to a refugee who has been recognised as a refugee under the Geneva Convention by a state [other than Ireland] and who has been granted asylum in that state and whose reason for leaving or returning to that state and for seeking a declaration [for refugee status in Ireland] does not relate to a fear of persecution in that state'.

[108] Section 13(6) of the Refugee Act, as amended in 2003. See Refugee Act 1996 (safe countries of origin) Order 2003, SI No. 422 of 2003.

[109] Immigration Bill 2002, Explanatory Memorandum (Dáil Éireann) Government amendments, footnote 72, p. 24.

[110] Section 13(7) Refugee Act as amended in 2003.

special procedure to be valid, it is a pre-requisite that the asylum applicant is notified in advance of the substantive investigation of the asylum application that this shorter time period may apply.[111]

The Immigration Act 2003 also provides for the prioritisation of certain classes of cases.[112] In practice, this entails the minister directing the Commissioner or the Tribunal to accord priority to certain classes of asylum applications.[113] Classes of cases can be prioritised by reference to any combination of the following factors:

(a) The grounds of application [for refugee status];

(b) The country of origin or habitual residence of applicants;

(c) Any family relationship between applicants;

(d) The ages of applicants and, in particular, of persons under the age of 18 years in respect of whom applications are made;

(e) The dates on which applications were made;

(f) Considerations of national security and public policy;

(g) The likelihood that applications are well-founded;

(h) If there are special circumstances regarding the welfare of applicants or the welfare of family members of applicants;

(i) Whether applicants do not show on their face grounds for the contention that the applicant is a refugee;

(j) Whether applicants have made false or misleading representations in relation to their applications;

(k) Whether applicants had lodged prior applications for asylum in another country;

(l) Whether applications [for refugee status] were made at the earliest possible opportunity after arrival in the State;

(m) Whether applicants are nationals of or have a right of residence in a country of origin designated as safe [in accordance with Section 12(4) of the Refugee Act, as amended];[114]

(n) If an applicant is a person [who is excluded from protection due to serious grounds for considering that he or she has committed crimes against peace, war crimes, crimes against humanity, a serious non-political crime outside the State prior to arrival or has been guilty of acts contrary to the purposes and principles of the United Nations].

---

[111] Section 13(9) of the Refugee Act, as amended in 2003.

[112] Section 12 of the Refugee Act, as amended in 2003.

[113] Section 12(1) and 12(2) of the Refugee Act, as amended in 2003. Prioritisation of individual cases is not permitted by the legislation. In amendments to the first and second schedules of the Refugee Act by the Immigration Act 2003 (the roles of the Commissioner and the Tribunal respectively), the Commissioner and the Chairperson of the Tribunal may prioritise their own caseloads in a more limited manner.

[114] Section 12(4)(b) Refugee Act, as amended in 2003. In order to designate a country of origin 'safe' it must be '(i) party to and generally comply with obligations under the Convention against Torture, the International Covenant on Civil and Political Rights, and, where appropriate, the European Convention on Human Rights; (ii) have a democratic political system and an independent judiciary and (iii) be governed by the rule of law'.

There is nothing in this section of the Refugee Act, as amended, to suggest that prioritisation will adversely affect the procedural rights of asylum applicants. The commitment to prioritising the cases of asylum applicants with special personal or family needs is particularly welcome. Prioritisation of caseloads ensures that the operations of the Commissioner and Tribunal work in tandem with government asylum policy. Comments made by the minister during the passing of the Immigration Act 2003 indicated a strong likelihood that asylum applicants who come from safe countries of origin, or residence, will be among the first classes to be prioritised.

Other countries have introduced 'safe country' or 'white' lists and it appears from this provision, and pronouncements by the minister, that Ireland will establish a similar scheme. The idea is to set up a procedural device whereby asylum applicants originating from countries that do not normally produce refugees be dealt with in a more expeditious manner. The overall aim is to preserve the integrity of the asylum process. But caution must be used before designating a country as 'safe'. The fact that the Minister for Foreign Affairs must be consulted before designation is a good safeguard. In practice, however, designation should be based on a broader range of sources, such as reports from international organisations (in particular UNHCR), non-governmental organisations and press reports.[115] Human rights organisations have urged that designation should not take place without parliamentary scrutiny.[116]

3 Appeals

a) Lodging an appeal with the Refugee Appeals Tribunal

The statutory task of the Tribunal is to hear appeals against recommendations of the Commissioner, if an asylum applicant exercises the right to appeal. The Tribunal has the power to affirm or set aside recommendations of the Commissioner.[117] In practice, most negative recommendations are appealed. In 2002, approximately 86 per cent of all recommendations made by the Commissioner were appealed to the Tribunal.[118]

---

[115] *Comments by the UNHCR Representation to Ireland to proposed draft amendments to the Immigration Bill 2002* (June 2003).

[116] Amnesty International, Irish Refugee Council, Irish Council for Civil Liberties and Irish Commission for Justice and Peace, *Submission to the Dáil Joint Committee on Justice, Equality, Defence and Women's Rights on Immigration Bill 2002*, 13 May 2003.

[117] Section 16(2) of the Refugee Act, as amended in 2003.

[118] The work of the Tribunal has become increasingly efficient. In 2002 there were 5,297 appeals received, 5,275 cases scheduled, 4,951 decisions issued, 5,551 completed appeals (includes withdrawals and 'no-shows') and 5,291 substantive appeals completed. In 2002, there was a 74% increase in appeal cases scheduled over 2001 (Annual Report of Refugee Appeals Tribunal, 2002).

Normally, asylum applicants are entitled to an oral hearing but in the case of appeals against recommendations pursuant to accelerated and Dublin Convention procedures, only written submissions are permitted. Experience to date is that the majority of appeals dealt with by the Tribunal are oral ones (95 per cent in 2002);[119] this is expected to change with the coming into effect of the accelerated procedures pursuant to Section 12 of the Refugee Act (as amended in 2003). An asylum applicant who has been given a negative recommendation by the Commissioner must apply formally for an oral appeal hearing. He or she does so by way of lodging a 'notice of appeal' to the Tribunal. The notice of appeal sets out the grounds of appeal and must be lodged within fifteen working days from the sending of notice of the Commissioner's recommendation.[120] For Dublin Convention cases the time limit for lodging a notice of appeal is ten working days and for appeals from the accelerated procedure the time limit is ten, or four, working days.

When a case is assigned to a member of the Tribunal, he or she ascertains whether the Commissioner should be asked to carry out further investigations or offer written observations on any aspect of the appeal.[121] Where an oral hearing has been sought, the Tribunal gives at least seven working days notice of the date of the scheduled hearing;[122] in practice, the Tribunal generally notifies applicants a few weeks before the hearing date.[123] At the oral appeal hearing, an asylum applicant is usually accompanied by a legal representative and an interpreter (if necessary). A presenting officer represents the Commissioner's office. Hearings take, on average, an hour and a half and they are held in private,[124] although UNHCR is entitled to attend.[125] Witnesses may, at the discretion of the Tribunal, be called to give evidence at an appeal hearing[126] and they are entitled to the same privileges and immunities as witnesses in court.[127] Among the changes made by the Immigration Act 2003 is to shift the burden of proof to the asylum applicant on appeal.[128] Thus, it is for the asylum applicant to show that the Commissioner's recommendation was wrong and that he or she is entitled to refugee status.

---

[119] A total of 2,456 live appeals were on hand at the end of 2002 at the Tribunal. Of these, only eight were appeals from manifestly unfounded recommendations and twenty-five were Dublin Convention appeal cases (Annual Report of the Refugee Appeals Tribunal 2002, p. 12).

[120] Section 16(3) of the Refugee Act, as amended in 2003.

[121] Section 16(6) and (7) of the Refugee Act, as amended.

[122] Regulation 9(2) of SI No. 342 of 2000.

[123] Annual Report of the Refugee Appeals Tribunal 2002, p. 57.

[124] Section 16(14) of the Refugee Act, as amended.

[125] Section 16(15) of the Refugee Act, as amended.

[126] Section 16(11) of the Refugee Act, as amended.

[127] Section 16(12) of the Refugee Act, as amended.

[128] Section 11A(3) of the Refugee Act, as amended in 2003.

A significant number of decisions and procedures of the Tribunal have been judicially reviewed by the High Court.[129] The accumulation of judicial reviews has clarified a number of aspects of asylum appeal procedures. For example, the High Court has ruled that the Tribunal cannot be compelled by an asylum applicant to call an interviewer (caseworker) from the Commissioner's office to be cross-examined at an appeal hearing. According to the Court's ruling, no injustice is done if the asylum applicant, prior to the appeal hearing, has all of the appropriate documentation including the reports and recommendations of the Commissioner. Moreover, the Court has held that the appeal hearing is a *de novo* investigative process and it is up to the Tribunal to form a view which is independent of the original interviewer.[130] However, if the Tribunal refuses to accede to a request from an asylum applicant to call a caseworker from the Commissioner's office to be cross-examined a reasoned judgment must be proffered.[131] In another case, the High Court did not grant leave to apply for judicial review based on the contention of an asylum applicant that frequent interruptions and unnecessary questions by the Tribunal constituted an unfair hearing. It was held that the test was whether the conduct of a Tribunal member could reasonably give rise in the mind of an unprejudiced observer to the suspicion that justice is not seen to be done. The Court found that on the facts of the particular case this test was not satisfied.[132] The High Court has also pronounced that the manner in which the Tribunal reaches decisions is satisfactory as long the Tribunal member (i) has regard to all relevant facts; (ii) has stated the facts upon which he or she has founded the decision and (iii) has given reasons as to why he or she does not consider the facts adequate to find a well-founded fear of persecution.[133]

b) Decisions of the Tribunal

In order to reach a decision the Tribunal is statutorily obliged to consider

- the grounds of appeal set out in the notice of appeal
- all oral submissions made during the interview

---

[129] According to its Annual Report 2002, since the commencement of its work, the Tribunal had been named in 203 judicial reviews and, in 2002, the judicial review unit of the Tribunal had seventy-nine cases on hand.

[130] *Nicolaev v. The Refugee Appeals Tribunal and the Minister for Justice Equality and Law Reform* (High Court), 8 July 2002.

[131] *OKAFU v. The Refugee Appeals Tribunal and the Refugee Applications Commissioner and the Minister for Justice, Equality and Law Reform* (High Court), 4 October 2002.

[132] *Afrim Hoti v. John S. Ryan, sitting as the Refugee Appeals Tribunal* (High Court), 24 April 2002, Smyth J.

[133] *Abdullah Ali Ali Khamis v. The Minister for Justice, Equality and Law Reform and the Refugee Appeals Tribunal* (High Court), 24 June 2002.

- supporting documentation and all other information provided to the Commissioner
- the report of the Commissioner
- any observations made by the Commissioner and/or UNHCR.[134]

The Immigration Act 2003 clarifies the nature of the Tribunal's decision-making powers as follows:

> [T]he Tribunal shall affirm a recommendation of the Commissioner unless it is satisfied, having considered [the notice of appeal, report of the Commissioner, observations by UNHCR, evidence adduced and representations made at the oral appeal hearing and any documents or reports furnished to the Commissioner during first-instance investigation], that the applicant is a refugee.[135]

Thus, if the Commissioner errs in the conduct of the investigation or in arriving at a particular finding on the basis of the facts disclosed during the investigation of the asylum application, this does not provide a sufficient basis for overturning the Commissioner's recommendation. The Tribunal must be satisfied that the error was at the essence of the Commissioner's recommendation, and that the applicant should be granted refugee status, if it wishes to set aside a recommendation of the Commissioner.[136]

It takes an average of seventeen weeks to process and complete appeals that involve an oral hearing.[137] If the Tribunal makes a decision that refugee status should be granted, the asylum applicant and his or her legal representative (if known) are notified in writing and a copy of the decision is also sent to UNHCR. As with positive recommendations made by the Commissioner, the minister is obliged to affirm the positive decision of the Tribunal.[138]

The Tribunal, in substantive appeal hearings, overturned approximately one in four of the negative recommendations made by the Commissioner in 2002. This statistic has been criticised by refugee organisations and the media. The Commissioner defended her office's decision-making procedures as follows:

> ...[d]ecisions by the Office of the Refugee Applications Commissioner at first stage were upheld on appeal in 77 per cent of all cases in 2002 and in 80 per cent of cases in the first five months of 2003. It should be noted

---

[134] Section 16(16) of the Refugee Act, as amended.

[135] Section 16(16A) of the Refugee Act, as amended in 2003.

[136] Immigration Bill 2002, Explanatory Memorandum (Dáil Éireann) Government amendments, footnote 101, p. 30.

[137] An internal Tribunal assessment from a sample of 1,623 cases between 1 January 2002 and 31 December 2002 (Annual Report of the Refugee Appeals Tribunal 2002, p. 28).

[138] Section 17(1) of the Refugee Act, as amended.

that these figures relate only to those decisions which were actually appealed. If decisions which were not appealed were also taken into account, together with those decisions reached following the applicant's failure to attend for interview, then the percentage of first-stage decisions upheld or unchallenged would in fact be far higher ... the above figures do not to my mind give rise to cause for concern and they most certainly do not suggest that increased processing has come at the expense of quality.[139]

The decisions of the Tribunal have not hitherto been published, which creates difficulties for lawyers seeking established case patterns. Published decisions would undoubtedly lead to greater transparency and consistency. Section 19(4A) of the Refugee Act (inserted by the Immigration Act 2003) allows for the publication of Tribunal decisions which the chairperson of the Tribunal considers to be of legal significance. Published decisions will be anonymised for the purposes of publication to protect the identity of asylum seekers. In 2002, the Tribunal ran a small pilot project to audio tape selected appeals hearings to assist with judicial review hearings.

4 Final stages

a) Successful asylum applicants

If a recommendation of the Commissioner or a decision of the Tribunal is in favour of an asylum applicant being granted refugee status, the finding is sent to the minister. The minister may decide, on the grounds of public policy or national security, to deny a person to whom a declaration has been granted the rights set out in sections 3, 9 and 18 of the Refugee Act as amended. These are the rights and benefits accorded to recognised refugees, the right to remain in the state and the right to family reunification respectively.[140] Such a person may also be required to leave the state.[141] If no considerations of national security or public policy apply, the minister issues a letter confirming that the asylum applicant should be declared to be a refugee. Section 3 of the Refugee Act sets out the rights of refugees, which are as follows:

1) right to work and carry on a business trade or profession on the same basis as Irish citizens
2) access to education and training like an Irish citizen
3) same medical care rights as Irish citizens

---

[139] *Irish Times*, letter to the editor from O'Neill, B., Saturday 14 June 2003, in response to an article by O'Brien, B., 'Asylum-seeker System in Dire Need of Reform', *Irish Times*, 7 June 2003. (www.ireland.com). See also Irish Refugee Council press release, 15 May 2003, on the launch of the Annual Report of the Office of the Refugee Applications Commissioner 2002. (www.irishrefugeecouncil.ie).

[140] Section 17(2)(a) of the Refugee Act, as amended.

[141] Section 17(2)(a)(ii) of the Refugee Act as amended.

4) same social welfare rights as Irish citizens
5) same rights of residence and travel to and from the state as Irish citizens
6) same freedom of religion and regard to religious education of children as Irish citizens
7) same access to courts as Irish citizens
8) same right to join trade unions and freedom of association as Irish citizens.

b) Unsuccessful asylum applicants

If an asylum seeker has failed the asylum process and has no other legal basis for remaining in the state, he or she is liable to be deported. The Immigration Act 1999 sets out the procedures for deportation.[142] It falls on the Commissioner and the Tribunal to consider whether an individual fits the description of a 'refugee' as defined by the Refugee Act.[143] There are no other bases, such as connections to the state or humanitarian considerations that the Commissioner and the Tribunal may consider. Such deliberations are solely within the remit of the minister at the deportation stage.

Deportation orders are not automatically made once an unsuccessful asylum seeker's file is sent to the Department of Justice, Equality and Law Reform. Section 3 of the Immigration Act 1999 deals with the process that must be undertaken by that department in every individual's case. Section 5 of the Immigration Act deals with the enforcement of deportation orders.[144]

When the minister is considering the making of a deportation order, the potential deportee is notified and given fifteen working days to make representations as to why deportation should not be enforced.[145] The notification also informs the person that he or she may leave the state voluntarily. There are a number of matters that the minister is required to take into account, insofar as they are made known, before a decision to make a deportation order is made. These are set out in section 3(6) of the Immigration Act 1999:

---

[142] Section 17(5) of the Refugee Act, as amended, in conjunction with Section 3(2)(f) of the Immigration Act 1999 forms the legal basis for the deportation of failed asylum seekers.

[143] Section 2 of the Refugee Act, as amended.

[144] Section 5 of the Immigration Act was amended by Section 10 of the Illegal Immigrants (Trafficking) Act 2000 which gave Gardaí extended powers to detain a deportee and require a greater degree of co-operation from the deportee in the deportation process. In a challenge to the constitutionality of the Illegal Immigrants (Trafficking) Bill under an Article 26 reference to the Supreme Court (Article 26 of the 1937 Constitution gives the President a power to refer a Bill to the Supreme Court to test its constitutionality before signing it into law) these amendments were held as not repugnant to the Constitution. See *In Re Article 26 and the Illegal Immigrants (Trafficking) Bill 2000* [2000] IR 360.

[145] Section 3(3)(a) of the Immigration Act 1999.

a)   age
b)   duration of residence in the State
c)   family and domestic circumstances
d)   nature of connection with the State
e)   employment record
f)   employment prospects
g)   character and conduct both here and abroad (including criminal convictions)
h)   humanitarian considerations
i)   any representations made
j)   the common good
k)   considerations of national security and public policy.

When a deportation order is made the deportee and his or her legal advisor are sent notification of the making of the order, which includes a requirement that the person present him/herself to an immigration official or member of the Gardaí at a named time and place. Included may be other requirements such as a request for the production of travel documents, obligation to reside at a particular place or periodic reporting to a Garda station.[146] A failure to co-operate in the deportation process is an offence and may result in detention with a view to deportation.[147] Normally, such detention cannot exceed eight weeks. However, if a person detained pending deportation is also on remand awaiting trial on other matters or is serving a prison sentence, detention can exceed eight weeks. Similarly, if a person is awaiting the outcome of a court challenge to the deportation order the detention period may also exceed eight weeks. In that case, the court may make an order for the person's release from detention subject to conditions. The effect of a deportation order is that a deported person may not legally re-enter Ireland unless the order is formally revoked.[148]

---

[146] Section 3(9)(a)(i) of the Immigration Act 1999, as amended by the Illegal Immigrants (Trafficking) Act 2000.

[147] Section 3(1A) and Section 5 of the Immigration Act 1999, as amended by the Illegal Immigrants (Trafficking) Act 2000.

[148] Although not all were unsuccessful asylum seekers, the total number of deportees for 2001 was 365, for 2002 it was 521 and for 2003 (as at 20 October 2003) it was 428 (source: Department of Justice, Equality and Law Reform).

CHAPTER 6

UNHCR, International Refugee Protection and Ireland

Pia Prütz Phiri*

Introduction

Providing asylum is an established tradition in every part of the world, including Ireland. However, in a modern European context Ireland is unique in many ways, being for all intents and purposes a recent asylum country. Ireland received 39 asylum seekers in 1992, but until 1996 had not received in excess of 1,000 applications. By the end of the decade Ireland was receiving 7,724 asylum applications in a single year, with a growth in subsequent years to date to approximately 11,000 applications annually. In 2003 Ireland assumed fifth position on the table of asylum applicants per 1,000 inhabitants in industrialised countries.

Historically, Ireland's absence from the asylum arena compared with other European countries has stemmed from geographical, political and economic isolation. Ireland was spared the experience of large refugee flows on or through its territory in the advent and aftermath of World War II, and although protection was offered to a small number of Jewish refugees during the period, it has been generally recognised that there was a failure in providing protection.

Ireland's contribution to the international protection of refugees mostly followed the events of World War II, although it was ostensibly absent from the historic debates on refugee protection in the early 1950s as the international community first embarked on the task of designing the specific guarantees set out in the 1951 Convention Relating to the Status of Refugees. Ireland became a party to the Convention in 1956, and subsequently to its 1967 Protocol a year later in 1968.

Periodically over the years, from the 1950s onwards, Ireland welcomed refugees on resettlement-type programmes, including Hungarians in 1956, Chileans and Vietnamese in the 1970s, and

---

* The opinions expressed in this chapter do not necessarily reflect the views of UNHCR.

Bosnians and Kosovars (under a Humanitarian Evacuation Programme) in the early and late 1990s respectively. Significantly, in 1956, the year of the revolt in Hungary, Ireland signed the 1951 Refugee Convention. Yet, despite establishing itself as a country of refuge following 1956, the phenomenon of spontaneously arriving refugees was only visible in Ireland from the mid-1990s.

Today, at an international level, a dynamic relationship exists between UNHCR and Ireland. As a member of UNHCR's governing body, the Executive Committee to the High Commissioners Programme (ExCom), and as a top-twenty donor to refugee programmes worldwide, Ireland has a significant stake in the UN's refugee agency. In recent years UNHCR has sought the assistance of Ireland Aid in meeting the funding requirements for emergency as well as established refugee programmes. Significantly, UNHCR has been one of three priority agencies for Ireland. Based on the level and the nature of the Irish funding, which is predictable and flexible to UNHCR's needs, we consider Ireland one of our model donor countries. Ireland contributed US$ 6,245,600 to UNHCR in 2002, placing it sixteenth on the list of UNHCR's top donors. The contribution translates as US$ 1.7 per citizen. Ireland's funding has been on average about 0.3% of UNHCR's annual expenditure over a number of years.

The commitment of Ireland to UNHCR as a priority UN agency and the close support offered by Ireland as an executive member of the agency has assisted in meeting the varied and difficult needs of refugees in many parts of the world. That relationship has been developed in a domestic context also since 1997–98 on foot of UNHCR establishing a formal office presence in Ireland. The level of co-operation extended to UNHCR has been exceptional and forms the basis of open and constructive dialogue on a range of national asylum policies.

UNHCR's involvement in the development of national asylum law and policy

There was no UNHCR presence on the ground in Ireland effectively until the summer of 1997. All asylum matters pertaining to Ireland were covered competently by a UNHCR branch office for the United Kingdom and Ireland, based in London. UNHCR officials from as early as the mid-1980s undertook numerous missions to Ireland to provide advice and negotiate agreements with the Irish authorities on asylum. In 1985, UNHCR and Ireland formed an agreement based on a letter from the Irish Department of Justice to the UNHCR representative in London, Mr von Arnim, in respect of implementing the 1951 Refugee Convention and liaising with UNHCR in asylum matters. Until the advent of the Refugee Act in 1996, the 'von Arnim' letter (as it was known) acted as *de facto* asylum law in Ireland.

Due to growing numbers of applications from asylum seekers in Ireland in 1996, the Irish authorities funded UNHCR to assist in assessing 400 asylum cases in London. This was an interim measure, until procedures were adopted in Dublin and training could be provided to Irish officials. Co-operation with Ireland has remained high and as intensive as ever.

During the period prior to 1997 UNHCR funded a legal project in the Irish Refugee Council to provide advice and assistance to refugees and asylum seekers in Dublin. UNHCR believed it was a crucial period during which to support the growth of local non-governmental organisations because Ireland was still in the process of developing legal procedures and reception standards.

Although the Refugee Act was signed into law in 1996, laying the groundwork for statutory procedures, the provisions of the Act were not all implemented immediately. As an interim measure, a set of administrative procedures was introduced by the Department of Justice, Equality and Law Reform on 10 December 1997 and remained until the Act became effectively operational in November 2000. The administrative measures operated between 1997 and 2000 were, like the 'von Arnim' letter, communicated by the Department of Justice, Equality and Law Reform to Ms Hope Hanlan, UNHCR's representative in London, and were known generally as the 'Hope Hanlan' letter. Although the branch office in the United Kingdom had been consulted on the letter before it was officially received, various comments by the office were not incorporated and this gave rise to concerns. The 1997 administrative procedures relied in part on key legislative provisions from the Refugee Act which were in force at this time.

UNHCR's presence in Ireland

With the increasing commitment by the Irish authorities to establish a functioning asylum system in 1997, the newly arrived representative in London seriously considered the establishment of a liaison office in Ireland, which, as mentioned above, materialised eventually in April 1998. For the first few months of its establishment, the office closely monitored the asylum procedures. It was based inside the Department of Justice, Equality and Law Reform for the first seven months, followed by a move, still within the Department, to the Refugee Applications Centre on Lower Mount Street in October 1998.

In March 1999, UNHCR moved out of the Department's building to independent premises to allow for the expansion of other services at the 'one-stop-shop' in Lower Mount Street. The office remained in close contact with the asylum procedure through training all newly recruited staff to various services, by observing decisions and attending interviews. As a consequence of the Refugee Act, UNHCR is informed of all decisions in the procedure.

Ireland began to grapple seriously with the reality of asylum from 1997 onward. Given the limited expertise on the ground, and a service confined to a small number of officials and academics, the need to promote refugee law in Ireland was all too evident to UNHCR at the time. UNHCR sent two short-term missions in 1997 prior to establishing its office in Ireland in 1998. The first mission was spearheaded by a staff member who arrived in Ireland for a three-month stay from Mauritania in June 1997. The first office in Dublin was a live-in apartment overlooking Temple Bar Square. The main policy tasks at the time involved liaison with the Department of Justice, Equality and Law Reform on refugee status determination for individual cases and promoting the implementation of the Refugee Act, which had been passed in the previous year but remained unimplemented.

Following the first three-month mission, UNHCR decided that a further presence was required to continue close liaison with the Department. A second short-term mission of two months was authorised. This time, as mentioned previously, UNHCR was based in the Department building in Stephen's Green. The first UNHCR official to set up office in Room 124 of the Department attracted the interest of the media, appearing prominently in his first week in Dublin on the front page of the Irish Times (3 November 1997). The article led with the line 'The United Nations High Commission for Refugees (UNHCR) has responded to the huge increase in asylum-seekers coming to Ireland by appointing its first representative'.

Four months after this mission, in April 1998, UNHCR established a more permanent liaison office in Ireland. The intervening period prior to April 1998 was interspersed by weekly missions from the UNHCR branch office in London (which was covering Ireland). A newly appointed senior liaison officer arrived from Myanmar on 6 April 1998 to assume his post, accompanied by the deputy representative from London. Following introductory meetings with senior Department of Justice, Equality and Law Reform officials, a general meeting was organised with all the representative refugee non-governmental organisations on 7 April. The liaison officer's post was funded by the Irish government for a period of one year. The positive reception received by the office from the first day was welcome and vital.

Since 1998, UNHCR has maintained a continuous presence in Ireland, with a change of the head of the mission in July 2000, followed four months later by my arrival. The liaison office, which existed from 1998, was covered and supported by the UNHCR branch office in the United Kingdom. The representative, deputy representative, refugee law training officer and public information officer rotated on mission to Ireland at different points throughout the period 1997–2001.

On my arrival at the liaison office in Ireland there was no training support from the branch office in London. To a large extent this dictated the immediate tasks I undertook, because the Irish authorities were rapidly moving ahead with the establishment of the Office of the Refugee Applications Commissioner and the Office of the Refugee Appeals Tribunal (November 2000), in addition to the hiring of staff in these offices requiring UNHCR training. For the first year of my new appointment, the training of staff members from the two offices was among the major priorities of the liaison office in Dublin. In combination with the challenge of training large numbers of new staff, I also had to supervise a range of protection matters. In March 2001, UNHCR appointed a legal assistant to UNHCR's liaison office.

The liaison office was separated from the UNHCR office in the United Kingdom in July 2001, following a period during which the office was independently undertaking protection, administration and public information functions without the support of UNHCR's branch office in London. The representative in the United Kingdom at the time made the decision to support the independence of UNHCR Ireland from the United Kingdom office. UNHCR's liaison office in Dublin was designated a fully fledged branch office in its own right in 2002. The original post of senior liaison officer was retitled accordingly over time to reflect the status and capacity of the office, first to head of office and subsequently to representative.

The staffing has changed during the years, and the liaison office in Dublin has been fortunate to have dedicated and committed staff, consultants and interns. During the first stages of the office the team consisted of the head of mission and two consultants with functional support provided by the branch office refugee law training officer and public information officer, both based in London. The office currently consists of the representative, three staff members in the areas of protection, public information and administration, and one international UNHCR project staff member, funded by the Department of Justice, Equality and Law Reform. These changes to the office structure, including a small increase in staffing, have provided us with the capacity and credibility to carry out the functions under our charge.

An emerging asylum system

The government has quickly and effectively since 1997 established a functioning asylum system. This system was pulled together by a few key government officials and we have witnessed vast improvements in the system in a short few years, including credibly mandated agencies such as the Office of the Refugee Applications Commissioner and the Office of the Refugee Appeals Tribunal. Today, Ireland's asylum system is performing at a greater efficiency than a number of other EU asylum systems. By the end of 2001 a backlog of 12,500 pre-existing asylum applications was brought to conclusion. In 2002, despite 11,000 new applications, by the end of the year only 7,750 were awaiting the outcome of their cases from the asylum authorities.

The fact that there is no longer a public perception that Ireland's asylum system is spiralling out of control is evidence that a solid and fair system is beginning to take shape. From UNHCR's perspective, the asylum process will inevitably require more time, investment and refinement, but it cannot be seen as less than a success so far.

An effective system catering for the return of individuals found not to be in need of international protection to their countries of origin will be necessary to ensure the integrity of the asylum system. All involved including non-governmental organisations, lawyers and other asylum advocates recognise that this is an essential element of a fully functional asylum system.

Working with NGOs in Ireland

During UNHCR's initial presence in Ireland, there were frequent misunderstandings of its role, working methods and mandate, particularly as the liaison office was initially based in the Department's premises on Stephen's Green. However, UNHCR's impartial and independent role of supervision and monitoring was increasingly accepted as time elapsed. UNHCR is an organisation that sometimes has to walk a tight line in order to bring opposing views on refugee issues together, but the agency's mandate nevertheless has the singular purpose of guaranteeing the protection of refugees.

UNHCR has promoted constructive dialogue in all asylum matters to assist in creating a positive protection environment for refugees. Where concerns and difficulties exist we have encouraged practical solutions, believing that it is refugees who will suffer in a vacuum of opposing views and disengagement. From the outset of our presence in Ireland we recognised the need for engagement between the government and refugee-supporting NGOs. We have encouraged the reconciliation of disparate interests, often succeeding in fostering solid co-operation among key stakeholders to achieve the standards that benefit refugees and promote their protection.

In recent years UNHCR has seen the real possibility of partnerships forming between the authorities and the voluntary sector, in particular in the area of refugee integration. This will be valuable especially because initiatives on refugee integration require a concentrated effort on the ground in communities and this is an area where the voluntary sector has a dynamic presence.

The public view of asylum

Over the years UNHCR has felt that there is genuine empathy for refugees among the majority of the Irish public, and it fully understands that inevitably there will be some concern over potential abuse of the asylum system by persons not in need of international protection. UNHCR has undertaken initiatives to explain in public statements that an efficient and fair asylum process is the way forward. Being restrictive in the admission of asylum seekers would jeopardise refugees in need of assistance and protection.

Whilst there has been real progress in the public sphere in understanding the need to provide asylum, it is discouraging to continue to encounter negative arguments on the cost of asylum or statistical arguments on unsuccessful applicants.

One of the challenges that UNHCR has encountered in Ireland is to overcome asylum myths that engender racism. Asylum in many ways has dominated the political and social discourse on multicultural changes that have occurred in Ireland. Asylum hit the headlines in the mid-1990s and peaked as an election concern in 1997 in tandem with Ireland's large-scale integration into the global economy, a process that had accelerated throughout the 1990s. As a result of the economic boom, Ireland witnessed an upsurge in the numbers and diversity of immigrant workers and tourists visiting its shores. Key issues surrounding racism and multiculturalism had not been discussed in Ireland to any significant degree prior to this period.

The country underwent a period of rapid social change from the early 1990s, from a situation in which relatively few non-Irish people lived and worked in Ireland, to the late 1990s where a new Ireland was visible on the streets in towns and cities around the country. During that crucial period, asylum dominated every newspaper in Ireland. It is easy to see why there might be a sense that 'floods' of asylum seekers had entered the country, but the fact is that large numbers of non-nationals were in the country for other reasons that never made the news headlines. The phenomenon became so exaggerated that there was a time when anyone appearing different on the street was immediately identified by some as an asylum seeker. The important distinction between refugees and other immigrants was often overlooked. For this reason it has been very important for UNHCR to try to disseminate facts on asylum seekers and refugees in order to promote an understanding of the reasons why they seek safe haven in Ireland.

The formation and escalation of hostile public views about asylum in Ireland was often due to the unavailability of credible and informed opinion. During the general election in 1997, newspapers, in particular the tabloids, declared that a 'flood' of asylum seekers was 'inundating'

Ireland. Politicians, who seemed to be unprepared for the emergence of asylum as an election issue and hesitant to predict which way their constituency might be swaying, were either conservative in their appraisal of the prevailing situation, avoided asylum in order not to involve themselves in an issue tempting discussions on racism, or sometimes used asylum as an election platform calling asylum seekers 'bogus' and 'fraudsters'. The election debate on asylum was predominantly centred in Dublin because no asylum seekers were dispersed outside the capital before 1999.

However much fears of inundation were unfounded, a number of myths abounded. We unfortunately still continue to see refugees referred to in terms of 'floods' and 'hordes' despite the fact that this is an obvious exaggeration or manipulation of asylum figures. This perception reduces sympathy for the refugee cause and can have a catastrophic impact on the political action undertaken by successive governments in the area of asylum.

In 2002, there were close to two million asylum applications in industrialised areas, including Europe, North America, Australia, New Zealand and Japan. Europe received just over one million applications. Ireland received just over 11,000 of these applications. Of the twelve million refugees in the world, Europe hosts 2.2 million refugees, and Ireland 5,400. By comparison, six million tourists visited Ireland in 2002 and up to 40,300 work permits were provided to non-EU nationals.

The immediate public response to the emergence of spontaneous asylum seekers in the 1990s requires more analysis than is afforded by this short chapter; however there was certainly a sense of discomfort in political and social spheres, in particular over the growth of asylum during the boom period of the Irish economy. This led to a generally negative perception of refugees as 'economically-motivated'.

Few arguments favouring an economic theory on the development of asylum in Ireland have taken into account that the last decade of the twentieth century was a period of unrelenting suffering for millions around the world. It was almost inevitable that an upsurge in people fleeing persecution would result in greater numbers seeking asylum in Ireland and elsewhere. Of the numerous reported wars throughout the 1990s, such as the Gulf War in 1991, hundreds of other conflict situations went unreported, including inter-state wars, and civil conflicts based on ethnic divisions.

It is regrettable when refugees are seen as 'bogus' and 'spongers' and not people forced to leave their homes for fear of their lives and because of attacks on their freedom, including severe and systematic violations of their human rights. But unfortunately this negative perception is widespread and in Europe at least we are continuously confronted by the image of asylum seekers as 'spongers', 'cheats' and 'illegals'. This has inflicted unaccountable damage on international efforts to protect refugees, particularly in industrialised nations.

UNHCR and partners such as the National Consultative Committee on Racism and Interculturalism (NCCRI) and Know Racism have produced public information and awareness campaigns to promote debate on these issues. There is a continuing need to produce information and integrated awareness programmes in all sectors of society.

UNHCR and dispersal

Asylum was predominantly an issue confined to Dublin until late 1999, but a decision of the government to introduce the dispersal and direct provision regime for asylum seekers saw it develop into a broad national issue. For the first time since the issue of asylum gained prominence, the decision to introduce dispersal demonstrated a planned approach to the reception of asylum seekers within clearly defined parameters.

The unexpected surge in numbers seeking asylum in Ireland from 1997 to 1999 produced an accommodation crisis for the authorities in the Dublin region. The shortage was exacerbated to such a degree that queues were beginning to develop outside the Refugee Applications Centre in mid-late 1999. At the peak of the crisis, asylum seekers were arriving at UNHCR's office for assistance in finding accommodation. Recognising the difficulties facing the authorities UNHCR was supportive of dispersal, encouraging the involvement of the voluntary sector as a vital counterpart in positively implementing the decision.

Dispersal and direct provision spurred the development of an inter-departmental agency under the aegis of the Department of Justice, Equality and Law Reform. As a result, the Directorate for Asylum Support Services was established and later the Reception and Integration Agency (RIA). Under the Reception and Integration Agency we witnessed the cross-fertilisation of different departmental areas of expertise, leading to a more comprehensive response to asylum seekers. The development of the Reception and Integration Agency has resulted in a focus on reception and integration as issues separate from the legal policy being pursued in the area of asylum.

The dispersal and direct provisions scheme has not been free of asylum myths, such as that expressed in the statement 'asylum seekers are treated more favourably than Irish nationals'. But contrary to the many tabloid headlines, asylum seekers under the dispersal/direct provisions programme never received health board money for mobile phones and cars, only for clothes and other basic items. Asylum seekers were provided residence in hostel accommodation, where they received food and a payment of €19.10 per week. They were not allowed to work and are dependent on state welfare. Recognised refugees by comparison were provided with rights and entitlements similar to Irish nationals.

Dispersal has been successful and of immense benefit in the national debate in Ireland on asylum. As a consequence of the programme, communities outside Dublin have developed support groups and local activities around the new arrivals, enhancing national support for the principles of refugee protection.

UNHCR and resettlement

Since 1999 Ireland has operated an annual resettlement quota for ten cases, including dependent family members. This has been a model area of co-operation between UNHCR and the Irish government. UNHCR has submitted cases for Ireland, which are selected by the Department of Foreign Affairs in consultation with the Department of Justice, Equality and Law Reform. Recommended cases are resettled to Ireland as a result.

Although this process has developed over time, UNHCR is promoting the adoption by Ireland of a larger quota and one that will equally cater for emergency resettlement cases. There are visible signs of UNHCR's progress in this area with the Minister for Justice, Equality and Law Reform incorporating a provision on resettlement in the Immigration Act 2003. This provision will allow the minister to enter into agreement with the Minister for Foreign Affairs to provide for future potentially expanded resettlement quotas.

Outlook on refugee integration in Ireland

Ireland has travelled a tremendous distance in terms of establishing a credible asylum system, complete with a resettlement programme. The emphasis on refining asylum legislation, establishing and building institutions, streamlining procedures, training staff, implementing a reception programme, drafting an integration policy, and contributing to the development of European instruments on asylum, has all taken place within the space of five years. During this period Ireland has maintained high protection standards, by virtually shunning the practice of detention, by sensitising staff to the needs of children and women, including the determination of cases involving gender-related persecution. A free legal aid scheme was agreed with the Legal Aid Board, and safeguards in procedural aspects of refugee status determination have been fair. Considering the rapid progress that was required in the area since the mid-1990s, Ireland has made unparalleled progress and is a model that a number of newly emerging Eastern and Central European countries favour. Inevitably, because of the steep incline in asylum developments in Ireland, a number of important areas remain to be developed, including the area of refugee integration.

UNHCR has been lobbying for refugee integration since before the development of a national policy on the issue, and made a written submission at the initial stages of the formulation of government policy as well as an oral presentation before an inter-departmental committee in early 1999.

Refugee integration is one of the most pressing issues affecting refugees at present in Ireland. It will never be possible for many refugees to return home and so a systematic integration programme will be a vital stepping stone for their meaningful contribution to Ireland. Even if refugees return home some day, an investment in their futures will not be lost because long-term ties will be established between countries through the friendships and relations formed while refugees were provided asylum in Ireland. Integration is an issue in which government, the voluntary sector, refugees and civil society all share responsibility. Problems will arise if there is a failure to address integration at an early stage, although the effects may not be visible for another fifteen years.

Integration, as the government's published policy states, is a 'two-way process'. UNHCR would strongly agree with this vision of integration. Refugees arriving in Ireland must be prepared for change, as too must the host community. But change cannot be imposed. It should be stimulated through a process of interaction, acceptance and mutual compromise, by the building of understanding and consensus among communities.

In other countries we see the shutters coming down on refugees. We see the emergence of the far right promoting stereotypes of refugees, cultural isolation and demands for conformity to the host society. These actions lead to discrimination, racism and xenophobia which are among the main barriers to refugee integration. In Ireland the debate on refugee integration so far has received a welcome start, particularly with the government being to the forefront at an early stage with a clear and balanced policy on this important matter. Ireland has also adopted and implemented many measures in the area of equality, anti-discrimination and anti-racism, which are as important to refugees as to other old and new communities in the country.

Irish presidency of the European Union 2004

In 2004 Ireland will assume the presidency of the European Union and with it an important chapter in the life of European asylum law. The year 2004 will be particularly crucial because it has been designated the period for the completion of the principal asylum *acquis* (the EU's central body of laws and regulations to govern asylum) for the harmonisation of asylum law in Europe. Although UNHCR does not expect that harmonisation will immediately deliver the reward of a unified, cohesive and broad asylum front in Europe, we nevertheless see 2004 as potentially an historic year for the region, and Ireland will have a prominent role in the final packaging of the asylum directives.

CHAPTER 7

Supporting Asylum Seekers

Peter O'Mahony

Introduction

Until the mid 1990s Ireland was rarely seen as a country of potential refuge for people who were forced to migrate from their home countries, except by occasional groups of refugees who were accepted into Ireland by government decision. Even where such decisions were made those who were offered asylum were not guaranteed the levels of support needed to help them to make a meaningful life in their new country.

Asylum seekers in Ireland are effectively living in a 'limbo'. They do not have the right to work[1] or to make many of the most basic day-to-day decisions for themselves and their families. Often they will have left behind all natural support networks of family and friends and, while they may well be multilingual, language barriers are a real problem for many who are facing into an uncertain future outside their country of origin.

Asylum seekers require support at a number of levels – food and shelter, access to healthcare, psychological and counselling services, language training, legal representation and support in adapting to, and integrating into, a different cultural environment. Questions arise as to how these various types of support should be provided and who should be responsible for their provision. Options include the State, church groups, nongovernmental organisations, voluntary groups and, more recently, individuals from refugee and asylum seeking communities themselves. This chapter examines some of the issues.

---

[1] Section 9(4)(b) of the Refugee Act 1996. However, on 26 July 1999 a once-off political decision was taken to permit asylum seekers who had made their applications in Ireland twelve months prior to 27 July 1999, and who were still awaiting a decision on their asylum application, to work. This right was also extended to those who had applied for asylum in Ireland on or before 27 July 1999, and who would subsequently be in Ireland for twelve months awaiting an outcome on their application.

Historical background

A comprehensive history of Ireland's contribution to the resettlement of worldwide refugee populations has yet to be written. However, what literature there is on the subject suggests that the overall approach of the Irish authorities to accepting and accommodating refugee populations displays an official mindset that views such people as temporary guests rather than as new communities that would become permanent features of Irish society.

Prior to the late 1990s, Irish experience of immigration was for the most part confined to a relatively small number of refugees and other non-nationals who had settled here. Those who were granted asylum in Ireland at this time were permitted to enter the country as pro-gramme refugees (i.e. they arrived following a formal invitation from the Irish government and were deemed to be in need of protection prior to their arrival in Ireland). A handful of Jewish refugees fleeing Nazi persecution and widespread anti-semitism in Europe did succeed, with the help of the Irish-Jewish community, in obtaining refuge in Ireland in the years immediately preceding World War II. However, requests that Ireland take larger numbers of Jewish refugees during and after the war were refused, mainly on the pretext that they would be an undue burden on a weak Irish economy. In total, Ireland admitted approximately sixty adults between 1939 and 1945, followed by 147 Jewish war orphans in 1947, all of whom were relocated abroad within twelve months.[2] It has since been shown that official anti-semitism, internationally widespread at that time, was a factor in Ireland's refusal to accept a larger number of refugees fleeing Europe.[3]

What is of particular interest is the fact that the Irish authorities sought to set definite limits on the periods for which protection would be offered. Onward resettlement to a third country was encouraged and, where possible, onward resettlement agreements and guarantees were sought with third countries. In effect, the attitude of the Irish authorities was to limit as much as possible the numbers accepted into Ireland and to seek assurances that the period during which Ireland would provide refuge would be finite. During the period 1939–45 and in the immediate aftermath of World War II Ireland was to achieve singular success in effecting these policies.

The story of the Hungarian refugees granted protection in Ireland in 1956 following the uprising against Soviet communism in Hungary bears testament to the Irish policies of minimising numbers and ensuring onward resettlement. A commitment by the Irish government to taking 1,000 Hungarian refugees was hastily abandoned soon after the initial 500 or so had arrived when the reality of meeting their needs became

---

[2]   Keogh, D. (1998), *Jews in Twentieth-Century Ireland,* Cork: Cork University Press.
[3]   *Ibid.*

clear.[4] Within two months of their arrival, the Irish government was 'anxious that every effort be made to have the refugees accepted into Canada, or some such country of immigration'.[5] By 1957 most of the Hungarian refugees had relocated to Canada.

The arrival of Chilean, Vietnamese and Bosnian programme refugees in Ireland in the 1970s and 1990s appeared to mark some change in the Irish approach. This change, however, was short-lived. The Irish intake of these refugees is not noteworthy for its scale: 120 Chileans were admitted in 1973, 212 Vietnamese in 1979 (this had grown to 582 by 1998) and approximately 1,000 Bosnians in the early 1990s. However, the acceptance by the Irish government of these programme refugees marked a shift away from the earlier policy of onward resettlement insofar as it appears to have been based on the understanding that they would settle permanently in Ireland.

In 1999 it became evident that a policy of accepting programme refugees as permanent settlers in Ireland was not deeply embedded in the thinking of the Irish authorities when approximately 1,000 Kosovar refugees arrived. When the first instalment arrived the then Minister for Justice, Equality and Law Reform, announced that a figure of 1,000 would be the limit that Ireland would accept.[6] Interestingly, unlike the case of the Chilean, Vietnamese and Bosnian programme refugees, the arrival of the Kosovar refugees occurred at a time when asylum applications in Ireland had significantly increased. In these circumstances the attitude of the Irish authorities to programme refugees appeared to harden and policies that were temporary and minimalist were quickly reasserted. In effect, the permanent resettlement of refugee numbers in Ireland was predicated on their numbers remaining small.

Unexpected and unwanted guests? – asylum seekers in modern Ireland

Asylum applications in Ireland 1992-2003

1992	1993	1994	1995	1996	1997	1998	1999	2000	2001	2002	2003 (to 30 October)
39	91	362	424	1,179	3,883	4,626	7,724	10,938	10,325	11,634	7,158

Source: Office of the Refugee Applications Commissioner, www.orac.ie

---

[4]   Fanning, B. (2002), *Racism and social change in the Republic of Ireland,* Manchester: Manchester University Press.

[5]   *Ibid.* p. 91.

[6]   Department of Justice Press Release 10 May 1999, 'O'Donoghue welcomes Kosovar Refugees to Ireland' http://www.justice.ie/80256996005F3617/vWeb/wpJWOD4TFL66.

Commentators have attested to the expressions of near hysteria and thinly disguised hostility on the part of some Irish politicians in the face of significantly increased numbers of asylum applications in Ireland. As noted by one commentator:

> (a)fter the initial surprise, when the numbers started rising, the official reaction was to blame, stigmatise and then criminalise the new arrivals.[7]

Arguably, the hostile reaction of official Ireland towards asylum seekers served as the impetus for a radical reshaping of a nascent Irish asylum policy.

Ireland's reaction to international migratory flows, at least until the mid-1990s, seemed for the most part to consist of supporting EU measures aimed at regulating unsolicited migration. There is no evidence to suggest that Ireland was acting out of self-interest at this time. Rather, it appears that the Irish position was to agree to measures deemed necessary to address problems affecting the EU as a political/ geographical entity but which were otherwise of no particular concern to Ireland. In the mid-1990s, however, domestic asylum issues became more pressing.

Prior to this time, despite Irish governmental support for changes in EU asylum procedures, Irish immigration controls did not become more restrictive until the numbers seeking asylum in Ireland began to increase. This did not reflect an Irish unwillingness to adhere to tighter EU immigration controls. Rather, it signified the fact that Ireland was not attracting asylum seekers or irregular migrants in any significant numbers and had not become a major gateway to the EU for would-be immigrants. This was also true for the Republic of Ireland's internal border with Northern Ireland. Controlling subversive activity, and not immigration, continued to be the almost exclusive focus of border controls between the Republic and Northern Ireland. The lack of focus on immigration controls suggests that there was no anticipation by the Irish authorities that the pattern of asylum-seeking in the EU would impact on Ireland.

Moreover, the introduction of the Refugee Act 1996, which was generally recognised by human rights groups in Ireland as being more liberal and progressive than many asylum laws within the EU, also occurred at a time when asylum applications were significantly increasing in Ireland. This nonchalant Irish attitude towards asylum seekers was surprisingly set against a backdrop of increasing concern in the EU at the spectre of mass immigration and the development of EU policies and practices aimed at restricting entry to Europe. There is merit in the view that the Irish authorities were blind to the impending changes in

---

7   Cullen, P. (2000), *Refugees and Asylum Seekers in Ireland,* Cork: Cork University Press, p. 1.

Ireland's pattern of inward migration even when those changes were already underway. Such unpreparedness did not, however, augur well for the reception of increased numbers of asylum seekers in Ireland.

By 1997 the number of persons seeking asylum in Ireland was subject to an increasingly strong focus from both Irish politicians and sections of the Irish media. This new attention did not promote a welcoming attitude and overall quite a negative public perception emerged. Although the initial response of 'official' Ireland to levels of asylum seekers was significant by Irish standards, such attitudes were relatively muted when compared with other EU countries. For example, similar trends to the rise of far-right parties in Austria, Belgium, France and the Netherlands have not been witnessed in Ireland to date.

The extent to which the Irish authorities were caught by surprise was evident in the delay in commencing the Refugee Act 1996, which was unworkable in the new context of increasing asylum appli-cations. In this regard it appeared that progressive legislation relating to asylum seekers was dependent upon Ireland having a low level of asylum applications. The logic of this approach was that increased asylum applications would be matched by a diminution of the protec-tions afforded to asylum seekers.

Measures were quickly introduced as the levels of asylum applications increased in the late 1990s. In 1997, amendments to the Aliens Act 1935 were introduced which increased the powers of immigration officers by allowing them to check the documents of persons arriving to the state from the UK and Northern Ireland.[8] In 2000, Irish immigration officers were posted on ferries between France and Ireland and passengers without proper papers were refused permission to board. These measures had the effect of denying would-be asylum seekers the opportunity to apply for asylum in Ireland.[9]

State support structures in Ireland

Welfare benefits and the policy of direct provision

During the asylum determination process, asylum seekers are entitled to basic economic and social rights. In November 1999, the Directorate for Asylum Support Services was set up within the Department of Justice, Equality and Law Reform to locate and provide accommodation for asylum seekers throughout Ireland. This policy of 'dispersal' was introduced to address the shortage of available accommodation in

---

[8] S.I. No. 277 of 1997 Aliens (Amendment) (No.3) Order 1997.
[9] Connolly J. and Lean M., 'Pre-Emptive Exclusion of Asylum Seekers? Disturbing Evidence of a New Policy: A Briefing Paper', December 2000 in Connolly J. and Lean M., *Refugees and Asylum Seekers – A Challenge to Solidarity*, a joint policy document of the Irish Commission for Justice and Peace and Trócaire, Dublin (Updated March 2002).

Dublin but also to enable Ireland to fall into step with EU states that had introduced similar policies.[10] [11]

The Reception and Integration Agency, which operates under the aegis of the Department of Justice, Equality and Law Reform, replaced the Directorate for Asylum Support Services in April 2001. The role of the Reception and Integration Agency is to plan and co-ordinate the provision of services to both asylum seekers and refugees. It also implements integration policies for refugees and persons who are granted leave to remain in the state.

In conjunction with the introduction of the dispersal policy, the state introduced its policy of 'direct provision', which meets the basic needs of food and shelter. Apart from being accommodated with full board, asylum seekers are entitled to €19.10 per adult and €9.60 per child per week. All costs for asylum seekers, such as meals, heat, light, and laundry are paid for directly by the state. Once-off payments can also be made under the Supplementary Welfare Allowance Scheme to provide for exceptional needs such as clothing. Asylum seekers may also be entitled to avail of other social welfare schemes such as 'Child Benefit', 'One Parent Family Payment', 'Disability Allowance', 'Back to School Clothing and Footwear' and 'Non-Contributory Old Age Pension' schemes. Asylum seeker children have the same right to access primary and post-primary school as Irish children and adult asylum seekers are entitled to state-funded English language training courses (through Vocational Education Committees). In addition, asylum seekers may access the health services on the same basis as Irish people.

Since direct provision was introduced, the Reception and Integration Agency has provided accommodation for approximately 30,000 asylum seekers. There are three main reception centres and two overflow accommodation centres (capacity 670) in the Dublin area and approximately 60 accommodation centres in 24 counties in Ireland. Asylum seekers remain in the Dublin-based reception centres for a period of 1-2 weeks where they are offered health screening and where their family profiles and needs are determined. After this initial period, they

---

[10] Haughey, N., 'System designed to stem the flow of immigrants', *Irish Times*, 12 June 2003.

[11] The Free Legal Advice Services point out that 'the prime motivation for introducing the scheme of Direct Provision for asylum seekers was not in line with social welfare 'needs' ethos, but a cost-cutting measure driven by the [Department of Justice, Equality and Law Reform]. The question arises whether this department should have a legislative role in shaping social welfare policy having regard to the provisions of the social welfare code. One could argue that the [Department of Justice, Equality and Law Reform] is not the main policy provider in the area of social welfare law. It is therefore questionable whether social welfare objectives should be informed by another government department which has a marginal social welfare function'. Free Legal Advice Centres Report, *Direct Discrimination? An analysis of the scheme of direct provision in Ireland,* Dublin (2003), pp. 24, 25.

are allocated accommodation elsewhere in Ireland. The Reception and Integration Agency also operates two step-down self-catering facilities (in Drogheda and Tralee) with a total capacity of 96, which are geared towards assisting those granted refugee status to make the transition from direct provision to securing their own accommodation.

The dispersal and direct provision policies have been criticised by refugee organisations and some have called for a complete reversion to the old system whereby asylum seekers receive normal social welfare payments and rent allowance to enable them to pay for private accommodation. Other recommendations have suggested at least a revision upwards of the weekly payment of €19.10 for adults and €9.60 for children. These suggestions are normally accompanied by a call for the right to work for asylum seekers at least after six months of being in the asylum process.[12]

The Free Legal Advice Centres (FLAC) published a critical report on the system of direct provision in July 2003.[13] The report maintains that direct provision represents an unwarranted departure from the normal social welfare code. Irish social welfare legislation allows any person in the state whose means cannot meet his/her needs to benefit from the supplementary welfare allowance scheme (up to €124.80 per week; the amount and method of payment is at the discretion of the community welfare officer). The only reference to direct provision is in section 180(1) of the Social Welfare (Consolidation) Act 1993, which provides that 'in exceptional circumstances' a health board (ie community welfare officers) may address the needs of an individual by providing goods and services instead of cash payments, to which he or she might otherwise be entitled.[14] FLAC concludes that

> the decision to introduce the scheme [of direct provision] was based on a policy of deterrence rather than on any attempt to address the needs of asylum seekers as a class or as individuals. FLAC argues Section 180(1) cannot be interpreted as permitting a departmental decision to refuse [supplementary welfare allowance] and rent allowance payments to an entire category of people as a matter of policy.[15]

In its report, FLAC analyses the case law on the exercise of statutory

---

[12] Refugee Information Service, Annual Report 2002, p. 15 (www.ris.ie); Fanning, B., Loyal, S. and Staunton, C. (2000), *Asylum seekers and the right to work in Ireland,* study commissioned by the Irish Refugee Council (www.irishrefugeecouncil.ie), and Conference of Religious in Ireland (CORI) Justice Commission paper on its core policy objective on migration and interculturalism (www.cori.ie/justice/soc_issues/culture.htm).

[13] Free Legal Advice Centres report, *Direct Discrimination? An analysis of the scheme of direct provision in Ireland,* Dublin (2003).

[14] Section 180(1) Social Welfare (Consolidation) Act 1993.

[15] Free Legal Advice Centres report, *supra* note 13, Conclusion and Recommendations, p. 39.

discretion and concludes that the Department of Justice, Equality and Law Reform has unlawfully fettered the discretion of community welfare officers by the manner in which direct provision was introduced (i.e. by administrative circular and not statute) and the nature of the policy, which requires blanket, instead of individual assessment.

A further erosion of the welfare entitlements of asylum seekers occurred with the enactment of Section 13 of the Social Welfare (Miscellaneous) Provisions Act 2003.[16] This Section now provides a statutory footing for the exclusion of asylum seekers from entitlement to rent supplement. Until the Section came into force in May 2003, asylum seekers were entitled to apply to withdraw from direct provision on exceptional social or medical grounds. Such a decision lay with the discretion of community welfare officers and it is estimated that 10,000 asylum seekers have moved from direct provision to the normal social welfare system (ie supplementary welfare allowance of up to €124.80 per week, plus a rent supplement). While the community welfare officers retain the power under Section 182 of the Social Welfare (Consolidation) Act 1993 to make a grant of supplementary welfare allowance in cases of urgency, it is clear from the circular accompanying Section 13 of the Social Welfare (Miscellaneous) Provisions Act 2003 that Section 182 would rarely if ever apply to asylum seekers' situations. In its report FLAC recommends that Section 13 of the Social Welfare (Miscellaneous Provisions) Act be repealed.

The FLAC report also critically examines the legality of direct provision from an equality perspective and concludes that direct provision may come in conflict with the equality guarantees in the Constitution of 1937 and with the Equal Status Act 2000. Article 40.1 of the Constitution, which has been interpreted to include non-nationals, holds that all citizens shall, as human persons, be held equal before the law, with the limitation that the state may in its enactments have due regard to differences of capacity, physical and moral, and of social function. According to case law analysed in the report, a legitimate government objective must justify a difference in treatment of individuals and FLAC 'questions whether the discriminatory nature of the policy of Direct Provision can be justified in this respect'.[17]

The Equal Status Act 2000 requires that the provision of goods and services be delivered without discrimination on the grounds of, *inter alia*, race (defined to include national origin). FLAC points out that an Irish homeless person who is living in state-provided hostel accommodation will not be automatically denied rent supplement on the basis that s/he is not deemed to be in need of accommodation.

---

[16] Statutory Instrument No. 210 of 2003, 27 May 2003.
[17] Free Legal Advice Centres Report, *supra* note 13, Conclusion and Recommendations, p. 40.

However, due to a direction from the Department of Justice, Equality and Law Reform to the Department of Social, Community and Family Affairs, there is a presumption that hostel accommodation is adequate for asylum seekers.[18] Similarly, the reduced supplementary welfare allowance that homeless people in hostel accommodation receive differs depending on the standard of accommodation provided and consequential personal needs. In contrast, asylum seekers are paid a fixed figure of €19.10 per week in direct provision. These discrepancies, according to FLAC, may be in contravention of the Equal Status Act 2000. The Act does not permit a challenge to enactments by the government but the report argues that until May 2003 the direct provision scheme was entirely without legislative basis and is still only partially on a statutory basis (in relation to refusal of rent supplement).

The adoption of the policy of direct provision suggests that the hallmark of Ireland's new asylum policy was becoming one of prevention and deterrence. In these circumstances, there was little room for the development of policies aimed at supporting asylum seekers beyond providing for their basic needs. The net effect of these measures, combined with a determined resistance on the part of the Irish government to calls from trade unions and representative groups for employers and the unemployed for the right to work to be granted to asylum seekers after six months, has been to effectively guarantee the social exclusion of asylum seekers in Ireland.

It is in the area of social exclusion that the tension and conflict between the policies of central and local government are highlighted. At the level of central government asylum seekers are excluded from measures aimed at enabling integration into Irish society and from the key provisions of the partnership agreement 'Sustaining Progress' drawn up in 2003,[19] while the social inclusion policies of local government invariably include asylum seekers as one of their target groups. At best, this scenario encourages the interpretation that Irish asylum policy is fraught with unresolved tensions. At worst, it suggests that the Irish authorities are enforcing and enabling policies of prevention and deterrence through the *de facto* social exclusion of asylum seekers, while at the same time presenting the illusion of making earnest efforts at their integration.[20]

Dispersal

Accompanying the introduction of the direct provision policy was that of 'dispersal'. To compensate for the financial shortfall resulting from

---

[18] Circular 04/00 issued by the Department of Social, Community and Family Affairs.

[19] See www.ictu.ie/html/publications/SP/sp.htm.

[20] On best practice see the European Council on Refugees and Exiles (ECRE), *Updated Position on the Integration of Refugees* (2002).

the system of direct provision asylum seekers are allotted full board in hostels, hotels and other accommodation centres which are located nationwide. The primary responsibility to provide adequate accommodation to asylum seekers lies with the government until the end of the asylum process and the Reception and Integration Agency is the section within the Department of Justice, Equality and Reform which deals most directly with asylum seekers and refugees particularly on accommodation-related issues. The dispersal policy, as an accommodation-driven scheme, focuses on finding shelter and food and, consequently, there is little evidence to suggest that other needs are assessed.[21] Access to appropriately qualified and culturally sensitive healthcare workers, to legal advice and representation and to English language training has not been available to many asylum seekers living outside the Dublin area.[22]

The accommodation provided by the government through the Reception and Integration Agency is generally in shared accommodation, under the direct provision scheme. Long-term stays in such accommodation can lead to institutionalisation and loss of personal initiative, aversion to the host society as well as unnecessary dependency on state care.[23] There is an increasing body of evidence which suggests that there are important links between health problems and prolonged stays in communal accommodation.[24] It is unsurprising that some asylum seekers unilaterally migrate back to urban areas to be with family and other support networks.[25]

---

[21] See Article 11(1) of the International Covenant on Economic, Social and Cultural Rights 1966. 'The States Parties...recognise the right of **everyone** to an adequate standard of living for himself and his family including adequate food, clothing, and housing, and to the continuous improvement of living conditions'. Stapleton J., *Direct Provision and Dispersal – 18 Months On*, October 2001, The Irish Refugee Council.

[22] Cassidy, E. 'Asylum seekers denied vital services', *Irish Examiner* 19 June 2003 quoting Moore, B., chairman of SONAS, an EU-supported asylum seeker support group: 'While there are already a range of state organisations providing specialist services to asylum seekers, along with a number of local voluntary groups, there are huge gaps in the services which need to be filled, especially outside of the greater Dublin area'.

[23] ECRE (1997), *Position on the Reception of Asylum Seekers*, p. 5 (quoting from a refugee policy document of The Norwegian Ministry of Local Government and Labour, 1995): *Experience has shown that those who master their life in exile, often are better qualified for managing the transition that is involved in re-establishing oneself in the country of origin. Thus there is no contradiction between measures facilitating an active, self-reliant life in Norway, and measures aimed at facilitating repatriation.*

[24] See for example, Dibelius C. (2001), *Help or Hindrance: Accommodation and the Integration of Refugees and Asylum Seekers in Waterford City*, Dublin: Clann Housing Association; and Fanning B., Veale A. and O'Connor D. (2001), *Beyond the Pale: Asylum Seeker Children and Social Exclusion in Ireland*, Irish Refugee Council.

[25] FLAC report, *supra* note 12, p. 35.

Medical practitioners, recognising the potential damaging effect that this system has on asylum seekers' mental health have recommended that hundreds be granted financial assistance to find private accommodation.[26] In spite of this, the Social Welfare (Miscellaneous Provisions) Act 2003 provides that asylum seekers may no longer move to private accommodation, unless exceptional circumstances prevail.

Legal advice and representation

The asylum process must establish whether or not persons claiming asylum need and are entitled to protection from persecution in their country of origin. The implications are clear. An incorrect decision – that a person does not need international protection when, in fact, s/he is a refugee – could be fatal for the person concerned. International, and domestic, law and standards stress the importance of fairness and predictability in the asylum process and that all asylum seekers must have effective access to the process.[27] It is a basic principle of natural justice that every person is entitled to fully put his/her case before an impartial decision maker, with legal assistance, when fundamental values such as life, personal integrity and freedom are at stake.

By their nature, asylum laws and procedures affect many individuals who are not well versed in the law of the host state. They frequently do not speak the national language and, due to past experiences, are often particularly distrustful of persons in authority.[28] Most asylum seekers are not aware of the intricacies of the procedure and issues of burden of proof. They might not be aware that they have to give a complete recount of their history, failing which they may be considered lacking in credibility and statements made afterwards might be considered false or concocted.

Early and continued access to competent legal advice and representation is critical to a fair and just asylum process. The ultimate

---

[26] Guerin, P. (2001), *Refugees and Asylum Seekers in County Monaghan: Population Profile Needs and Analysis*, County Monaghan Partnership and The Office of Community and Enterprise, Monaghan County Council, p. 28.

[27] For example, UNHCR Executive Committee Conclusion No. 93 (LIII) (2002), *Conclusion on Reception of Asylum Seekers in the Context of Individual Asylum Systems*; UNHCR Executive Committee Conclusion No. 82 (XLVIII) (1997), *Safeguarding Asylum*; UNHCR Executive Committee Conclusion No. 7 (XXVIII) (1977), *Determination of Refugee Status*. See also ECRE, *Guidelines on Fair and Effective Procedures for Determining Refugee Status* (1999).

[28] Para 190 of the UNHCR Handbook on Procedures and Criteria for Determining Refugee Status under the 1951 Convention and the 1967 Protocol relating to the Status of Refugees: 'It should be recalled that an applicant for refugee status is normally in a particularly vulnerable situation. S/he finds himself/herself in an alien environment and may experience serious difficulties, technical and psychological, in submitting his/her case to the authorities of a foreign country, often in a language not his/her own'.

rationalisation for the provision of free legal assistance is to be found in the principle that justice should be equally accessible to all.[29]

The right to legal representation is secured indirectly in Ireland, through the Refugee Act. Section 11(8) of the Act requires that the Office of the Refugee Applications Commissioner inform the applicant of his or her right to legal representation. In February 1999 the Refugee Legal Service (RLS) was established under the auspices of the Legal Aid Board to provide independent legal assistance at all stages of the asylum process to persons applying for asylum in Ireland. The RLS is based mainly in Dublin, but has satellite offices in Cork and Galway and also provides outreach services around the country. At the initial stage of the asylum procedure, the main function of the RLS is to assist applicants with pre-interview advice and in the production of post-interview written submissions. This work is carried out not by qualified solicitors but by caseworkers, who are not required to have formal legal training.

For those dispersed outside Dublin it has, in the past, proven to be extremely difficult to access legal representation. A survey of asylum seekers in County Kerry established that although 95% of the respondents accepted the importance of accessing legal advice, 80% of the asylum seekers questioned had not spoken to a lawyer since coming to Ireland.[30] Furthermore 60% of the asylum seekers did not know how to access legal advice. Similarly, a needs assessment of refugees and asylum seekers in County Monaghan found that there was a lack of legal expertise in County Monaghan regarding asylum law.[31] Primarily as a result of the expansion of the Refugee Legal Service there has been a marked increase in the proportion of asylum seekers who have been able to access legal advice.

As asylum and refugee law is a relatively new area of law for Irish solicitors and barristers, it is essential that individuals who practice in this area undertake adequate training. The quality and experience of legal representation for asylum seekers remains variable – from excellent to highly questionable. However, irrespective of the quality of an asylum seeker's legal representative, s/he should never be penalised for the actions of the legal representative. If, through no fault of the asylum seeker, a legal representative does not adequately represent his/her interests, the asylum seeker should be allowed to access alternative legal representation and to continue the asylum case.

---

[29] Article 7 of the Universal Declaration of Human Rights, although not legally binding, declares that: 'All are equal before the law and are entitled without any discrimination to equal protection of the law.' See also ECRE (2001), *Study on the availability of free and low cost legal assistance for asylum seekers in European States* (www.ecre.org).

[30] Collins, A. (2001), *Meeting the Needs of Asylum Seekers in Tralee,* Kerry Action for Development Education (KADE), April 2001.

[31] Guerin, P. *Supra* note 26.

At present there is still not a sufficient number of experienced refugee lawyers in many parts of the country and, as a result, asylum seekers who have been dispersed outside the Dublin region can face difficulties in accessing legal advice and representation. It has fallen on many support or voluntary groups to provide information regarding the asylum procedures in Ireland. Unscrupulous or uninformed advice by unqualified individuals can potentially be detrimental to an asylum seeker's application. The problems that this can cause have been identified and addressed in other states, such as the UK.[32]

Healthcare

There is no provision in the Refugee Act for healthcare for asylum seekers but, in practice, they are issued with a medical card which entitles them to free access to general medical practitioners and to free hospital and dental care on equal terms with Irish citizens. However, there is a lack of access to appropriately qualified and culturally sensitive care workers to assess how the specific concerns of asylum seekers (e.g. guilt and anxiety about family members, uncertainty about the future, and adaptation to a new culture) have negatively impacted on their health.

It is important to recognise that when dealing with asylum seekers there is a high possibility that they will have suffered mental, physical or sexual abuse prior to arrival in Ireland. It is also necessary to understand that

> while [on arrival] a refugee's initial emotional reaction may be a sense of relief, this is only short-lived. They are then confronted with a bewildering set of demands and challenges, combined with feelings of loss and concern for the welfare of those left behind.[33]

Support for vulnerable groups

A number of groups are particularly vulnerable and thus may need extra or specialist supports. Some examples are women, victims of torture and separated children.

Women

The UNHCR estimates that 75-90% of the world's refugee population are women. However, in Ireland, women account for approximately one-third of all asylum seekers. It has been argued that women

---

[32] In the UK the Immigration and Asylum Act 1999 Part V established a scheme to regulate immigration advice. The Act created the Office of the Immigration Services Commissioner to carry out this function.

[33] Quote by Dr Maeve Stokes, senior psychologist, St Brendan's Psychiatric Hospital, Dublin, in Clark, J. (2001) *Healthcare for Refugees*, www.irishhealth.com, p. 6.

refugees are at the same time vulnerable and indomitable. Described as 'the most affected refugee group' when uprooted by conflict, 'women, whether raped, secluded, unable to feed their children, or abducted, are victims of war and suffer physically, psychologically and spiritually'.[34]

Women are frequently persecuted for reasons similar to those of men. However, the persecution of women may differ, both in terms of form and motivation, from that commonly experienced by men. Women are often, for example, the targets of sexual violence for political ends. Women in such cases have often faced difficulties in showing that they are victims of persecution – rather than targets of random violence – despite the fact that it is widely accepted that rape and sexual violence are commonly used as weapons of war.[35] The difficulties are exacerbated by the trauma resulting from such experiences and the cultural factors that may inhibit the woman from speaking freely about her experience. Consequently, great care is required when adjudicating on claims involving sexual violence. Gender-specific violence should not be evaluated differently from other forms of violence that are considered as amounting to persecution. Another form of gender-related harm is where women face penalties for transgressing social mores in their country of origin. The case of Amina Lawal, a Nigerian woman who was sentenced to death by stoning for adultery, is an example.[36]

Asylum seeking women require specific forms of support throughout the process.[37] Claims by asylum seeking women should be assessed on their own merits, and independently of male family members, if requested. Asylum seeking women should therefore be informed, in private, on arrival of their right to make an independent application and to be interviewed without the presence of other family members. Women fleeing persecution may be uncomfortable talking to men about their experiences, and female interviewers along with female interpreters should therefore conduct interviews. Women asylum seekers should be helped to obtain a female legal representative.

Particular problems concerning the physical safety of women arise in direct provision centres because communal accommodation lacks privacy and may increase the risk of sexual or other violence against them. Single asylum-seeking women should not be accommodated in

---

[34] Hans, A. (1997), 'Sri Lankan Tamil Refugee Women in India', *Refuge* 16(2), pp. 3-9.

[35] UN World Conference on Women, 'Beijing Platform of Action', 1995, Strategic Objective E5; see also Sachs, L., *Sexual Violence as a Tool of War* (1999), UNHCR Conference, Refugee Women – Victims or Survivors?, Dublin 19 November 1999, p. 34.

[36] See www.mertonai.org/amina/?Factnet last viewed 2 August 2003.

[37] Irish Council For Civil Liberties Women's Committee (2000), *Women and the Refugee Experience: Towards a Statement of Best Practice*, Dublin. See also Irish Refugee Council Guiding Principles on Asylum-Seeking and Refugee Women (July 2001), and UNHCR Guidelines on the Protection of Refugee Women (July 1991).

predominantly male communal accommodation. It must also be remembered that such accommodation centres may be unsuitable, even on a short-term basis to meet the needs of women with families, women expecting babies and women who have suffered trauma.[38]

Localised, accessible and culturally sensitive specialised support in the form of counselling and mental health services should be offered to all asylum-seeking and refugee women, because they may have been traumatised by their experiences. The potential physical and mental health implications for women who are separated from their families and cultures must be recognised. This has implications beyond the individual woman, not least given that the well-being of mothers is closely linked to the well-being of children.

Furthermore, asylum-seeking and refugee women potentially face multiple discrimination when trying to access employment. The failure to provide childcare, the patriarchal structure of Irish society, the trend for women to be pushed towards low-paid, part-time employment and cultural differences about the role of women are all factors which may act as barriers to employment and training.

Victims of torture

A particularly vulnerable group among asylum seekers and refugees are those who were victims of torture or cruel and inhuman treatment prior to leaving their own country. Refugees and asylum seekers are likely to be more vulnerable to mental health problems due to the often-traumatic circumstances in which they had to flee their countries of origin. In addition, the journey to seek refuge may itself have involved experiences that served to compound the initial trauma. Stressful conditions faced in the host country and high levels of uncertainty and insecurity regarding the future can also serve to aggravate the effects of earlier traumas.

Accessing existing mental health services can often be difficult for people seeking refuge due to a range of cultural and linguistic differences. To overcome these difficulties it is important that statutory services develop culturally appropriate and sensitive methods for dealing with such vulnerable groups. In Ireland the Centre for the Care of Survivors of Torture (SPIRASI) was established in 2001. It is a non-governmental organisation that specifically works with survivors of torture in Ireland. Although SPIRASI has received some income from the European Refugee Fund, it does not have any guaranteed state funding. The centre provides a medical referral service, counselling, physiotherapy and other complementary therapies. The centre also

---

[38] Goodchild, S. and Ober, L., 'Rape claim highlights risk to female refugees', *Independent on Sunday,* 27 July 2003.

prepares medico-legal reports to substantiate claims of torture during the asylum determination process.

Separated children

In recent years, the phenomenon of separated asylum-seeking children has grown within Europe. According to the Separated Children in Europe Programme, separated children may be seeking asylum in Ireland as a result of fear of persecution or lack of protection arising from human rights violations, armed conflict, or disturbances in their country of origin. They may be the victims of trafficking for sexual or other exploitation, or they may travel to Europe to escape conditions of serious deprivation.[39]

Separated Children are defined as children under eighteen years of age who are outside their country of origin and separated from both parents or from their legal/customary primary caregiver.[40] The number of separated children arriving in Ireland between 1998 and 2002 was 1,226. Under the Refugee Act the local health board is legally responsibility for ensuring the best interests of unaccompanied minors.[41] Separated children need special support and attention because, in addition to their distress and uprooting, they lack the necessary family support in a crucial phase of their life.

Separated children, like all children, are more susceptible to illness and injury than adults. But they also lack the physical protection and psychological and emotional support they need. Without such support there is a great danger that their full development will be disrupted.

In the short-term, separated children can be overwhelmed by the practicalities of fleeing their home, arriving in Ireland exhausted from the journey, and suffering the shock of dislocation from their family and environment. Frequently they disembark into an alien culture, where they are unable to speak the language and express their views. In the period following their arrival they are faced with a complex asylum procedure which they may find difficult to understand. The same definition of a refugee applies in Ireland, regardless of the age of the applicant. This being so the Irish asylum authorities have responded very well over the past two years to the increase in the number of separated children arriving in Ireland. Both the Office of the Refugee Applications Commissioner and the Refugee Appeals Tribunal have specially trained staff to deal with separated children. The Refugee Legal Service also has specially trained staff to work with separated children.

---

[39] Separated Children in Europe Programme (www.separated-children-europe-programme.org).
[40] Separated Children in Europe Programme, Statement of Good Practice.
[41] In conjunction with the Child Care Act 1991.

Unfortunately separated children are forced to enter into independent life prematurely without family and community supports usually available to them.

> In psychological terms, all experience loss to a greater or lesser degree, loss not only of family and friends but also of a defined identity, of a belonging; all experience culture shock and post-migratory stressors associated with new language, different lifestyles and customs.[42]

The emergence of asylum-seeker/ refugee support groups

In effect, the Irish government delegated much of the responsibility for earlier programme refugees to the voluntary sector.[43] This dependence on the voluntary sector has remained the chief feature of meeting the needs of asylum seekers and refugees in Ireland. The Red Cross oversaw the reception of Hungarian refugees in 1956. Care of the Chilean refugees in the 1970s was left to a voluntary committee specifically formed for that purpose. Although the welfare needs of Vietnamese refugees in the 1980s were overseen by a government resettlement committee, it mainly limited its work to their initial reception.

The establishment of the government funded Refugee Agency in 1991 marked the emergence of an attempt to co-ordinate the resettlement of programme refugees in Ireland. The Bosnian and Kosovar refugees of 1992 and 1999 respectively were the chief beneficiaries of the Refugee Agency. In 2000 the Refugee Agency merged with the Directorate for Asylum Support Services to become the Reception and Integration Agency. Since its inception the primary focus of the Reception and Integration Agency has been almost exclusively concerned with the reception and accommodation of asylum seekers through the dispersal and direct provision schemes.

Effective programmes aimed at enabling the full integration of those recognised as refugees remain underdeveloped with most refugees being left to fend for themselves once they exit the asylum process. While there have been some attempts to create a co-ordinated government approach for dealing with programme refugees it has largely been left to the community and voluntary sector to provide support to the much larger number of recognised refugees (approximately 2000 were recognised in 2002).

It was not until the early 2000s that Ireland saw the emergence of asylum-seeker and refugee support groups across the country. Their

---

[42] King, D., *Unaccompanied Minors, An Information Booklet,* Barnardos and Centre for Social and Educational Research, Dublin Institute of Technology, p. 11.

[43] Fanning, B. (2002), *Racism and Social Change in the Republic of Ireland,* Manchester: Manchester University Press, p. 95.

establishment occurred largely as a local response to the nationwide dispersal of asylum seekers. Support groups were usually formed by local people as a humanitarian response to the arrival of asylum seekers in their communities. In some cases support groups emerged through local partnership organisations, churches or as offshoots of existing community and voluntary organisations. Integrating Ireland, a national network of refugee, asylum-seeker and immigrant support groups, was established in 2000 and this, and other fora, have successfully helped to bring some networking to the large numbers of disparate groups.

Initially these humanitarian efforts consisted of befriending and welcoming new arrivals. Over time, however, support groups found themselves in the unenviable position of attempting to fill the gaps in state-provided services. To this end, support groups effectively became the mediators between asylum seekers and officialdom in Ireland and have not only sought to provide some social and cultural supports to asylum seekers but have been engaged in the provision of information relating to statutory services, the asylum process, accessing legal representation and in attempting to address a host of difficulties faced by asylum seekers.

Despite the government's dependence on refugee and asylum-seeker support groups, such groups are either under-funded or not funded at all. Groups in receipt of funding are small in number and limited in their capacity to meet the needs of their constituency. Apart from some small specific project funding from the Irish government the money that has been available to such groups has come from the European Refugee Fund. Huge competition for money from the European Refugee Fund, combined with the short-term nature of the funding (1-3 years), has seen some asylum-seeker and refugee projects close down while others continue to face a very uncertain future. Arguably, this stiff competition for scarce resources is also serving to hinder the emergence and development of refugee community organisations.

Conclusion

The asylum issue evolved most dramatically in Ireland in the late 1990s and early 2000s. While it took some time for the infrastructure to be put in place some laudable progress has been made. However, the task of supporting asylum seekers remains only partly addressed. Ireland needs to accept the reality that asylum seekers, in numbers similar to that of recent years, will continue to arrive. The response by the state must be on the basis of this reality and must take into account that many of those who seek refuge in Ireland will become long-term residents here. It must also seek to respond comprehensively and in a co-ordinated manner to all the essential needs, ensuring that resources are well managed, that asylum seekers are appropriately supported and that integration is facilitated.

CHAPTER 8

Too Fast to be Safe?: Regular/Irregular Asylum Determination Procedures

Siobhan Mullally

Introduction

The use of accelerated asylum procedures reflects an increasing concern among states to limit access to the institution of asylum. Both in Ireland and elsewhere, an expanding category of asylum claims can now be channelled through procedures that lack the procedural safeguards necessary to guard against *refoulement.* Underpinning the use of accelerated procedures is a culture of disbelief and a desire to dispense with asylum claims with ever increasing speed. Securing effective protection to those fleeing persecution has become a secondary concern, as the prevention of abuse dominates asylum discourse. As Irish experience of accelerated procedures shows, the twin objectives of fairness and efficiency are more likely to be met by a single well-resourced regular asylum determination procedure.[1] Accelerated procedures, though superficially attractive, will often create more problems than they solve.[2] This chapter examines the use of accelerated asylum procedures in Ireland. As in other jurisdictions, the growth of asylum applications in recent years has led to increased restrictions on access to regular asylum determination

---

[1] See: Mullally, S. (2002) 'Manifestly Unfounded Asylum Claims in Ireland and the Right to Fair Procedures, 8(4) *European Public Law,* pp.525-543; *Ibid.* (2001) *Manifestly Unjust: A Report on the Fairness and Sustainability of Accelerated Procedures for Asylum Determinations,* Dublin: Irish Refugee Council.

[2] Justice, ILPA, ARC (1997) *Providing Protection: Fair and Effective Asylum Procedures,* London: ILPA, p.10. In Ireland, for example, if a determination of manifestly unfounded is overturned on appeal, the asylum applicant is re-interviewed and if a negative decision is given, she may have a second appeal. The initial use of an accelerated procedure turns out to lengthen the procedure even further. See: Ingoldsby, B., 'The Refugee Act and its Amendments', paper delivered at the Bar Council Seminar: Refugee and Asylum Law in Ireland, King's Inn, January 2001, pointing to the need for careful and discriminating use of accelerated procedures, p.7, available at http://www.justice.ie, accessed on 10 May 2003.

procedures. These restrictions have taken the form of greater use of accelerated procedures, limited rights of appeal, and more stringent time limits. Until recently, accelerated procedures were applied primarily in the context of manifestly unfounded asylum claims. Under the amendments introduced by the 2003 Immigration Act, however, the manifestly unfounded procedures have been brought to an end, to be replaced by yet more complex provisions for the use of accelerated procedures.[3]

The trend towards an increasing use of such procedures is not unique to Ireland.[4] The concern with efficiency, speed and the prompt removal of unsuccessful asylum applicants is now a constant in many refugee determination systems.[5] The UNHCR has not opposed the use of accelerated procedures as such. As early as 1983, the UNHCR Executive Committee acknowledged that a limited category of asylum claims could be processed through accelerated determination procedures.[6] The category of claims to which such provisions could apply were those that were deemed manifestly unfounded, that is they were 'so obviously without foundation as not to merit full examination at

---

[3] Immigration Act 2003, s.6 (amendments to the Refugee Act 1996).

[4] Van Selm, J. 'Access to Procedures: "Safe Third Countries", "Safe Countries of Origin", and "Time Limits"', Background paper for the Third Track discussions held in Geneva, June 2001, as part of the Global Consultations on International Protection (paper commissioned by UNHCR and the Carnegie Endowment for International Peace).

[5] See generally: Mullally, S. (2002) *supra* note 1, p.539. On the use of accelerated procedures in the Netherlands, see: Human Rights Watch *Fleeting Refuge: The Triumph of Efficiency over Protection in Dutch Asylum Policy*, available at: http://www.hrw.org/ reports/2003/netherlands0403/ accessed on 10 May 2003. In Canada, accelerated procedures are used in cases found to have 'no credible basis'. S.106, Immigration and Refugee Act, 2001. See: UNHCR Comments on Bill C-11, Submission to the House of Commons Standing Committee on Citizenship and Immigration, 5 March 2001, available at http://www.web.net/~ccr/c11hcr.PDF, as viewed on 8 January. 2002; Amnesty International Brief on Bill C-11, March 2001, available at http://www.amnesty.ca/ Refugee/Bill_C-11.PDF. In the UK, the extension of rights of appeal under the 1993 Asylum Act coincided with the introduction of accelerated appeals procedures for cases 'certified' as being without foundation under the 1951 Convention or otherwise 'frivolous' or 'vexatious'. Asylum Act, 1993, Sched. 2, para. 5. The consequences of certification were twofold: (a) the application was subject to accelerated appeals procedures and (b) the applicant was denied a right of appeal to the Immigration Appeals Tribunal. See generally: Harvey, C. J. (2000) *Seeking Asylum in the UK: Problems and Prospects,* London: Butterworths. In the US accelerated procedures have taken the form of 'expedited removal proceedings, s.235 Immigration and Nationality Act. See: Lawyers Committee for Human Rights (2000) *Is This America? The Denial of Due Process to Asylum Seekers in the United States,* New York: Lawyers Committee for Human Rights; Musalo, K. et al. (2000) *Report on the First Three Years of Implementation of Expedited Removal,* Center for Human Rights and International Justice, University of California, Hastings College of Law, also available at: (2001) *Notre Dame Journal of Law, Ethics and Public Policy 1* (special issue).

[6] UNHCR ExCom Conclusion No.30, 1983, The Problem of Manifestly Unfounded or Abusive Applications for Refugee Status or Asylum.

every level of the procedure'.[7] As part of its *Global Consultations* on international protection, the UNHCR has recently reiterated its position that the concept of a manifestly unfounded asylum claim is a useful case-management tool, particularly in states dealing with a significant caseload of asylum applications. However, it has again pointed out that a simplified, single procedure may prove fairer and more efficient.[8] This *caveat* has been largely ignored, however, with states opting instead for the quick-fix solution of accelerated procedures.

Within the EU, the shift towards a harmonised asylum policy has brought with it increasing emphasis on speed in the determination of asylum claims. The proposed European Council Directive on minimum standards on procedures in member states for granting and withdrawing refugee status includes extensive provisions for the use of accelerated procedures,[9] raising concerns that access to regular determination procedures may become the exception rather than the norm.[10] Linked with the expanding scope of accelerated procedures is a growing concern with the prevention of abuse and a shift away from the primary purpose of the asylum process – the provision of effective protection. This shift in asylum discourse reflects a politics of exclusion within the EU and a fortress mentality that feeds on an irrational fear of, and a lack of trust in, the 'other'.[11] It is this lack of trust, and not requirements of efficiency, that underpins the increasing shift towards accelerated asylum procedures.

More than a decade ago the UN High Commissioner for Refugees commented that Europe was at a crossroads.[12] We could, he said, build new walls, knowing that walls did not stop those who were fleeing persecution in the past. Or we could help to bridge the abyss which

---

[7] *Ibid,* para (d).

[8] UNCHR Asylum Processes (Fair and Efficient Procedures), Global Consultations on International Protection, 2nd meeting. EC/GC/01/12 31 May 2001 para. 24-26. See also: Comments by the UNHCR Representation in Ireland to proposed draft amendments to the Immigration Bill, 2002, June 2003 (Introductory Comments).

[9] COM (2002) 326 final/2, 03.07.2002. Article 23 of the proposed Council Directive provides that member states may adopt or retain accelerated procedures for the purpose of processing inadmissible applications, manifestly unfounded and other unfounded applications, repeat applications and in taking decisions on entry at border points. Inadmissible applications include those applications for which there is a 'safe third country' or 'first country of asylum'. The concept of a manifestly unfounded claim includes claims originating from 'safe countries of origin' and claims in relation to which exclusion clauses may apply. See: Article 29. In addition, asylum claims that are deemed to be 'abandoned' or that are 'late' may be channelled through accelerated procedures. See: Article 32(f), read in conjunction with Articles 16 and 20.

[10] See: JUSTICE, Proposed Directive on Minimum Standards in Asylum Procedures, evidence submitted to the European Union Committee, Sub-Committee E inquiry, January 2001.

[11] See generally Ward, I. (2002) 'Identifying the European Other', *International Journal of Refugee Law,* Vol.14, no.2/3, pp.219-237.

[12] Quoted in Spencer, M. (1995) *States of Injustice,* London: Pluto, pp.98-99.

now separates East from West and North from South. At the beginning of the twenty-first century, Europe, it seems, has chosen to build new walls, limiting access to asylum procedures designed to guarantee protection. Ireland, historically a land of emigration, has chosen to follow this path, building its own walls and allowing maxims of speed and efficiency to trump protection needs.

Accelerating the asylum process: the Immigration Act 2003

The Immigration Act 2003 includes extensive amendments to the 1996 Refugee Act. The provisions relating to the use of accelerated proce-dures in manifestly unfounded claims have now been replaced by a complex set of procedures to be applied to designated categories of asylum claims. New provisions on burden of proof, credibility and the duty to co-operate, draw on the repealed provisions relating to manifestly unfounded claims, ensuring a continuing emphasis on the credibility of the asylum applicant in the determination process. As amended, Sections 12 and 13 of the 1996 Refugee Act include lists of asylum claims which may be 'prioritised' or channelled through accel-erated procedures, subject to a direction in writing from the Minister for Justice, Equality and Law Reform to this effect. As with the previous manifestly unfounded process, where the provisions on accelerated procedures apply, appeals will take place without an oral hearing and will be subject to reduced time limits. As yet it is unclear whether the 'prioritising' of cases under Section 12 will be linked with the use of accelerated procedures. The UNHCR has welcomed the commitment to prioritise particular caseloads for processing, and has noted in particu-lar the possibility of prioritising 'manifestly well-founded' asylum claims or claims involving special considerations concerning the welfare of the asylum applicant or her family.[13] It has also expressed concern, however, that prioritisation should not be linked with the use of accelerated procedures. At present the categories of prioritised cases listed overlap with those cases that may be subject to accelerated pro-cedures, suggesting that at least certain categories of prioritised cases will be denied the normal safeguards of the determination process. The involvement of the minister in the designation of cases for priori-tisation also suggests that prioritising is not being introduced solely to enhance the managerial capacity of the Refugee Applications Commissioner or the Refugee Appeals Tribunal, but to ensure that the Commissioner and Tribunal follow governmental policy on asylum.

Section 13(6) of the Refugee Act (as amended) lists the categories of cases to which accelerated procedures may apply, subject to an order in

---

[13] See: Comments by the UNHCR Representation in Ireland to proposed draft amend-ments to the Immigration Bill 2003, June 2003.

writing from the minister. There is substantial overlap between the cases listed and the now repealed provisions on a manifestly unfounded claim. Echoing the most frequently used provisions of the manifestly unfounded process,[14] Section 13(6)(a) provides that accelerated procedures may be applied where there is 'either no basis or a minimal basis for the contention that the applicant is a refugee'. In its submissions on the Immigration Bill, the UNHCR argued that for the sake of consistency the terminology used in its Executive Committee (EXCOM) Conclusion No. 30 on manifestly unfounded claims[15] should be adopted, viz: 'that the application is not related to the criteria for the granting of refugee status laid down in the 1951 UN Convention [...] nor any other criteria justifying the granting of asylum'. This recommendation, suggesting the need to take into account the broader protection needs of the asylum applicant was, however, ignored. The terminology used in s.13 (6)(a) is also inconsistent with the proposed European Council Directive on Minimum Standards, which defines manifestly unfounded claims as those claims that are 'obviously not relevant' to the 1951 Convention,[16] narrowing the categories of claims that may be determined as manifestly unfounded and subject to accelerated procedures. Under the Refugee Act (as amended), however, accelerated procedures may now be triggered despite the applicant establishing a 'minimal basis' for the contention that she is a refugee.

The emphasis on the credibility of the asylum applicant, previously evident in the definition of a manifestly unfounded claim, is retained in newly inserted s.13 (6)(b). Under paragraph (b), false, misleading or contradictory statements by an applicant may lead to the conclusion that her claim is 'manifestly unfounded'. The term manifestly unfounded as used in this provision would seem to be intended to have a literal rather than a specifically legal meaning. No reference is made to the previous statutory definition of a manifestly unfounded claim or to relevant international standards. However, the continuing emphasis on the credibility of the applicant, both in the provisions on accelerated procedures and elsewhere in the Refugee Act, suggest the continuing influence of the manifestly unfounded concept. For the first time, detailed provisions on the assessment of credibility and the criteria to be taken into account in making such assessments are included in the Refugee Act. These include questions such as whether or not the applicant provided a 'full and true' explanation of how she travelled to the state. The asylum determination process in Ireland has frequently been criticised because of the emphasis placed by adjudicators on the applicant's route of travel to the state. This continuing emphasis on the mode of travel and arrival in the state reflects a preoccupation with

---

[14] See sections 12(4)(a)-(c) of the Refugee Act 1996.
[15] *Supra* note 6.
[16] *Supra* note 9, article 29(a).

immigration control, rather than protection. As the UNHCR pointed out in commenting on the credibility provisions, travel and arrival are not material to refugee status determination and should not form the sole basis of a credibility assessment.[17] The remaining provisions on credibility echo the now repealed definition of a manifestly unfounded claim. Credibility assessments must take account of factors such as the destruction of identity documents or the use of forged documents, without reasonable explanation. Much will turn here on how the test of reasonableness is applied by adjudicators and the extent to which the benefit of the doubt is given to the applicant. At the time of drafting the amendments to the Refugee Act the UNHCR pointed out that the corollary of the duty to co-operate was the principle of the benefit of doubt. A proposal to include a specific provision concerning the benefit of the doubt principle was, however, ignored.[18] Again, the overriding concern with the prevention of abuse won out.

As many commentators have noted, over-emphasis on the credibility of the applicant can undermine the effectiveness of protection afforded by the asylum system.[19] The ordinary guidelines for assessing the credibility of a witness are not easily transferred to the refugee determination process. In many cases there is a failure to understand the complex political, social and cultural contexts from which asylum applicants are fleeing. The adjudicator's own cultural background may hinder an impartial assessment of an asylum claim.[20] As a US court noted, '[W]hat sounds peculiar in one country may be the norm in another'.[21] Non-evidence-based assumptions about diverse cultural contexts need to be closely scrutinised. Within the context of accelerated procedures and limited rights of appeal, however, such close scrutiny may not be possible. Communication difficulties may also arise within the asylum process. It is widely recognised that asylum hearings frequently generate mistranslations and miscommunications.[22] An asylum-seeker may not have the capacity, without assistance, to articulate clearly and comprehensively why she has left her country of origin. Trans-cultural communication barriers and psychological complications may impair an asylum applicant's capacity to speak about traumatic experiences.[23] The UN Committee Against Torture has pointed out that '...complete accuracy in the application for asylum is seldom to be expected of victims of torture'.[24] As Merkel LJ has concluded elsewhere,

---

[17] *Supra* note 9.
[18] *Ibid.*
[19] See: Byrne, R. (2000), 'Expediency in refugee determination procedures', *35 Irish Jurist,* p.159.
[20] See: Mullally, S. (2001) supra n.1, p.92.
[21] *Chouchkov v. INS,* 220 F.3d 1077, 1083 n.15 (9th Cir. 2000).
[22] See: *Maini v. INS,* 212 F.3d 1167, 1176 (9th Cir. 2000).
[23] Byrne, R. (2000) *supra* note 19.
[24] Communication No.41/1996, *Kisoki v. Sweden,* 8 May 1996, para.9.3.

credibility should not be impugned simply because of vagueness or inconsistencies in recounting peripheral details, 'since memory failures are experienced by many persons who have been the objects of per-secution'.[25] Communication difficulties are exacerbated where there is fear or distrust of officialdom, or where there are other factors at play, such as the quality of interpreters or the availability of legal aid.[26] The UNHCR has argued that assessments of credibility are too complex to be dealt with in the context of accelerated asylum determination procedures. All too often, however, negative credibility determinations have led to asylum claims being fast-tracked, without adequate consideration given to the merits of the claim. Under the amendments introduced by the 2003 Immigration Act assessments of credibility are likely to continue to lead to 'fast-tracking' of asylum claims, increasing the risk of *refoulement*.

According to the explanatory memorandum attached to the 2003 Immigration Act, findings of the type listed in Section 13(6) of the Refugee Act (as amended) will be a basis for accelerating the appeals process, where a negative recommendation is made by the Commissioner, but will not be a basis for the recommendation itself. However, given the emphasis on credibility in the amended provisions of the Refugee Act and the extent to which credibility determinations have influenced the asylum process to date, it is likely that the findings listed in Section 13(6) will play a role in the substantive decision of the Commissioner.

Accelerated procedures may also be used where the possibility of a safe third country arises. The amendments introduced by the Immigration Act include detailed provisions on the safe third country concept, drawing heavily on the proposed European Council Directive on Minimum Standards. As we shall see, these provisions, yet again, lower the threshold of protection afforded to asylum applicants.

Accelerated procedures and 'safe third countries'

The concept of a 'safe third country' is referred to both in the provisions for 'prioritising' asylum claims and in the provisions on accelerated pro-cedures. These provisions would seem to concern asylum applicants to whom a safe third country agreement or the Dublin Convention have not been applied at the admissibility stage.[27] Given that provision is

---

[25] *Subarsan Kopalapillai v. Minister for Immigration and Multicultural Affairs* [1997] 1510 FCA (24 December 1997).

[26] UNCHR Asylum Processes (Fair and Efficient Procedures) May 2001 supra n.8, para.28. In Ireland, concerns have repeatedly been expressed at the difficulties faced by asylum seekers in accessing legal aid and translation facilities. See Almirall, L. and Lawton, N, *Asylum in Ireland: A Report on the Fairness and Sustainability of Asylum Procedures at First Instance* (Dublin: Irish Refugee Council, 1999).

[27] See generally s.22 of the Refugee Act 1996 (as amended).

made for the use of the safe third country concept at admissibility stage, it is unclear why it is necessary to also include this concept within the accelerated procedures provisions. Under s.13 (6)(d) an asylum claim may be accelerated where the Commissioner finds that the applicant had lodged a prior application for asylum in another state party to the Geneva Convention, whether or not that application had been determined, granted or rejected. In such cases, a presumption against the applicant's claim for asylum will also operate, under the newly inserted provisions on 'burden of proof'. The special accelerated procedures, introduced in s.13 (8) of the Refugee Act, allowing for a four-day time limit, are likely to be used in the context of safe third countries. With such a limited time for appeal, the risk of *refoulement* is greatly increased.

Previously a claim could be determined as manifestly unfounded where the applicant had already submitted a claim in a state party to the 1951 Convention, and the Commissioner was satisfied that it was 'properly considered'.[28] The UNHCR had proposed that this section be amended to ensure that an application would only be determined as manifestly unfounded if it had been 'properly considered' by a third state, in accordance with the 1951 Convention and 1967 Protocol. The UNHCR's proposal was intended to guard against the presumption that a state is a 'safe third country' simply by virtue of being a state party to the Geneva Convention. It would also have provided an additional safeguard against *refoulement*. This proposal, however, was ignored. The amendments introduced by the 2003 Immigration Act seem to lower the threshold of protection even further. To trigger the accelerated procedures it is enough that an application has been submitted in another state party to the Geneva Convention. There is no requirement that the application was properly considered or that the requirements of the Convention were adhered to. Neither is there any reference to the safe third country concept, as used in the context of admissibility procedures, or to the criteria to be used in designating a third country as safe. The UNHCR recommended the inclusion of a specific reference to the safe third country requirements, as set out in s.22 (5)(a) of the 1996 Refugee Act (as amended). However, no action was taken on this recommendation, raising the possibility of inconsistencies between the safe third country concept as used in the provisions on admissibility, prioritisation and acceleration.

The safe third country concept as used in the context of the admissibility procedures includes certain safeguards designed to guard against *refoulement*. These safeguards draw on the safe third country concept as used in the proposed European Council Directive on Minimum Standards, and will be subject to review once the Directive enters into force.[29] Under the amended Section 22, the minister, in

---

[28] S.12(4)(i).
[29] *Supra* note 9, Annex I.

consultation with the Minister for Foreign Affairs may draw up a list of safe third countries. The factors to be taken into account in designating a third country as safe include:[30]

i)   whether the country is a party to and complies generally with its obligations under the Geneva Convention, the Convention against Torture (CAT) and the International Covenant on Civil and Political Rights (ICCPR)

ii) whether the country has a democratic political system and an independent judiciary

iii) whether the country is governed by the rule of law.

The reference to compliance with a state's obligations is a welcome one, because it requires consideration of what happens in practice in state parties to the Geneva Convention, the CAT and the ICCPR. This requirement goes beyond the proposed European Council Directive on Minimum Standards, under which a safe third country may not even have ratified the Geneva Convention.[31] To guard against *refoulement,* however, it is not enough that a state 'generally' complies with its international law obligations. Asylum determination requires an individualised assessment of the merits of each claim. References to a state's general record of compliance, together with the use of lists of safe third countries, is likely to undermine the individualised nature of the determination process.

The European Council for Refugees and Exiles has noted that without safeguards the 'safe third country' concept poses 'a serious risk to the institution of asylum and to the fundamental principle of *non-refoulement*'.[32] The recent amendments to the 1996 Refugee Act – increasing the burden of proof on the applicant where a safe third country issue arises, restricted time limits and reduced rights of appeal – all combine to heighten the risks arising from the use of the safe third country concept.

Dublin convention, admissibility and accelerated procedures

The 'safe third country' concept has been used primarily within the EU as a 'burden-sharing' tool, leading in 1990 to the adoption of the Dublin Convention.[33] The implementation of the Dublin Convention

---

[30] S.22(5)(b).

[31] *Supra* note 9, Annex 1, para. 1(A)(2).

[32] Comments from the European Council on Refugees and Exiles (ECRE) on the working document of the European Commission: 'Towards Common Standards on Asylum Procedures', April 1999, available at: http://www.ecre.org/eu_developments/procedures/index.shtml, accessed on 10 May 2003.

[33] Convention Determining the State Responsible for Examining Applications for Asylum Lodged in one of the member states of the European Communities. In March 2000, the European Commission issued a Staff Working Paper entitled: Revisiting the Dublin Convention. The paper called for a Community instrument to replace the Dublin Convention, on the ground that the Convention was 'not functioning as well as had been hoped.' See: van Selm, J. supra n., p.31 para. 75.

met with many obstacles, however, with few applicants being transferred under the Convention regime. A process of reforming the
Convention regime has now been completed, and in February 2003,
the Dublin Regulation was adopted, with the intention of ensuring a
more effective transfer mechanism between EU member states.[34] One
of the stated aims of the Dublin Regulation is to make member states
'answerable' to all other member states for their 'failure' to control
entry into their territories. The mechanism devised in the Dublin
Convention and followed through in the Dublin Regulation attempts to
shift responsibility for determining asylum applications towards those
states with extended land and sea borders in Southern and Eastern
Europe – the principal migration entry points. These are the very states
with the most under developed asylum determination systems in the
EU. Given the protection needs of asylum applicants, and requirements of efficiency, it would be more logical that the member state in
which an asylum application is lodged would be the state responsible
for determining a claim. This solution would meet with both requirements of fairness and efficiency. At the heart of the transfer mechanism,
however, is a concern to restrict entry into the territory of the EU and
to 'punish' states that fail to police their borders. Again we see a concern with security and control taking priority over protection needs.

Under the proposed European Council Directive on Minimum
Standards a claim for which another member state has 'acknowledged
responsibility' may be deemed inadmissible and subject to accelerated
procedures.[35] The use of accelerated procedures in such cases pre-
sumes that other member states are 'safe third countries'. As previous
experience has shown, however, this presumption is not always well
founded. Despite increasing moves towards harmonisation of asylum
policy between EU member states, considerable discrepancies persist
both in the levels of protection provided to refugees and in the
definition of persecution applied in national determination systems.
This has led to difficulties in applying the 'safe third country' concept.
As the *Adan* and *Aitsegur* cases have shown,[36] the determination of

---

[34] Council Regulation (EC) No 343/2003 of 18 February 2003, establishing the criteria
and mechanisms for determining the member state responsible for examining an asylum application lodged in one of the member states by a third-country national. OJ
L 50/1 25.2.2003.

[35] Supra n.9, Article 25(a).

[36] *R. v. Secretary of State For The Home Department, Ex Parte Adan, R v. Secretary of State
For The Home Department Ex Parte Aitseguer* [2000] UKHL 67; [2001] 2 WLR 143; [2001]
1 All ER 593 (19th December 2000)). The House of Lords concluded that France and
Germany could not be defined as safe third countries because of their failure to recog-
nise that non-state agent persecution came within the scope of the 1951 Convention. The
UN Human Rights Committee has also criticised the unduly narrow definition of perse-
cution applied by France and, in particular, its failure to recognise persecution by non-
state agents. Concluding observations of the Human Rights Committee: France. 04/08/97.
CCPR/C/79/Add.80 (Concluding observations on the third periodic report submitted by
France under Article 40 of the International Covenant on Civil and Political Rights).

whether an asylum application has been 'properly considered' requires a full examination of the substantive criteria applied and the determination procedures followed in a third country. This may not be possible within the context of accelerated procedures. It may also be difficult for an asylum applicant to rebut the presumption of 'safe third country' in relation to other member states. For minority communities, such as the Roma community, the dangers of *refoulement* in the context of such accelerated procedures are greatly increased. If it is now intended that the transfer mechanism will operate more effectively between member states, the requirements of protection against *refoulement* are all the more urgent. With stringent time limits – forty-eight hours in the Irish context – it is difficult to see how an asylum applicant can be assured of an effective right of appeal against a decision to transfer her application. Under the Dublin Regulation an appeal does not have a suspensive effect unless this is determined as necessary by a court of law.[37]

The Irish government has been quick to follow this lowering of the protection threshold. The amendments introduced by the 2003 Immigration Act remove the right to an appeal with suspensive effect in the context of safe third country or Dublin Convention cases. The removal of this right further limits the procedural safeguards applying in such cases. In the light of Ireland's recent incorporation of the European Convention on Human Rights (ECHR)[38] it also raises questions as to whether or not an effective remedy is provided against potential violations of the applicant's right to *non-refoulement*.

White lists and 'safe countries of origin'

The amendments introduced in the 2003 Immigration Act make provision for the use of accelerated procedures where an applicant is a national of or has a right of residence in a designated safe country of origin. Such claims may also be 'prioritised' under the newly inserted provisions on prioritisation of claims. As with the safe third country concept, the criteria to be taken account of in designating safe countries of origin include whether or not the country is a party to and 'generally complies' with obligations under CAT, the ICCPR and, where appropriate the ECHR. The requirement to take account of a state's compliance record improves upon the manifestly unfounded process according to which a claim could be determined as manifestly unfounded simply because the applicant was a national of or a resident in a state party to the Geneva Convention.[39] Many refugee-producing countries – including Sierra Leone, Angola and Liberia – are state parties to the Geneva Convention. Assessing a state's compliance

---

[37] Supra n.34, Article 20(1)(e).
[38] See: European Convention on Human Rights Act 2003.
[39] 1996 Refugee Act, s.12(4)(j).

record avoids the designation of such countries as safe. There is, however, a fundamental flaw in the safe country of origin concept as used in the 1996 Refugee Act. Refugee law is not about what happens 'generally'.[40] It is about the protection needs of individuals. The safe country of origin concept, particularly when combined with 'white lists', ignores the need for an individualised assessment of each asylum claim.

The use of so-called 'white lists' of safe countries of origin further erodes the protection afforded to individual applicants. Speaking to the Select Committee on the European Union in October 2002, the Minister for Justice, Equality and Law Reform, Michael McDowell TD, indicated his intention to introduce a list of safe countries of origin, in respect of which, he said, there would only be 'a very summary process' of asylum determination.[41] A summary process is unlikely, however, to ensure an individualised assessment of the merits of each claim. Commenting on the amendments introduced by the 2003 Immigration Act the UNHCR said that it shared the government's intention to design procedural devices such as the safe country of origin concept, so as to 'preserve the integrity of the asylum system'.[42] The integrity of the determination system should not be confused, however, with the efficiency and speed of the process. The UNHCR went on to point out that the use of this procedural tool should not increase the burden or standard of proof for the asylum seeker. The High Commissioner had no objection to the operation of a rebuttable presumption against applications originating from designated safe countries, provided that each claim would continue to be fully assessed on the basis of its merit. If a full individual assessment takes place, however, it is unclear how the procedural device of safe country of origin will contribute to the efficiency of the determination system. As the British-based NGO, Justice, commented:[43]

> Either the designation will be applied broadly, [...] without proper consideration of the individual case; or, [...], states will in any event have to consider the detailed circumstances of the individual claim [...] The first is unsafe; the second is unlikely to accelerate procedures and, if it leads to satellite litigation, may indeed lengthen them.

The UNHCR initially viewed the 'safe country of origin' concept as having a role to play in preventing or reducing backlogs and helping

---

[40] See: European Council for Refugees and Exiles. (2003) Comments on the Amended proposal for a Council Directive on minimum standards on procedures in member states for granting and withdrawing refugee status CO1/03/2003/ext/AB, available at: http://www.ecre.org/eu_developments/procedures/index.shtml, accessed on 10 May 2003.

[41] Michael McDowell, Minister for Justice, Equality and Law Reform, speaking at the Select Committee on European Affairs, Wednesday 9 October 2002.

[42] UNHCR's general comment on Amendment no.13, *supra* n. 13.

[43] Justice supra n.10, p. 13 para. 59.

to identify cases for expedited treatment.[44] Its widespread use by states, however, particularly in the form of so-called 'white lists' of safe countries has attracted much criticism. Designating a country as 'safe' may amount to a *de facto* geographical reservation to the Geneva Convention. This is clearly incompatible with the intent of the 1967 Protocol to the Convention and runs counter to broadly based international opinion in favour of applying the Convention without geographic restrictions.[45] It also works against an individual assessment of the merits of an asylum claim, preferring instead the sledgehammer approach to crack what Goodwin-Gill refers to as 'the very small nut of the occasional abuse of claim'. [46] In its *Global Consultations on International Protection* the UNHCR commented that the concept of safe country of origin might operate as an effective decision-making tool. However, the High Commissioner has also pointed to the need for individual assessments of each claim and for an effective opportunity to rebut any general presumption of safety.[47] Within the context of accelerated procedures, with limited rights of appeal, it is unlikely that such an opportunity will exist.

The history of 'white lists' in the UK has been particularly controversial, with countries such as Pakistan and Nigeria having been designated as 'safe', despite persistently poor human rights records in both countries. The Nationality, Immigration and Asylum Act 2002 reintroduces the concept of white lists of 'safe countries of origin'. At present the ten new member states of the EU are included in this list.[48] Applicants from these countries may have their cases certified as 'clearly unfounded' and as a result lose their right to an in-country appeal.[49] Additional countries may be added to the list by the Home Secretary, if he is satisfied that there is 'in general' no serious risk of persecution or contravention of the United Kingdom's obligations under the ECHR.[50] The general designation of a country as 'safe', of course, ignores the particular circumstances of the individual applicant.

---

[44] UNHCR Executive Committee, Background Note on the Safe Country Concept and Refugee Status 26 July 1991 (EC/SCP/68).

[45] *Ibid.*

[46] Goodwin-Gill (April 2001) cited in: House of Lords Select Committee on the European Union, *Eleventh Report on Minimum Standards in Asylum Procedures*, London: HMSO.

[47] UNHCR, *supra* n.8, p.9 para. 39.

[48] Nationality, Immigration and Asylum Act, 2002, s.94(4). The Minister for Justice, Equality and Law Reform announced on 12 September 2003 (press release) that the following countries would be designated as safe countries of origin, pursuant to an Order: Cyprus, Czech Republic, Estonia, Hungary, Latvia, Lithuania, Malta, Poland, Slovak Republic and Slovenia. These ten accession states will become members of the EU on 1 May 2004. Also for inclusion in the Order are Bulgaria and Romania, who are currently EU applicant states.

[49] *Ibid.* s. 94 (3).

[50] Nationality Immigration and Asylum Act, s.94(5).

Listing the ten new member states of the EU as 'safe countries of origin' ignores the concerns expressed by the European Commission in its *Reports on Progress towards Accession* which have highlighted ongoing human rights problems in new member states.[51] A recurring theme in these reports is the discriminatory treatment afforded to the Roma community.[52] At the time of drafting the 2002 Nationality, Immigration and Asylum Act, the Joint Parliamentary Committee on Human Rights[53] expressed serious concerns about the use of the 'safe country of origin' concept.[54] On the designation of the ten new member states as 'safe', the Committee had this to say:[55]

> ... In view of the well-authenticated threats to human rights which remain in the states seeking accession to the European Union, [...] a presumption of safety, even if rebuttable, presents a serious risk that human rights would be inadequately protected. We consider that the presumption of safety is unacceptable on human rights grounds.

As to the absence of a suspensive right of appeal for claims that are certified as 'clearly unfounded', the Committee concluded that this would lead to inadequate protection against *refoulement,* and would, in some circumstances, deny an applicant the right to an effective remedy.[56]

The proposed European Council Directive on Minimum Standards sets out a list of principles to be applied in designating countries as 'safe'.[57] These provide, *inter alia,* that the non-derogable rights set out in international human rights law are 'consistently observed' and that the country provides for 'generally effective remedies against violations of these civil and political rights'.[58] Again, we see the individualised nature of asylum determination being undermined. Although the proposed Directive provides that the particular circumstances of the applicant must be taken into account,[59] in practice an opportunity to rebut the presumption of safe country of origin will arise only after a decision has been made at first instance. At this point an applicant may not have enough time to provide the evidence required and may not

---

[51] See, for example, European Commission, *Regular Report on Hungary's Progress Towards Accession,* COM (2002) 700 final, Brussels 9.10.2002, pp.30-33.

[52] See: Lord Avebury, HL Debs, 17 October 2002, cc. 1027-1029. See also: UNHCR 'No place of refuge for Roma', responding to the proposed designation of new member states as 'safe countries of origin', 24 October 2002.

[53] Joint Committee On Human Rights: *Twenty-Third Report,* 22 October 2002, available at: http://www.publications.parliament.uk/pa/jt200102/jtselect/jtrights/176/125502. htm, accessed on 10 May 2003.

[54] This view was shared by the House of Lords Select Committee on the European Union, supra n.46.

[55] Supra n.53, para.35.

[56] *Ibid.* paras.32-33.

[57] Supra n. 9, Articles 30, 31 and Annex II.

[58] *Ibid.* Annex II.

[59] *Supra* n., Article 31.

even be permitted to remain in the state, given the absence of a suspensive right of appeal.[60]

Accelerated procedures and exclusion clauses

At present the provisions on accelerated procedures in the 1996 Refugee Act do not include any reference to exclusion clauses. However, provision is made for the 'prioritising' of claims, in relation to which exclusion clauses apply.[61] The prioritising of such claims is a welcome development, provided of course that the principle of 'inclusion before exclusion' is applied. Given the increasing preoccupation with security and control, however, adherence to this principle cannot be guaranteed.

The definition of a manifestly unfounded claim in the proposed European Council Directive on Minimum Standards includes, for the first time, applications submitted by persons who are *prima facie* excluded from refugee status by virtue of article 1(F) of the 1951 Convention. Given the complex nature of cases arising under exclusion clauses and the need for a precise legal analysis of questions involving individual criminal responsibility, this addition to the concept of a manifestly unfounded claim is particularly worrying.[62] It is widely recognised that exclusion clauses are of an exceptional nature, to be applied scrupulously and restrictively because of the potentially serious consequences for the individual applicant.[63] Accelerated procedures do not allow for such scrupulous application.[64] They also run contrary to basic principles of procedural fairness, particularly as they apply in the context of the criminal process. As presently drafted, the proposed Directive creates a rebuttable presumption in favour of exclusion, placing an unduly heavy burden on the applicant and one that runs contrary to international standards. In effect, applicants are required to prove their innocence.[65] The UNHCR has repeatedly urged states to adopt a restrictive approach to exclusion clauses, and to follow the general principle of 'inclusion before exclusion'.[66] On the standard of proof to be applied, the High

---

[60] *Ibid.* Article 40.
[61] See: s.12(1)(n) (as amended).
[62] See: ECRE supra n.40, p.20.
[63] See: UNHCR. *Summary Conclusions: Exclusion from Refugee Status*, Lisbon Expert Roundtable: Global Consultations on International Protection 3-4 May 2001, EC/GC/01/2Track1, 30 May 2001, para.4.
[64] See: Lawyers Committee for Human Rights (2000) 'Safeguarding the Rights of Refugees under the Exclusions Clauses', *International Journal of Refugee Law*, vol.12, pp.317-345, p.324.
[65] *Ibid.* p.325.
[66] Supra n.63, para.15. See also: UNHCR Press Release 'Ten Refugee Protection Concerns in the Aftermath of September 11th, 1 December 2001; *Ibid. Preliminary Observations: European Commission Proposal for a Council Framework Decision on combating terrorism*, COM (2001) 521 final 2001/0217 CNS, October 2001.

Commissioner has pointed out that 'serious reasons' should be interpreted, as a minimum, to mean clear evidence, sufficient to indict, bearing in mind international standards.[67] The test laid down in the proposed Directive lowers this standard of proof, requiring only a *prima facie* exclusion to trigger the accelerated process. Again, this undermines the procedural safeguards necessary to guard against *refoulement*.

Due process and the right to fair procedures

The use of accelerated asylum determination procedures potentially increases the risk of erroneous decisions. Against this background, the need for stringent procedural safeguards becomes ever more pressing. This need, however, has not yet been met in Ireland. Under the amendments introduced by the 2003 Immigration Act, asylum seekers' procedural rights are further eroded. The new provisions on accelerated procedures introduce two distinct sets of time limits. The time limit of ten working days for appeals applies to cases covered by Section 13(6) of the Refugee Act (as amended). Under the special procedures set out in Section 13(8), however, a further reduced time limit of four working days may apply to designated cases.[68] The application of these special procedures is subject to a direction in writing from the minister. An additional safeguard is introduced with regard to the use of the Section 13(8) procedures, requiring that the applicant and her solicitor be notified in advance of the investigation that the reduced time limit will apply.[69] Without such notification, of course, it would be difficult if not impossible for an applicant to comply with the four-day time limit. In essence, once an applicant receives such a notification, she would be well advised to begin preparing her appeal.

It is likely that Section 13(8) procedures will be applied to applications falling under the 'safe third country' or 'safe country of origin' provisions of the Refugee Act (as amended), and to cases where applicants are accommodated or detained at 'one-stop' reception centres. The use of accelerated procedures in this way is closely modelled on similar procedures in the UK, where asylum applicants from designated countries of origin are detained at 'fast-track' reception centres and their claims subject to accelerated determination procedures.[70] While the use of one-stop reception centres may improve access to legal advice and to interpreters, 'fast-tracking' designated groups of asylum claims undermines the individualised nature of asylum determination, increasing the risk of *refoulement*.

---

[67]   Ibid, para.17. See also: Lawyers Committee for Human Rights supra n.64, p.328.
[68]   S.13(8) of the Refugee Act 1996.
[69]   *Ibid.* s.13(9).
[70]   *Ibid.* s.22(2)(j).

The absence of an oral hearing on appeal has been one of the most controversial elements of the accelerated procedures in the Irish context. The amendments introduced by the 2003 Immigration Act continue to limit appeals under the accelerated procedures to a written hearing only. Commenting on the accelerated procedures introduced by the 2003 Immigration Act, the UNHCR expressed concern with the lack of any possibility for, at a minimum, the Tribunal and its members to request an oral hearing, where such a hearing was considered necessary in order to reach a fair decision. The failure to provide an oral hearing on appeal, in the context of the manifestly unfounded process, was the subject of judicial review proceedings in *Z. v. Minister for Justice, Equality and Law Reform.*[71] *Z.*, a Russian national, claimed that if returned to Russia he would face persecution on grounds of his Jewish background and his Communist party affiliations. His application for asylum was determined as manifestly unfounded at first instance and this determination was upheld on appeal.[72] He subsequently sought leave to apply for a judicial review of the determination, arguing, *inter alia,* that the absence of a right to an oral hearing on appeal infringed his right to fair procedures, protected as a 'personal right' under Article 40.3 of the Constitution.[73] In granting leave to apply for judicial review, the High Court was influenced by the findings of the US Supreme Court in *Goldberg v. Kelly.*[74] In that case, Brennan J held that the right to be heard must be tailored to 'the capacities and circumstances of those who are to be heard'.[75] There is little to suggest, however, that the *dictum* of Brennan J had any lasting impact on the High Court. In a judgment delivered on 17 July 2001, Finnegan J concluded that the absence of an oral hearing on appeal did not violate *Z.*'s constitutional right to fair procedures.[76] Though recognising that the 'credibility and veracity' of an applicant often lies at the heart of a decision that an application is manifestly unfounded, he nonetheless chose to ignore Brennan J's conclusion that written submissions are a 'wholly unsatisfactory basis' for such decisions. Because a 'single oral procedure' was provided for at interview stage, he concluded that both the

---

[71] [2001] IEHC 70 (29th March 2001).

[72] Paragraphs 14(a), (b) and (c) of the Hope Hanlan letter were invoked. These correspond to sections 12(4)(a),(b) and (c) of the 1996 Act.

[73] Personal rights are guaranteed regardless of legal status. As Barrington J stated in *Finn v. Attorney General* [1983] IR 154 the personal rights protected under Article 40.3.2 derive, 'not from a man's citizenship but from his nature as a human being'. Although Article 40.3.2∞ refers specifically to the personal rights of citizens, Barrington J held that the 'whole scheme of moral and political values' accepted by the Constitution indicated the duty of the State to defend and vindicate the rights of non-citizens. The State, he held, does not create these rights, it recognises and promises to protect them.

[74] 397 U.S. 254.

[75] *Ibid.* at 268-269.

[76] *Z. v. Minister for Justice, Equality and Law Reform* [2001] IEHC 105 (17 July 2001).

constitutional requirements of natural justice and the standards laid down in the UNHCR Handbook on procedures and criteria for determining refugee status were satisfied.[77] In arriving at this conclusion, Finnegan J appears to equate the interview at first instance with an oral hearing. In doing so he ignores the shortcomings of the interview process, including the absence of a full right to legal representation at this stage. He also fails to examine the decision-making process at first instance. Under the current procedure the Commissioner arrives at a determination on an asylum application on the basis of a report drawn up by the interviewer and a further report and recommendation drawn up by an 'authorised officer' of the Commissioner.[78] Neither the Commissioner nor the authorised officer participates in a 'face-to-face' hearing with the applicant. The absence of such a hearing is particularly problematic where the final determination requires an assessment of the applicant's credibility. As Goodwin-Gill has noted, decisions made on the basis of a transcribed interview are likely to be replete with error. There is no substitute for bringing the decision-maker 'face-to-face' with the applicant.[79] A similar decision-making process was the subject of challenge before the Canadian Supreme Court in *Singh et al v. M.E.I.*[80] There, the applicant's claim to refugee status had been denied without a full oral hearing before any of the bodies empowered to adjudicate on the merits of the claim. Giving judgment for the Court, Beetz J held that where the right to liberty and security of the person depended on findings of fact and credibility, the opportunity to make written submissions was insufficient to satisfy the requirements of 'fundamental justice'.[81] The right to an oral hearing, he said, was a 'universal rule of equity'.[82]

Z. had also argued that the refusal to grant him an oral hearing on appeal was a violation of Article 6(1) of the ECHR. However, the High Court concluded that as the ECHR was not yet incorporated into domestic law, it could not give rise to justiciable rights and obligations and could not raise any 'substantial grounds' for judicial review.[83] It is, in any case, unlikely that Article 6(1) would have been of much assistance to Z. The European Court of Human Rights has repeatedly held that the concept of 'civil rights and obligations' referred to in

---

[77] *Ibid.* para.11. Finnegan J also held that the UNHCR Handbook was a 'legitimate aid' to interpretation of the Convention.

[78] Sections 11 and 13 of the 1996 Refugee Act.

[79] Goodwin-Gill, G (2001) supra n.46.

[80] [1985] 1 S.C.R. (Federation of Canadian Sikh Societies and Canadian Council of Churches Interveners).

[81] At issue in the case was the scope of the protections afforded by the Canadian Charter of Rights and Freedoms (section 7) and the Canadian Bill of Rights (section 2(e)).

[82] The Court cited with approval the dictum of Rinfret C.J. in *L'Alliance des Professeurs Catholiques de Montréal v. Labour Relations Board* [1953] 2 S.C.R. 140, at p.154.

[83] Supra n.76, per Finnegan J, para.37.

Article 6(1) does not include decisions relating to the deportation or expulsion of 'aliens' because these are covered separately in Protocol No.7 to the Convention.[84]

Z.'s appeal to the Supreme Court centred on two main questions: (a) whether the determination of manifestly unfounded was unreasonable, irrational and therefore *ultra vires* and; (b) whether natural and constitutional justice required an opportunity for an oral hearing on appeal.[85] The Court concluded that while it was unreasonable to find that Z.'s claim did not show 'any grounds' for the contention that he was a refugee, his claim nonetheless failed because it was unrelated to 'a fear of persecution', and because there were 'insufficient details or evidence' to support the claim. In the Court's view, Z.'s difficulties in Chechnya could be ascribed 'to the fortunes of war rather than to persecution or a failure of State protection'.[86] This finding displays a lack of understanding of the complex legal issues raised by non-state agent persecution. While a failure of state protection is essential to satisfying the test of persecution, the issues raised in a case such as Z.'s cannot be adequately dealt with in the context of accelerated procedures. Certainly Z.'s case would not seem to fall within the UNHCR definition of a manifestly unfounded claim as one that is 'clearly fraudulent' or 'without any substance'.[87] On the question of a right to an oral hearing, the Supreme Court had little to say. As an oral hearing had already taken place at the interview stage, there was, the Court concluded, no infringement of Z.'s right to natural and constitutional justice. Again the Supreme Court failed to take account of the inadequacies of the interview procedure at first instance, equating the procedure with an oral hearing despite the absence of a full right to legal representation at this stage.

A question that was not considered in the Z. case is whether the absence of a right to an oral hearing on appeal negates the availability of an effective remedy within the meaning of Article 13 of the ECHR. A related question is whether the right to apply for judicial review against a determination of manifestly unfounded constitutes an effective remedy. Following Ireland's recent incorporation of the ECHR (*albeit* in a limited form), such questions are likely to arise before the courts with increasing frequency. The protection of Article 13 of the ECHR is engaged where there is an 'arguable claim' that the applicant's Convention rights have been violated. In *Vilvarajah v. UK*[88] the Court was satisfied that the remedy of judicial review allowed the refusal of

---

[84] See: Protocol No. 7 to the Convention for the Protection of Human Rights and Fundamental Freedoms, ETS no.117, adopted 24.XI.84, Article 1. *Maaoiu v. France* (2001) 33 EHRR 42.

[85] [2002] IESC 12 (1st March 2002).

[86] *Ibid.* p.32.

[87] *Supra* n.6.

[88] 14 (1991) EHRR 248.

refugee status to be submitted to the 'most anxious scrutiny.' In *R v. Secretary of State for the Home Department, ex parte Turgut*,[89] Simon LJ held that the duty of the court, in a case involving an alleged violation of Article 3 of the ECHR, was to subject the asylum determination to 'rigorous examination'. In the Irish context, however, it is questionable whether a determination of manifestly unfounded can be subject to rigorous examination, either by the Refugee Appeals Tribunal or by the courts in the context of judicial review proceedings. The Illegal Immigrants (Trafficking) Act 2000 imposes restrictions on the right to apply for a judicial review of deportation or expulsion orders. Section 5 of the Act reduces the time limit within which an application for a judicial review can be made – from three months to fourteen days. It also requires that there are 'substantial grounds' for challenging the validity of the deportation or expulsion order in question. These restrictions must be read together with the judgment of the High Court in *Camara v. Minister for Justice, Equality and Law Reform*.[90] There, the High Court concluded that the Refugee Appeals Authority (as it then was) is a specialist administrative body and one to which 'curial deference' is due. Taken together, these judgments greatly restrict the right of access to the courts and with it the possibility of reviewing the procedures applied within the asylum determination process. They also raise serious questions as to whether the remedy of judicial review in the Irish context constitutes an effective remedy for the purposes of Article 13. In *Jabari v. Turkey*[91] the European Court of Human Rights found Turkey to be in violation of its Convention obligations under Articles 3 and 13. In the context of the judicial review proceedings at national level, the presiding court had limited itself to a review of the issue of 'the formal legality' of the applicant's deportation rather than the 'more compelling question of the substance of her fears'.[92] In judicial review proceedings in Ireland, all too often we see a reluctance to engage in a substantive examination of protection needs.

The proposed European Council Directive on Minimum Standards raises the risk of eroding procedural safeguards even further. The right to an appeal with suspensive effect is guaranteed only in the context of regular asylum procedures.[93] Within the context of accelerated procedures, member states are given discretion as to whether asylum applicants will benefit from this guarantee, raising the risk that 'irreversible harm' may be done to the applicant if she is refused the right to remain in the territory of the member state.[94] The requirement

---

[89] [2001] 1 All ER 719.
[90] Unreported judgment delivered on 26 July 2000.
[91] *Jabari v. Turkey* 2000 ILM 1309.
[92] *Ibid.* para.40.
[93] *Supra* n.9, Article 40(1) and (2).
[94] See: European Court of Human Rights, *Cruz Varas and Others v. Sweden*, 14 EHRR 1.

that a court of law would have the competence to rule on the suspensive effect of an appeal introduces an additional layer of complexity into what is intended to be an accelerated and simplified procedure. Member states are permitted to derogate from this requirement in certain cases, including on grounds of 'national security or public policy'.[95] Permitting such derogation runs contrary to the requirements of international refugee and human rights law requirements, and is contrary in particular to the requirements of a combined application of Articles 3 and 13 of the ECHR. In *Chahal v. UK*[96] the European Court of Human Rights held that the requirement of an effective remedy necessitated independent scrutiny of the risk of treatment contrary to Article 3, 'without regard to what the person may have done to warrant expulsion or to any perceived threat to national security of the expelling State'. The proposed Directive itself may fall short of the requirements of Articles 3 and 13. In Ireland the right to an appeal with suspensive effect has been removed in the context of Dublin Convention and safe third country cases, subject to an order to this effect.[97] Again this adds an additional layer of complexity to the determination process, raising the possibility that an asylum applicant will be transferred to a safe third country, may appeal this decision and may subsequently be returned, if the appeal is successful. Again we see that apparently accelerated procedures can lead to more time-consuming, expensive appeals.

Concluding remarks

Ireland has a long history of seeking refuge on distant shores. It does not have such a long or worthy tradition of extending protection to those arriving at its shores. Ireland has also prided itself on its commitment to the human rights movement and its liberal rights-based traditions. How we treat those who are 'strangers' to the state's legal traditions, languages and 'ways of life' will test that commitment and the potential of those traditions.[98] If their full potential is to be realised, maxims of efficiency should not be allowed to trump the fundamental rights of those seeking asylum from persecution. The use of accelerated procedures in refugee determination systems reflects a concern with efficiency and with the speedy removal of unsuccessful claimants. It also represents a triumph for statist concerns and for the discourse of security and control. Recognising asylum as an aspect of human rights

---

[95] *Supra* n.9, Article 40(3)(d).

[96] [1997] 23 EHRR 533.

[97] S.22(2)(b) (as amended).

[98] See: Article 26 and the Illegal Immigrants (Trafficking) Bill 1999, Re [2000] IESC 19; [2000] 2 IR 360 (28 August 2000) p. 37; Mullally S (2001) 'The Irish Supreme Court and the Illegal Immigrants (Trafficking) Bill, 1999', in *International Journal of Refugee Law*, vol. 13, pp.354-362.

law highlights the potential dangers of accelerated procedures and the failings of a system that places a higher value on speed than on the need for effective access to protection.

Accelerated procedures are designed to conserve legal and administrative resources for the determination of 'genuine' refugee claims. In practice, however, valuable resources are diverted into lengthy appeals and time-consuming, expensive judicial review proceedings. Accelerated procedures often turn out to be not so accelerated after all. The twin objectives of fairness and efficiency would be better served by a regular, well-resourced, refugee determination procedure, one that considers each claim on its merits, within a reasonable time period, and a procedural framework that 'scrupulously observes' the requirements of natural and constitutional justice and international human rights law. Populist measures, designed to bring immigration under control, have led to the erosion of asylum seekers' substantive and procedural rights. An asylum seeker without valid documentation, or unable to recount her story of persecution with 'sufficient detail', may find herself subject to accelerated procedures. The proposed European Council Directive on Minimum Standards allows Ireland and other member states to expand the use of accelerated procedures even further. Ireland has quickly taken advantage of this possibility, further reducing time limits and rights of appeal in the context of 'super fast' determination procedures. As the Irish Refugee Council has noted, the 2003 Immigration Act contributes very little to developing a fair and transparent immigration process in Ireland.[99] The introduction of substantial amendments to the Act, at a late stage in the parliamentary process, allowing little time for submissions from relevant human rights groups, reflects the government's refusal to adopt a rights-based approach to asylum law and policy.[100] As Amnesty International noted: *Céad Míle Fortress*.[101]

The UNHCR has said that in the limited cases where accelerated procedures may be employed by states, procedural safeguards must be 'scrupulously observed'.[102] Where the consequences of a flawed decision may imperil life or liberty, a special responsibility lies on the decision-making process.[103] In the context of accelerated determination procedures in Ireland, however, there is little to suggest that this responsibility will be fulfilled.

---

[99] 'Amendments to the Immigration Bill 2002', Press Release, 17 June 2003, available at: www.irishrefugeecouncil.ie, as viewed on 28 July 2003.

[100] See letter submitted to the Joint Committee on Justice, Equality, Defence and Women's Rights, by the Irish Refugee Council, Amnesty International, the Irish Commission for Justice and Peace, the Irish Council for Civil Liberties, 23 June 2003.

[101] 'The Immigration Bill 2002 – Céad Míle Fortress', *Urgent Action*, 1 July 2003, available at: http://www.amnesty.ie/act/ua/bill2002.shtml, as viewed on 18 July 2003.

[102] UNHCR, Dublin office, *supra* n.8.

[103] *Bugdaycay v. Home Secretary* [1987] A.C. 514, *per* Lord Templeman.

CHAPTER 9

Judicial Review and the Asylum Process

Siobhan Stack and Bill Shipsey

Introduction

The purpose of judicial review is to allow the High Court to exercise its supervisory jurisdiction in relation to inferior tribunals and decision-makers. The balance to be struck by the Court is, as always, to ensure that the decision-maker acts lawfully while refraining from usurping his role. The rise in the numbers of asylum applications in recent years has led to a large number of applications for judicial review of the decisions made in the course of those applications, necessitating a separate High Court list to deal with them and, while the general principles of judicial review apply in these cases as in any other, inevitably a number of issues specific to the asylum and immigration context have emerged.

One of these concerns the access of the asylum seeker to the courts in the first place. There appears to be a general trend towards the use of procedural barriers designed to prevent judicial review becoming a barrier to public administration, and in particular to delaying the implementation of legally valid decisions. Asylum and immigration law is but one of the areas in which various procedural barriers have been introduced,[1] the apparent objective being to allow the decisions made in the asylum and immigration system to be implemented with certainty at as early a date as possible.[2] This is thought to be in the interests of the asylum seeker as well as furthering the cause of good administration.[3] On their face, the procedural barriers to the institution of judicial review proceedings would suggest that an asylum seeker's access to the courts has been significantly restricted. However, with the possible exception of the matter of the availability of an appeal, the

---

[1] By Section 5 of the Illegal Immigrants (Trafficking) Act, 2000.

[2] The Supreme Court has inferred this purpose from the provisions of the Illegal Immigrants (Trafficking) Act 2000: see The Illegal Immigrants (Trafficking) Bill, 1999 [2000] 2 I.R. 360, at 392.

[3] *Ibid.*

legislative provisions, in and of themselves, do not appear to have materially restricted access to the courts.

A second, substantive, area of concern surrounds the application by the High Court of the usual legal principles governing grounds for judicial review. In general, there has been no modification of those principles in ease of the asylum-seeker, despite arguments to the effect that there ought to be a less stringent test of 'reasonableness' in the case of asylum decisions.[4] The relaxation of the current threshold which must be met by an applicant in seeking to establish that the decision under challenge is 'unreasonable' would be a very significant alteration in the law, leading to a reassessment by the High Court of the merits of the decision.[5]

While it seems that the High Court is demanding increasingly higher standards, particularly of the Refugee Appeals Commissioner and the Refugee Appeals Tribunal, in its concern that a flaw in the decision-making process will lead to a threat to the applicant's fundamental human rights, there has been no alteration as of yet of the general principles of judicial review.

Obtaining leave

In all judicial review applications, the leave of the High Court is required before the proceedings can be instituted. If the challenge is to a decision made in the asylum and immigration system, the application for leave is subject to a number of procedural hurdles which do not apply in the ordinary case. First, the application must be brought within fourteen days of the notification of the decision. Although the Court has discretion to extend the time, this is substantially shorter than the usual six month time limit.[6] Secondly, in order to obtain leave to apply for judicial review, the applicant must establish 'substantial grounds' rather than merely showing that he has a stateable case. Thirdly, the application for leave must be made on notice to the

---

[4] See for example the arguments of the applicant as they appear in the judgment in *Zgnat'ev. v. Minister for Justice* [2002] 2 I.R. 135. The debate was commenced by Hogan, 'Judicial Review, the Doctrine of Reasonableness and the Immigration Process' (2001) 6 *Bar Review* 329-332. For a very recent analysis, see Higgins, 'If Not O'Keeffe, Then What?' (2003) 8 *Bar Review* 123-127.

[5] It should be noted that the High Court cannot substitute a positive decision for the negative decision being challenged. An application for judicial review involves an application for *certiorari* which merely quashes the decision, but does not amount to a declaration that the applicant is a refugee. The application is normally remitted back to the decision-maker for further determination.

[6] However, it should be noted that the status of the six month time limit set out in Order 84 of the Rules of the Superior Courts, 1986, as a general time limit is being gradually eroded by the imposition of shorter time periods for challenges to particular decisions. For example, the Planning and Development Act 2000 now provides for an eight-week time period within which to institute judicial review procedures.

Minister for Justice, Equality and Law Reform, who is entitled to be heard on the application for leave and frequently files a replying affidavit where the facts averred to in the verifying affidavit filed on behalf of the applicant are in dispute. Fourthly, the right of appeal to the Supreme Court is severely restricted.

The restrictive intent of these provisions is apparent when one considers that an application for leave to apply for judicial review of most administrative decisions can be made up to six months after the making of the decision (although there is an obligation to act 'promptly' within that time), is made *ex parte*[7] and the applicant is required only to disclose a stateable case. If the applicant fails in either the application for leave or the substantive application for judicial review, he/she may appeal to the Supreme Court under the procedures applicable to any other case.

So if one were simply to look at the procedural barriers in Section 5, one would assume that the asylum seeker has a greatly restricted right of access to the courts. In practice, this is not the case at all, with the exception of the right of appeal to the Supreme Court. We will look at each barrier in turn, but the common background to the discussion of each is the practical necessity of listing leave applications in asylum matters for hearing, and the delays in the High Court lists which prevent an early hearing of those applications. It will be seen that the procedural barriers introduced by Section 5 have the effect of increasing the length and complexity of leave applications, thereby necessitating the formal listing of those applications.

Leave applications generally are not such complex matters. Because an application under Order 84 is *ex parte* and requires the applicant only to demonstrate a stateable case, there is no need for a list: provided a judge is made available the application can be made at any time. A judge is made available each Monday, and if the application is particularly urgent, the application can be made to any judge who is available to hear it during the week. Since the threshold is low and there are no opposing submissions to be heard, such applications tend to take very little time and therefore the courts can easily accommodate them. If no stateable case is made out, the application is refused, and although the refusal of leave may be appealed to the Supreme Court the nature of the application generally means that the application can be disposed of expeditiously in that court also. The purpose of the leave application, which is to prevent the institution of vexatious proceedings which would unjustifiably delay the implementation of administration decisions, is achieved. If leave is granted, well, a High Court judge has found an arguable case, so it can hardly be regarded

---

[7] That is, without putting the proposed respondent to the proceedings on notice or allowing him to make submissions.

as not worthy of consideration and that in itself justifies some delay in implementation of the decision.

In contrast, applications for leave to challenge asylum and immigration decisions take a long and winding path through the court list. Once a notice of motion is issued seeking leave to apply for judicial review, the Court will give interim relief[8] preventing the state from executing the decisions already made, including deportation orders. It is possible for an unstateable case to remain in the court lists for up to a year, with no entitlement in the state to execute the deportation order or to progress the asylum application. To explain how this can happen, it is necessary to consider the practical effect of each of the procedural barriers contained in Section 5.

The requirement of putting the minister on notice

The requirement of serving the minister must remove a large part, if not all, of the benefit to the minister, Commissioner or Tribunal, of the fourteen day time limit. The necessity to hear the rebutting arguments of the minister requires an extended time for hearing of the application for leave. Even allowing for the additional time which would be required if the need for a higher threshold is accepted, the requirement that the minister should be served in all cases prolongs the delay in assigning a hearing date to a very significant degree. The minister has two roles in an application for leave. First, he may file a replying affidavit in order to controvert matters of fact deposed to in the applicant's verifying affidavit. Secondly, he may simply make submissions to the effect that the applicant has failed to disclose substantial grounds.[9]

While it is of course open to the minister not to file any replying affidavit, the necessity to serve him means that the application cannot be heard immediately but must have a date fixed for hearing in the separate list which is reserved in the High Court for asylum matters. Ultimately, as in any judicial review, leave may be refused so that, in theory, there were never any proceedings. It hardly reflects well on the legal system that a public authority of any kind should be restrained for several months from acting on foot of a decision in respect of which proceedings were never – technically – brought.[10]

The Law Reform Commission has recently recommended that the matter of whether the minister ought to be served should be for the discretion of the High Court judge before whom the application for

---

[8] Recognising the inevitability of interim relief, and in an effort to reduce costs and prevent additional delays, the authorities almost always offer undertakings not to execute or implement the decisions or orders pending determination of the proceedings.

[9] *Vidrashku v. Minister for Justice* (Unreported, High Court, Finlay-Geoghegan J, 17 October 2002).

[10] Simons, 'Judicial Review under the Planning Legislation – The Case for the Abolition of the Leave Stage', (2001) 8 IPELJ 55.

leave is initially made returnable and that that discretion should be exercised in favour of joining the minister only in exceptional cases.[11] In fact, the manner in which the minister has been singled out by Section 5 is unusual in that if the challenge is to a decision under the Refugee Act 1996 then very often the appropriate respondent to the substantive application will be either the Refugee Applications Commissioner or the Refugee Appeals Tribunal. The Court has a discretion under Section 5 to require that 'any other person' be joined, and presumably this discretion is intended to allow the Commissioner or the Tribunal to be joined. It would seem appropriate to put the Commissioner or the Tribunal on notice of the leave application where it is their decision under challenge, because they would be best placed to controvert or depose to matters of fact; the role of presenting arguments to rebut the applicant's submission that 'substantial grounds' have been disclosed can then be discharged by the minister. In practice this is not done, because all of the relevant decision-makers are represented by the Chief State Solicitor, who briefs counsel to deal with all matters arising in the leave application.

The effect of imposing a higher threshold on the applicant

The full implications of requiring an applicant to meet the higher test of 'substantial grounds' have probably not yet been explored. 'Substantial grounds' are 'reasonable', 'arguable' and 'weighty', and must not be 'trivial or tenuous'.[12] In order to establish that such grounds for review exists, it might be thought that the applicant would be entitled to discovery even prior to the grant of leave. While the High Court has rejected the contention that there is any heightened entitlement to discovery on the basis that the minister is a notice party to the leave application, an entitlement to discovery on the usual principles has been established.[13] Prior to leave, that entitlement is somewhat restricted as it has been held that the proposed respondents to the application (other than the minister) are third parties insofar as the leave application is concerned, so that only the more restrictive right to third party discovery is available.[14] Where 'substantial grounds' rather than merely a stateable case have to be established, the temptation to apply for discovery will be very strong. That application would have to be heard prior to the leave application, thereby delaying further the determination of the matter of leave.

---

[11] See LRC CP 2, 2003, 'Consultation Paper on Judicial Review Procedure', at p. 57.

[12] *McNamara v. An Bord Pleanála* [1995] 2 I.L.R.M. 125.

[13] *Ayaya v. Minister for Justice* (Unreported, High Court, Finlay-Geoeghegan J. 2 May 2003). The entitlement to discovery as against the minister was found to exist on the basis that an application for leave was a 'matter' within the meaning of Order 31 of the Rules of the Superior Courts, 1986, which allows for the making of discovery by any party to any 'cause or matter'.

[14] *Ayaya* at p. 7.

In addition, while the higher threshold has so far been coupled with a requirement of serving the minister so that it has not been possible to assess its effect on the length of the hearing, it is likely that the imposition of the higher threshold, in itself and without any requirement of putting the minister on notice, tends to lengthen the leave hearing, thereby requiring a formal listing of the leave application.

The time limits for bringing an application for leave

So far, we have concentrated on the effects of Section 5 on the ability of the High Court to determine the leave application expeditiously. However, Section 5 also contains very grave restrictions on an applicant's ability to have recourse to the courts. The short time limits coupled with the very limited right of appeal are very real barriers to an applicant. The fourteen day time limit can be extended where the applicant is able to show 'good and substantial reason' for his failure to act within the time limit. The principles applicable in an application to extend time have been set out by the High Court and Supreme Court in *G.K. v. Minister for Justice, Equality and Law Reform*.[15] The core principle appears to be that the applicant must show that he himself moved with all reasonable diligence. However, the question of whether an applicant may be vicariously liable for the defaults of his legal advisers has not yet been settled. It was suggested by the High Court in *G.K. v. Minister for Justice, Equality and Law Reform* that an applicant would be liable for such defaults, but the authorities cited related to private law actions brought by Irish citizens who would have an adequate alternative remedy against their legal advisor in negligence if their primary action was held to be barred. There being no such avenue of redress for an asylum seeker, it seems likely that the courts will refine the principles involved so as to extend time where the default is on the part of the applicant's adviser and he himself has prosecuted his application with all reasonable diligence.

Restriction on the right of appeal

The most serious restriction of all, however, is the extremely limited basis upon which an unsuccessful applicant can appeal. While the restriction formally applies in an equal manner to both parties, it generally affects the applicant to a much greater degree. The purpose of an appeal for the applicant carries consequences of obvious individual concern. For the authorities, the purpose of an appeal will usually be to seek clarification of the law. Section 5 stipulates that there is to be no appeal unless the High Court certifies that its own decision involves 'a point of law of exceptional public importance' and 'that it is in the

---

[15] See *G.K. v. Minister for Justice, Equality and Law Reform* [2002] 2 I.R. 418 (S.C.) and [2002] 1 I.L.R.M. 81 (H.C.).

public interest' that an appeal should be taken to the Supreme Court. These criteria are cumulative[16] and exclude any question which does not transcend the facts of the case, thereby removing any right to appeal on grounds which are specific to the applicant's case. On this point at least, Section 5 achieves its objective of providing certainty.

However, that objective is advanced at the cost of the public interest in the clarification of the law by a collegiate court of final appeal. The grounds in Section 5 are exceptionally restrictive, requiring identification of a point of law of *exceptional* public importance and thereby relegating many points of law, even ones of general (though unexceptional) importance, to a status where they are unworthy of consideration by the Supreme Court. Therefore, if the point of law transcends the facts of the case, this is not sufficient to fully take into account the use of the word 'exceptional' in Section 5 and a certificate will not be forthcoming.[17] This seems to be an excessive restriction of the right of appeal, because it would seem to be in the public interest that any point of law of public importance which transcends the facts of the case ought to be canvassed in the Supreme Court. The guidance so far available from decisions in asylum cases indicates that where there is uncertainty among decision-makers as to the state of the law, that is a matter which would support certification for an appeal.[18] However, questions of statutory interpretation which are of public importance will not attract a certificate.

In addition to any principled objection to the restriction on appeal, Section 5 may also be criticised for being clumsy in its effects. Once a single point of law of exceptional public importance is identified, Section 5 ceases to govern the appeal, which is then taken in accordance with the ordinary procedures for appeal. As a result, all issues can thereafter be canvassed on appeal.[19] This could lead to the very unsatisfactory position of an applicant succeeding on appeal on a ground which was individual to his case, even though the vast preponderance of applicants had no right to appeal because they had failed to identify a point of law of exceptional public importance.

In addition, the Law Reform Commission has remarked that the necessity of applying to the High Court for a certificate may lead to arbitrariness and injustice.[20] There is a reasonable perception that this

---

[16] *Raiu v. Minister for Justice, Equality and Law Reform* (Unreported, Finlay-Geoghegan J, 26 February 2003), applying *Kenny v. An Bord Pleanála (No. 2)* [2001] 1 I.R. 704 which considered an identical provision in the planning legislation. Although the criteria are cumulative, it is difficult to imagine that the High Court would not consider it to be in the public interest that the Supreme Court should have the opportunity to adjudicate upon a point of law of exceptional public importance.

[17] *Ibid.*

[18] *Ibid.*

[19] *People (Attorney General) v. Giles* [1974] I.R. 422; *Kenny v. An Bord Pleanála (No. 2)* [2001] 1 I.R. 704.

[20] LRC CP 20-2003, 'Consultation Paper on Judicial Review' at p. 78.

is the case, because the current practice in the High Court – though it does not necessarily follow from Section 5 – is that the application for a certificate is heard by the judge whose determination is sought to be appealed. The Law Reform Commission has therefore recommended that the application for a certificate should itself be subject to appeal to a single Supreme Court judge, who could review any refusal.

Conclusion

On balance, Section 5 produces two very unfortunate results, neither of which advance the inferred legislative objective of allowing for the early implementation of decisions. First, Section 5 significantly delays the determination of leave applications, thereby preventing the state from enforcing or relying upon decisions and orders against which no stateable challenge can be raised.[21] At the same time, it substantially restricts the right of appeal to the Supreme Court, thereby depriving that Court of the opportunity of developing the law in this area, as well as depriving asylum seekers of the opportunity of an appeal.

Effective review by the courts: what does 'anxious scrutiny' mean?

The Supreme Court has accepted that in judicial review of decisions made in the asylum and presumably the immigration processes, the courts must subject the decision in question to 'anxious scrutiny'.[22] However, the implications of this approach have not been explored in any meaningful way.[23]

In the only reported case where reference is made to this approach, it was raised by the applicant in an attempt to urge upon the court a test for irrationality which was lower than the test which is generally applicable, i.e. whether the decision flew in the face of reason and common sense or, alternatively whether there was any basis for the decision in question. This is the so-called *O'Keeffe* test.[24] However, that attempt failed in *Zgnat'ev.*, the Supreme Court there applying the conventional test, notwithstanding its acceptance that the courts should approach the decision with 'anxious scrutiny'. More recently, four of the seven judges of the Supreme Court in *Lobe v. Minister for Justice*[25]

---

[21] Furthermore, the minister now incurs significant expense by way of legal fees in defending leave applications. Although the minister is successful in a majority of applications, there is no realistic prospect of his recovering his costs from unsuccessful applicants.

[22] *Zgnat'ev. v. Minister for Justice, Equality and Law Reform* [2002] 2 I.R. 135.

[23] See especially McGuinness CJ in *Zgnat'ev*, at p. 236.

[24] See *O'Keeffe v. An Bord Pleanála* [1993] 1 I.R. 39, where the dicta of Henchy J in *State (Keegan) v. Stardust Injuries Compensation Tribunal* [1986] I.R. 642 was approved.

[25] (Unreported, Supreme Court, 23 January 2003.)

either doubted the appropriateness of the usual test or expressly reserved their position in relation to it. Accordingly there is some considerable uncertainty as to the status of the *O'Keeffe* test in asylum cases. It is notable that the decision in *Zgnat'ev* expressed some doubt as to whether the concept of 'anxious scrutiny' would alter the basic test of unreasonableness, and in this respect the origin and development of the concept in England is enlightening.

The English case law on 'anxious scrutiny'

The phrase 'anxious scrutiny' was first introduced in the case of *R. v. Secretary of State for the Home Department, ex p. Bugdaycay*[26] where Lord Bridge stated:

> I approach the question raised by the challenge to the Secretary of State's decision on the basis of the law stated earlier in this opinion, namely that the resolution of any issue of fact and the exercise of any discretion in relation to an application for asylum as a refugee lie exclusively within the jurisdiction of the Secretary of State subject only to the court's power of review. The limitations on the scope of that power are well known and need not be restated here. Within those limitations the court must, I think, be entitled to subject an administrative decision to the most rigorous examination, to ensure that it is in no way flawed, according to the gravity of the issue which the decision determines. The most fundamental of all human rights is the right to life and when an administrative decision under challenge is said to be one which may put the applicant's life at risk, the basis of the decision must surely call for the most anxious scrutiny.[27]

The *Bugdaycay* case itself, however, does not involve any change in, or more specifically any dilution of, the test first propounded in *Wednesbury*,[28] which may be regarded as equivalent to the *O'Keeffe* test applied in Ireland. Lord Bridge's view of the case to be established by the applicant was set out by him in very conventional terms.

Nevertheless, the *Bugdaycay* case was cited in support of a dilution of the *Wednesbury* test in a series of human rights cases throughout the 1990s, leading to judicial pronouncements of a reasonableness test which is specific to human rights cases, though perhaps with few positive results for applicants. The pronouncements at least have provided encouragement for Irish lawyers who advocate an alternative to the stringent *O'Keeffe* test in asylum cases. However, there are two very significant factors which suggest that many of the English cases are not a sound guide for future Irish developments.

First, some of the leading English cases concerned decisions of a

---

26 [1986] 1 WL.R. 155 (CA); [1987] A.C. 514 (H.L. (E)).
27 [1987] A.C. 514 at 531.
28 [1948] 1 K.B. 223.

different nature to that challenged in *Bugdaycay* in that they concerned the exercise of discretionary powers so as to restrict the acknowledged rights of the applicants. They were not determinations of fact and/or assessments of risk which were designed to ascertain whether the applicant's human rights were at risk in the first place.

Secondly, there is a critical difference between the Irish and English legal systems, which means that the English cases must be read with extreme caution. In the circumstances of the *Brind* and *Smith* decisions, discussed below, an Irish lawyer would be able to mount a constitutional challenge to the decision and to the legislation pursuant to which it was made. The decision would then be tested by reference to the principle of proportionality which has been developed by the European Court of Human Rights and adopted by the Irish courts.

An English lawyer, prior to the Human Rights Act 1998, had no option but to apply to the court to exercise its power of judicial review. *Brind* is best viewed as an attempt to introduce the principle of proportionality into English law as a ground of judicial review. Of the established grounds of judicial review, that most suitable for the importation of the principle of proportionality was unreasonableness. *Reg. v. Home Secretary, ex p. Brind*[29] concerned a challenge to the Secretary of State's directives issued to the BBC and to the Independent Broadcasting Authority restraining broadcasting of any words spoken by the representative of certain organisations or any words supporting or soliciting support for those organisations. Lord Bridge dismissed the challenge on the basis that the applicant's complaints fell short of demonstrating that a reasonable Secretary of State could not reasonably conclude that the restriction was justified by the important public interest of combating terrorism.[30]

Notwithstanding the respects paid to the concept of 'anxious scrutiny', the House of Lords unanimously decided that the test of proportionality was not an independent ground for review but was at best an aspect of *Wednesbury* 'unreasonableness', although they left the door open for an incremental development of a new principle of proportionality.

In *Reg. v. Ministry of Defence, ex p. Smith*,[31] unlike in *Brind*, the sympathies of the Court of Appeal were undoubtedly with the applicants. The applicants were members of the defence forces, each of whom had been discharged solely on the ground of their homosexual orientation. The decisions of the respondent were the result solely of a blanket policy preventing anyone of homosexual orientation from serving in the armed forces, and there was no suggestion of any wrongdoing by any of the applicants.

---

[29] [1991] 1 A.C. 696.
[30] At p. 749.
[31] [1996] Q.B. 517.

Counsel for the applicants put forward the following test which was accepted by the Court of Appeal and by subsequent cases as a correct distillation of the principles set out in *Bugdaycay* and *Brind*:

> The court may not interfere with the exercise of an administrative discretion on substantive grounds save where the court is satisfied that the decision is unreasonable in the sense that it is beyond the range of responses open to a reasonable decision-maker. But in judging whether the decision-maker has exceeded this margin of appreciation the human rights context is important. The more substantial the interference with human rights, the more the court will require by way of justification before it is satisfied that the decision is reasonable in the sense outlined above.[32]

Notwithstanding Bingham MR's approval of this test as being correct in law, he went on to reject the proposition that the *Wednesbury* test was inappropriate:

> The greater the policy content of a decision, and the more remote the subject matter of a decision from ordinary judicial experience, the more hesitant the court must necessarily be in holding a decision to be irrational .... Where decisions of a policy-laden, esoteric or security-based nature are in issue even greater caution than normal must be shown in applying the test, but the test itself is sufficiently flexible to cover all situations.[33]

The extent to which *Smith* must be regarded as rejecting any contention that the *Wednesbury* test is not the correct test of irrationality in cases involving fundamental human rights is disclosed by two factors. First, it was accepted by all of the judges in both the Divisional High Court and the Court of Appeal that the applicant's human rights had been invaded in a distasteful and (in the non-legal sense) unjustifiable way. Notwithstanding this, the court was reluctant to intervene in a 'policy-laden' decision, and if it did not do so on the facts in *Smith* then the chances of intervention in any other case must be slim.

Secondly, while the court knew from the material before it the substance of the advice on which the policy was based and the assertions contained in it, it did not know the details of the experience which informed that advice. The applicants complained that there was no evidence before the court showing the basis for the decision, and therefore the decision was unlawful. The response of the Court was to reject any presumption that, no such evidence being before the court, the policy was without any rational basis. This is a very telling ruling because it appears to run counter to the effect of the 'anxious scrutiny' approach as evidenced by the decision in *Bugdaycay* itself.

In *Bugdaycay*, relief was granted by Lord Bridge on the basis that

---

[32] At p. 554.
[33] At p. 556.

the decisions of the Secretary of State 'appeared'[34] to have been made without taking into account past breaches by Kenya of its Article 33 obligations and by Lord Templeman because there was 'a suspicion'[35] that the dangers and doubts involved in sending the applicant back to Kenya had not been adequately considered and resolved. The phrases quoted have been selected to demonstrate that both judgments appear to have been based on an uncertainty which was resolved in favour of the applicants. This is not the usual approach in applications for judicial review, the burden being on the applicant to establish grounds for review on the balance of probabilities. The uncertainty evident in the judgments in *Bugdaycay* suggests that the court in fact placed an evidential burden of proof on the respondent.[36]

The true implications of the decision in *Bugdaycay* were acknowledged by Simon Brown LJ in *Smith* when, after citing the passage from Lord Bridge's judgment already set out above, he stated:

> [T]hose dicta ... do not impinge on ... the relatively limited impact which ... the restriction of fundamental human rights ... has upon judicial review. Rather they emphasise that within the limited scope of review open to it the court must be scrupulous to ensure that no recognised ground of challenge is in truth available to the applicant before rejecting his application. When the most fundamental human rights are threatened, the court will not, for example, be inclined to overlook some perhaps minor flaw in the decision-making process, or adopt a particularly benevolent view of the minister's evidence, or exercise its discretion to withhold relief.[37]

One might have thought that, even allowing for the application of the *Wednesbury* test, the courts might have granted relief in *Smith* if they were simply scrutinising the decision of the Secretary of State to ensure that no conventional ground of challenge was available to the applicant. The arguments of the applicant appear to have been directed at this possibility, as they involved the submission that there was no evidence before the Secretary of State to support his decision. As such, the argument would appear to fall either within *O'Keeffe* concepts of unreasonableness – that there was no basis for the decision – or within that part of the proportionality test which requires a rational connection between the objective pursued and the means chosen to pursue it.

---

[34] [1987] A.C. 514, at p. 534.
[35] [1987] A.C. 514, at p. 538.
[36] For a similar reading of *Bugdaycay*, see Barrington, E., 'Asylum Applications and Judicial Review', in an unpublished paper delivered at a TCD Conference entitled 'Judicial Review: All the Recent Developments in Irish Law and Practice' on the 29 March 2003.
[37] At p. 537.

Those arguments dissected the basis for the policy as set out in the affidavits filed on behalf of the Secretary of State, and Bingham MR at least seems to have accepted that the Select Committee which upheld the ban did not require or receive any evidence of actual harm done by sexual orientation alone or by private homosexual activity outside the context of service life, and that the Committee did not consider whether the objectives of existing policy could be met by a rule less absolute in its effect than that which was then applied. However, it does seem to have been established to the satisfaction of the Court of Appeal that the blanket ban reflected the overwhelming consensus of service and official opinion in the United Kingdom.

The decision in *Smith* rests on the notion that the court should, where the decision challenged is one 'of a policy-laden, esoteric or security-based nature', exercise greater caution in the application of the *Wednesbury* test,[38] because the courts recognise that they are not well-qualified to second-guess such a decision. The inference to be drawn not just from the arguments of the applicants in *Smith* but from the views of the judges, was that while the Secretary of State could point to the advice and views of those involved in the defence forces as a basis for his decision, he could not disclose that this was a rational basis, or that the advice, opinion or views were capable of supporting his decision. The argument of the applicants that the advice or opinion was based solely on conjecture and/or prejudice seems unassailable. However, in applying the *Wednesbury* test in accordance with the more cautious approach suitable to the type of decision under challenge, the court accepted the basis put forward as rationally connected with the considerations to be balanced without actually inquiring into this matter.

One might say that it was for the applicant to seek to establish the objectionable or illusory nature of the purported basis for the decision, but, as already outlined, the approach in *Bugdaycay* itself would not support this approach. Henry LJ was more explicit than Bingham MR in his approach to this question, stating that:-

> We know from the material before us the substance of advice on which the policy was based and the assertions contained in it, but we do not know details of the experience which informed that advice. Hence the lawyers' criticism that the advice is not based on evidence. I would not at this stage of the debate assume that the views of the armed forces are not based on evidence, though that evidence is not before us.

Therefore, in a policy-based decision, it seems that the principle of 'anxious scrutiny' does not apply, notwithstanding the acceptance by the courts of the principle that a very strong justification will be required for interference with human rights. In reviewing the lawfulness of the

---

[38] See Bingham, MR at p. 556.

interference, the court is concerned merely to ensure that the reasons put forward are of a nature that would justify interference with established human rights.

The appropriate approach on judicial review of asylum decisions: no curial deference

The nature of the majority decisions made in the asylum and immigration process is such that the caution displayed in the *Smith* approach is not appropriate. Generally, the decisions involve fact-finding and risk assessment, questions which could not be said to be 'remote from judicial experience', and policy is introduced only at the final stage of granting humanitarian leave to remain under Section 3 of the Immigration Act 1999.[39]

The same reluctance should not be relevant, and is not apparent, where the decision challenged is not one made in the exercise of a discretionary power or policy-laden, but is closer to the type of decision-making process in which the judiciary are themselves experienced, i.e. fact-finding and decision-making of individual rather than general application.

The Court of Appeal alluded to this distinction in *R. v. Secretary of State for the Home Department, ex p. Turgut*[40] where the Court had to decide whether, on a challenge to the decision of the Home Secretary that the applicant would not be at risk of ill-treatment within the meaning of Article 3 of the European Convention of Human Rights, the Court could assume the role of primary fact-finder. Simon Brown LJ stated that:

> It is one thing to say that an administrative decision to deport will be rigorously examined and subjected to the most anxious scrutiny: quite another to say that the court will form its own independent view of the facts which will then necessarily prevail over whatever view has been formed by the Secretary of State.[41]

He then went on to state that the domestic court's obligation on an irrationality challenge in an Article 3 case was to subject the Secretary of State's decision to 'rigorous examination, and this it does by considering the underlying factual material for itself to see whether or not it compels a different conclusion to that arrived at by the Secretary of State'.[42] Simon Brown LJ made it clear, however, that this was 'not an

---

[39] The decision to grant or refuse such leave can only be made after the minister is of the opinion that there is no risk of *refoulement*. However, consideration of this matter again involves fact-finding and risk assessment.

[40] [2001] 1 All E.R. 719, C.A.

[41] *Ibid.* at p. 729.

[42] *Ibid.* at p. 729.

area in which the Court will pay an especial deference to the Secretary of State's conclusion on the facts'.[43]

Three reasons were given for this approach, the first being the particular character of the rights of the applicant under Article 3, which are absolute, and do not require a balance to be struck with some competing social need. The second reason was that the Court was hardly less well-placed than the Secretary of State himself to evaluate the risk once the relevant material is placed before it. As a third reason the Court said that, on the facts of the case, it must recognise the possibility that the Secretary of State had tended to depreciate the evidence of the risk and to rationalise the further material adduced so as to maintain his pre-existing stance rather than reassess the position with an open mind. In those circumstances, the 'discretionary area of judgment', i.e., the area of judgment within which the Court should defer to the Secretary of State as the person primarily entrusted with the decision, was a decidedly narrow one.

At least the first two reasons are relevant to all asylum cases. The rights in Section 2 of the Refugee Act 1996 are unqualified and do not require the risk of persecution to be balanced against any other consideration. Therefore the decision involves fact-finding and risk assessment functions, rather than the balancing of policy considerations against established rights.

Similarly the second factor – that the Court was hardly less well-placed than the Secretary of State to make the decision – will almost always be relevant. Decisions of the Commissioner generally comprise the Section 11 and Section 13 reports and the practice so far has been to append such country of origin information as is being relied upon, though possibly not everything actually considered in making the decision, to the reports themselves. In addition, the applicant's version of events is available in writing by means of the questionnaire and the transcript of the interview under Section 11.

A similar situation pertains to the decisions of the Refugee Appeals Tribunal in manifestly unfounded or accelerated cases or in those rare appeals in a substantive case where the applicant has not opted for an oral hearing. However, the vast majority of the decisions of the Refugee Appeals Tribunal on a substantive appeal are made after an oral hearing, of which no transcript is available. The High Court may be appraised of the evidence by means of a verifying affidavit which sets out the oral evidence tendered by the applicant in the course of his appeal and which exhibits the country of origin information submitted. While not as exact a replica of the evidence before the decision-maker as the first instance reports, the High Court can usually be satisfied as to its authority to identify all of the evidence before the

---

[43] *Ibid.* at p. 729.

Tribunal. In any event, the practice of the Tribunal is to set out in its decisions a précis of the evidence given by the applicant, and the submissions made, before proceeding to set out its findings, inferences and conclusions.

The third category of decision generally reviewed is that of the minister under Section 3 of the Immigration Act 1999 and while the decision is communicated to the applicant in the form of a letter, the documents recording the matters considered in making the necessary decision under Section 5 and under Section 3 are generally made available to the applicants.

The approach in *Turgut* would therefore seem to be the appropriate approach for the Irish High Court in the exercise of its judicial review jurisdiction, and indeed a careful reading of *Zgnat'ev. v. Minister for Justice*[44] discloses this approach in practice. It is submitted that this is in line with the 'anxious scrutiny' test as laid down in *Bugdaycay* and is instructive as to how that test should be applied in practice. It must also be doubtful whether the courts will continue to regard the notion of 'curial deference' as being relevant to asylum cases, given the competence of the courts in the exercise conducted by the Commissioner and the Tribunal.[45] Future affirmation of the *O'Keeffe* test is more likely to rest on notions of the proper jurisdiction of the courts whether the decision-making power has been granted to others, rather than on any peculiar respect based on expertise.[46]

The application of 'anxious scrutiny' in practice: importance of the duty to give reasons

The *Bugdaycay* case itself shows a willingness to draw an inference of illegality in favour of an applicant where there is an ambiguity as to the approach taken by the decision-maker. In fact, in *Bugdaycay*, the courts drew an inference of illegality from the lacunae in the records of the decision of the Secretary of State. However, that presupposes that the documentation can be produced by the applicant for scrutiny by the courts. Although discovery is available to an applicant prior to the granting of leave,[47] it cannot be used on a 'fishing expedition' basis. In other words the applicant must disclose some grounds for review prior to the application for discovery. Furthermore, at the leave

---

[44] [2002] 2 I.R. 135.

[45] Contrast the decision of the High Court in *Camara v. Minister for Justice* (Unreported, High Court, Kelly J, 26 July 2000) where the notion of 'curial deference' was specifically endorsed.

[46] Decisions under section 3 are somewhat different from asylum decisions and the prior decision on *refoulement* as these may involve considerations of public policy: see *Lobe v. Minister for Justice* (Unreported, Supreme Court, 23 January 2003) and *R (Mahmood) v. Home Secretary* [2001] 1 W.L.R. 840.

[47] *Ayaya v. Minister for Justice* (Unreported, High Court, Finlay-Geoghegan J, 2 May 2003).

stage the proposed respondents are generally not party to the proceedings and discovery would only be available on the more limited basis on which the court generally orders third party discovery.

The inevitable conclusion is that the duty of the decision-making authority to give reasons for its decision may be more onerous than the authorities suggest it might be.

Generally the duty of any public authority to give reasons for its decision has not been placed at a high level by the courts in this jurisdiction. In those areas of law which are subject to a specialised statutory procedure, it has been stated to be discharged by the giving of reasons which are 'proper, intelligible and adequate', although the degree of particularity depends on the circumstances of each case.[48]

Initial efforts by applicants to establish that the duty should be higher in the context of the asylum and immigration systems were unsuccessful. In *P. v. Minister for Justice* the Supreme Court flatly rejected the argument that the usual principles did not apply to the statutory duty of the minister to give reasons for his proposal to make a deportation order. The same approach was evident in the High Court decision in *Zgnat'ev v. Minister for Justice*[49] where the mere recital by the Refugee Appeals Tribunal of the equivalent of Section 12 (4) (a) (b) and (c)[50] was accepted by the Court as an adequate statement of reasons.[51]

These decisions and the law on the duty to give reasons have not been reviewed by the High Court in its judgments in asylum cases. Nevertheless, there seems to be a fresh attitude in the courts to this question, although no single decision establishes that the courts are looking to different principles. For example, in the case of *Bujari v. Minister for Justice*,[52] the High Court granted leave on the basis that

> there are substantial grounds for contending that the tribunal member was under an obligation as a matter of fair procedures in the assessment of the applicant's claim for refugee status to consider and assess the explanation given to him at the appeal oral hearing of the reason for which the applicant did not disclose at an earlier stage and was now disclosing that his father was a Serb collaborator and that this was the cause of his parents' killing and his fear of returning to Kosovo and that the failure to have done so invalidates the decision.

While expressed to be a decision based on fair procedures, the decision may be likened to *Bugdaycay* in that the High Court found that there were substantial grounds for contending that there had been a breach

---

[48] *O'Keeffe v. An Bord Pleanála* [1993] 1 I.R. 39, *Ní Éilí v. Environmental Protection Agency* (Unreported, Supreme Court, 30 July 1999).
[49] (Unreported, High Court, Finnegan J, 29 March 2001).
[50] The case was decided under the Hope Hanlan procedures which provided an identical definition of a manifestly unfounded application.
[51] At p. 13 of the judgment.
[52] Unreported, High Court, Finlay-Geoghegan J, unapproved at time of writing.

of fair procedures (in relation to which the Court was entirely guided by the *Handbook on Procedures and Criteria for Determining Refugee Status*[53]) as no assessment was found in the written decision of the Tribunal. Of course, that assessment might have been made in fact, though not disclosed in the written decision. The High Court, in an approach which is entirely consistent with that in *Bugdaycay*, was not prepared to presume that the assessment had in fact been made. If this is to be the approach of the High Court, then it will be incumbent upon the Commissioner and the Tribunal to deal specifically with each issue in the written decisions, or they will be presumed to have failed to undertake the necessary assessment. While both the Commissioner and the Tribunal issue reasonably detailed reasons for their decisions already, *Bujari* seems to require a very high degree of detail in those decisions so as to enable the High Court to scrutinise those decisions for illegality. Otherwise, the High Court seems to be willing to draw an inference that the decision was not lawfully made and will grant *certiorari*.

If such an approach were applied to the manner in which the minister notifies his decisions under Section 3 of the Immigration Act 1999, the effect on the form of notification would be dramatic. At present, the minister generally does not give detailed reasons for his decisions when notifying them to applicants. In particular, a decision to grant or refuse leave to remain in the state under Section 3 of the Immigration Act 1999, which automatically includes a consideration of *refoulement*, issues to the applicant in the form of a standard letter, containing standard reasons for the refusal of leave to remain. The giving of standard reasons has been upheld in *P. v. Minister for Justice*,[54] albeit in a case which did not raise any *refoulement* arguments. While it appears acceptable that detailed reasons would not be required in a standard immigration case, a higher duty seems appropriate in the context of consideration of *refoulement*. In fact *Bugdaycay* itself is directly on point and the notion of 'anxious scrutiny' would seem to require a detailed disclosure on the part of the minister insofar as *refoulement* is concerned.

Nevertheless, in *Baby O v. Minister for Justice*,[55] the Supreme Court rejected the argument that the judgment in *P. v. Minister for Justice* did not apply in *refoulement* cases. However, in practice, the minister frequently makes available the documentation recording the matters considered by him in examining an application for leave to remain in Section 3. In fact, the internal memoranda prepared on behalf of the minister were put in evidence in both *Lobe*[56] and *Ojo*.[57] So it seems

---

[53] (Office of the UNHCR, Geneva, 1992).
[54] [2002] 1 I.R. 164.
[55] [2002] 2 I.R. 169.
[56] (Unreported, Supreme Court, 23 January 2003).
[57] (Unreported, High Court, Finlay-Geoghegan J., 8 May 2003).

that, in practice, the minister feels obliged to disclose all of the matters considered so as to meet the evidential burden upon him in a challenge to a deportation order. It is submitted that this is in line with the notion of 'anxious scrutiny.'

Despite the current practice of the minister in making the internal memoranda available to the court, frequently at leave stage, it is possible that the notion of 'anxious scrutiny' requires the minister to furnish those memoranda to the applicant as a legal right when notifying his decision under Section 3 to the applicant. While the additional administrative burden on the minister would be light, because the memoranda are in practice prepared in all cases prior to the making of a deportation order, such a requirement would inevitably lead to more detailed scrutiny by the High Court of decisions on *refoulement*, and possibly the gradual development of more demanding standards of reasoning by the Court, as appears to have happened in relation to the decisions of the Refugee Applications Commissioner and the Refugee Appeals Tribunal.

Conclusion

This chapter has attempted to address the two issues of general concern to those involved in the practice of asylum and immigration law. No doubt a case will arise which will give the Supreme Court an opportunity to review the law on reasonableness, and specifically to consider the effect of the notion of 'anxious scrutiny.' Such a decision would be welcome, given the continuing uncertainty on the issue, and must be considered inevitable given the dicta casting doubt on the applicability of the *O'Keeffe* test in *Lobe*. However, the better view seems to be that the *O'Keeffe* test will survive as the applicable test in asylum cases.

The practical difficulties arising out of the operation of section 5 of the Illegal Immigrants (Trafficking) Act, 2000, require an entirely different solution, as amendment is obviously a matter for the legislature. However, even at this early stage of its operation, the arguments for amendment, in the interests of all concerned, appear to be unassailable.

CHAPTER 10

Media Response to Asylum

Harry McGee

Introduction

A couple of weeks before Ireland's general election in May 2002 a pamphlet was dropped through front doors in Dublin 1 and Dublin 7. Its contents were an incoherent mess, a rambling racist rant of the kind you sometimes hear from callers to Ireland's late-night radio talk shows. The anonymous author purported to represent the Irish People's Party (IPP), an outfit that was later – to put it in broad journalese – branded by the media as a 'neo-Nazi party'. The policies of the IPP, such as they were, were despicable, ascribing the worst criminal and predatory attributes to immigrants as well as indulging in some pathetic bar stool theorising about the purity of the Irish race. The pamphlet included a reference to the IPP internet site. The website was in essence a rehash of the pamphlet with one important addition. There was a link to a section that contained press cuttings in support of the arguments.

As a journalist who has long become inured to overweening claims made by the media about its own influence on society, I found myself experiencing a chastening bit of reading. There were many dozens of press cuttings stretching back over five years. The articles had been culled from the full range of newspapers in Ireland, including the most sober broadsheets. All context was compromised by the arm-lock of a virulently racist site and even the most balanced reports seemed somehow tilted. The vast preponderance, predictably, came from the red top morning and evening tabloids in their worst 'Daily Hate' modes. Scrolling through the clippings made for disconcerting reading. All the canards cropped up. There were what were referred to as the Nigerian and Romanian scam artists, criminal gangs, spongers, rapists and murderers. There were the stories of huge influxes and floods, of the country being inundated and over-run. Asylum seekers, many of the stories implied, were living in the lap of luxury at the expense of the state and, by corollary, elbowing out Irish citizens from receiving entitlements.

The clustering of these articles on asylum seekers provided a telling demonstration of how media treatment of an important issue can be manipulated – and essentially hijacked – for crude propagandistic purposes. But it also represents the extremity of a process where an institutional policy (not immune to hype and exaggeration) that purports to stop large numbers of 'bogus asylum seekers', 'illegal immigrants' and 'economic migrants' reaching our shores is, in turn, reflected in the media, which is – by its nature – Pavlovian, reactionary and declamatory.

Research on media treatment of immigration and race-related issues in EU countries carried out by the European Monitoring Centre on Racism and Xenophobia[1] found that

> once a negative discourse on migrants or ethnic minorities was established it tended to remain prevalent. It became a fixed 'repertoire', where event coverage (in printed media) followed a repetitive chain of statements, actions and conclusions ... This logic was so strong that print media could construct a reading of the events that differed from the way in which the single elements of information were presented to them.

The study also found that

> news contents (themes) are influenced by policy agendas ... A Danish study notes that the perspective of authorities was dominant in many news stories on ethnic minorities ... In Sweden, instances were found where media failed to counter the predominant views and interpretations of authorities, and trivialised and denied racism, with the aim of restoring the myth of a tolerant enlightened Sweden.[2]

In this chapter I will argue that the coverage in Ireland has followed that pattern and has, on the whole, cleaved to the official view of 'crisis' in the thrust of its coverage. Successive Irish governments have followed the lead of virtually every government in the European Union in their 'get tough' policy on immigration and have found a generally compliant media that has been only too willing to ride shotgun for their various crusades to keep 'bogus asylum seekers' as opposed to 'genuine refugees' from our shores.

A numbers game

A feature of Irish news coverage since the asylum and immigration issue first came to widespread prominence in 1996–97 has been how its emphasis on the number of asylum seekers coming into the country

---

[1] *Racism and Cultural Diversity in the Mass Media: An overview of good practices in the EU member states, 1995-2000,* Jessika ter Wal (ed.). Carried out by the European Research Centre on Migration and Ethnic Relations on behalf of the European Monitoring Centre on Racism and Xenophobia, Vienna, February 2002, p. 36.
[2] *Ibid.* pp. 36, 37.

has determined the tone and direction of coverage. When the numbers of people seeking asylum in Ireland began to rise dramatically during 1996 and 1997, the media, like the government, was confronted by a novel issue which brought with it a novel set of challenges when it came to coverage. Faced with a new phenomenon, much of the early coverage was negative and reactionary, with a tendency to appropriate the news angles and highly suggestive lexicon ('influx', 'economic migrants', 'bogus asylum seekers', 'illegal immigrants') that had become a staple for the treatment of the issue in parts of the British media. Coverage has undergone a slow evolution since then, marked by a decrease in the number of stories from a peak in 1999-2000 and a discernible trend towards balance and context – though news coverage of the numbers seeking asylum (and the associated costs to the Exchequer) remain predominantly negative in tone, reflecting the government's oft-stated policy to place restrictions on asylum seekers and deport those whose applications for refugee status have failed.

How has media coverage of this most important issue evolved over the course of the past decade? Before 1996, asylum and immigration were almost non-issues for the Irish media. Ireland had yet to reach a point in the country's economic fortunes where it would no longer be a country of net migration but one of net immigration. From time to time, think pieces would appear in newspapers pondering whether or not the Irish were racist. The well of research material amounted to a few drops of isolated anecdotal incidents that could not be said to comprise any pattern. The proposition was, to all intents and purposes, a hypothetical one based on instinctual rather than actual evidence.

Amnesty International Irish Section's newspaper clippings for the period 1991–93 contains few records, reflecting a low level of media coverage. In 1993, all but two of the excerpts deal with the case of a Libyan man held in prison for eighteen months after his application for refugee status had been refused and that of refugees from the Balkan war being accommodated in Ireland. That, of course, reflected the very low numbers of people who had applied for asylum in Ireland (a total of thirty-nine applied in 1992).

However small in scale as the phenomenon was then, it still revealed portents of what was to come. Several newspapers, particularly *The Sunday Press*[3], revealed the practice of the Department of Justice of detaining asylum seekers in prison while their claims for asylum were being assessed, or after their applications for refugee status had been turned down. *Sunday Press* reporter Des Nix wrote a series of articles highlighting the case of a Libyan man, Marey al Gutrani, who was detained in prison for the extraordinary span of eighteen months as he awaited the outcome of his appeal against

---

[3] See *The Sunday Press,* 24 January 1993.

deportation. There were no direct flights to Libya at the time because of United Nations sanctions imposed against the regime of Muammar Qaddafi. The official attitude seemed to be one of indifference and inertia.[4] In its editorial, *The Sunday Press* berated what it described as the 'shameful Irish treatment of refugees'.

> The Irish record on the treatment of refugees and asylum seekers is widely regarded as the worst in the [European Community]. Over the past two years, between 15 and 20 asylum seekers have spent periods of two months to one year in prison, awaiting deliberation on their claims. Often too, we hear of asylum seekers being hurriedly deported without access to either a lawyer, an independent non-governmental refugee organisation or the United Nations High Commission on Refugees.

Marey al Gutrani's case prompted a series of articles in newspapers that took a critical look at the state's policies (or to be more accurate, its lack of policies) on the asylum and refugee issues. The articles noted that, although Ireland was a party to the 1951 United Nations Convention Relating to the Status of Refugees, no legislation had ever been enacted to implement the provisions of the Convention.

The Department of Justice had developed a purely administrative procedure for dealing with asylum applications, based on a letter to the United Nations High Commissioner for Refugees in London, drafted in 1985. The procedure had very tenuous legal standing, lacked transparency, was bedevilled by delays and inconsistencies, and had no appellate mechanism. Two other cases were instanced – one involving a Chinese man, the other a man from Somalia – where ministerial orders were issued for their deportation notwithstanding the fact that neither had been given access to independent legal advice nor told that they had a right to seek such advice. It also emerged that some people seeking refugee status in Ireland were 'interviewed and deported within hours of arrival'.[5] The most controversial of those incidents occurred when a group of twenty-six Kurds who tried to make applications for asylum at Shannon airport in November 1992 were forcibly put back onto an Aeroflot flight by a large force of gardaí. *The Sunday World* reported:

> During the tense twelve hour drama there were distressing scenes as the refugees persistently begged to be allowed stay in Ireland. Eventually they boarded a flight to Canada where [they were granted] asylum.

The most pertinent feature of the media coverage during that period was its empathy for the asylum seekers and their treatment at the hands of the Irish authorities, in addition to its condemnation of the

---

4   *The Sunday Press*, 24 January 1993.
5   *The Irish Times*, 29 June 1994.

hopelessly inadequate and arbitrary approach taken by the state to its obligations under the 1951 Convention. The revelations that the state was imprisoning people who had committed no crime, and forcing others back onto planes without adequately assessing their claims for asylum, received wide and critical coverage between 1992 and 1994 – and was partly responsible for expediting the drafting of the Refugee Act 1996.

Newspaper editorial and op-ed columnists were not slow to point out the anomaly between what appeared to be the government's indifference to the plight of incoming asylum seekers and Ireland's own recent history of mass emigration. An *Irish Examiner* editorial in June 1994 was typical:

> We continuously grieve at the habitual loss of our young people to the New World. It is not so long since a Tánaiste proclaimed this diaspora inevitable by proclaiming 'the rock' too small to support all of its children. However, when that New World imposes immigration restrictions upon our emigrants, the inevitability is transformed to desperation, with many resorting to illegal alien status, particularly in the United States. In this context, it is difficult to accept anything less than compassion in relation to the way in which this state deals with refugees fleeing political or religious persecution, as our children have habitually fled economic hardship. Our record in dealing with asylum-seekers is less than worthy.

However, the debate of the early 1990s took place against the gently lapping sounds of what was then the backwater of Western Europe. The break-up of the Soviet Union, the conflagration of the Balkans, repression in Myanmar, the Gulf War and a series of bloody wars in Africa had caused a staggering increase in the number of asylum seekers. By the end of 1992, some 1.1 million people had applied for asylum in Germany; 112,000 in Britain; 212,000 in France and 189,000 in Sweden.[6] In comparison, a paltry thirty-nine people had applied in Ireland during 1992.

Numbers up, sympathy down

The first significant increase in the numbers of refugees occurred in 1994 when 362 people applied for asylum. Over 200 of these were Cubans who made applications at Shannon Airport where Aeroflot jets on transatlantic flights refuelled. However, as the so-called 'tide' of refugees began to increase, conversely the compassion that the media had shown began to ebb and flow.

On 1 November 1994, *The Evening Press* led with a story, employing language and semiotics that would become drearily familiar over the course of the following nine years. Headlined 'Cuba Refugees

---

[6]   *Newsweek,* 22 November 1993.

Flooding Here', the article warned that a 'Cuban refugee crisis [was] looming' because 'upwards of 200 Cuban refugees now staying in temporary accommodation in Ennis are beginning to stretch resources to the limit'. Read retrospectively it seems almost innocent. But it marked the first of the scare stories that were to become the staple of some sections of the Irish print media and Dublin late-night radio talk-in shows.

The first article to deal with the sudden leap in the number of applications during 1996 in an in-depth and considered manner appeared in *The Irish Times* in September 1996. Its author, Andy Pollak, identified a number of traits peculiar to the phenomenon, all of which were to haunt the debate in subsequent years. The numbers had increased exponentially during the first nine months of 1996. Applicants were left to exist in a kind of legal limbo while the Department of Justice, Equality and Law Reform processed their applications. Only a tiny proportion had been recognised as refugees or given leave to remain in 1996 and preceding years. A small number of Department officials had been assigned to deal with asylum applications and they had been overwhelmed by the increase in applications. It was for this reason that the process was taking an average of two and a half years to complete. Pollak posited several reasons for the increase.

> What appears to have happened is that Ireland has, for the first time, become known as a possible refugee destination, particularly among the agents who, for a price, often organise their flight from countries in Africa, the Middle East and the former Soviet empire.
>
> In the past Ireland would have been thought of in many of these countries as indistinguishable from the UK. However, as British rules governing the admittance of refugees became harsher in the 1990s and Ireland's profile in the world rose ... this country started to be mentioned on the international refugee grapevine as a safe place for people fleeing civil war and political persecution.
>
> In recent years the single country from which most asylum seekers have arrived is Romania, many of them economic refugees. Other larger groups have come from countries torn apart by civil war such as Somalia and Algeria; from Zaire, with its despotic government and strong Catholic presence; and the countries of the former Soviet Union with their multiple problems of civil strife and economic dislocation.[7]

Pollak's report presented the problem in a nuanced and context-laden way, an approach that has been adhered to by *The Irish Times* in its reportage since then. The same could be said – on the whole – for RTÉ and, to varying degrees, for other broadsheet newspapers, where 'influx' stories on the news pages have often been balanced by countervailing context stories on the analysis and opinion pages.

---

[7]   *The Irish Times,* 14 September 1996.

As the number of asylum seekers arriving into Ireland continued to increase during 1997, the focus of news stories began to hone in almost obsessively on the numbers coming in, the welfare benefits they might hope to enjoy, and the costs that the state would incur in housing and providing for them while their applications were being processed. 'Floodgates open as a new army of poor swamp the country' ran a headline in *The Sunday World* in May 1997. A month earlier, *The Sunday Tribune* reported, under a headline of: '£20 million cost to maintain refugees' that some asylum seekers 'admitted openly that they were attracted here by the generous benefits on offer, particularly at a time of major clampdowns on immigration in Britain and other European countries'.[8]

That the thrust of the coverage put up a mirror – albeit a grotesquely distorted one at times – to reflect the government's position on immigration is indisputable. The Irish political response to the immigration question has replicated that of other EU countries in an attempt to prevent the 'pull factor' – a phrase beloved of the former minister for Justice, Equality and Law Reform, John O'Donoghue. Pull factor essentially means anything that would make Ireland more favourable as a destination for asylum seekers than other countries. Examples include giving jobs to asylum seekers, allowing all Irish-born babies to be Irish citizens and allowing asylum seekers the freedom to find their own accommodation.

The wall that countries build to repel immigrants seems to get higher each year, as states vie to out-do each other in the macho stakes when it comes to clamping down on immigration. During a number of elections throughout Europe in the past two years, socialist governments have appropriated large tracts of the manifestos of anti-immigration parties in their countries in order to avert the electoral threat from the self-same anti-immigration parties. One particularly brutal suggestion was that jointly formulated by the British and Spanish prime ministers in May 2002 which mooted the idea of using financial clout (i.e. the withdrawal of aid) to coerce developing countries' governments into preventing migrants from leaving their countries of origin. The astute political writer from *The Observer*, Andrew Rawnsley, summarised the contradiction inherent in this get-tough approach.

> This defeats me, this logic of saving the country from lurching to the Right by lurching the Government to the Right. The result is a pernicious cycle of ever-inflating abuse hurled at migrants and ever quackier cures for the 'crisis'.

---

[8] *The Sunday Tribune,* 20 April 1997.

Stigmatisation of asylum seekers

The EU-wide survey of media treatment of racism and cultural diversity found the following.

> A common feature for all countries facing new immigration is the stereo-typical language used, in particular the metaphors comparing arrivals of asylum seekers to a natural disaster and military invasions in headlines, to represent immigration as a major threat. This was a common trend registered in Austria, Italy, Ireland, Finland, Sweden and Spain.[9]

It also found that a common link was often established 'between the ethnicity or the origin of groups, on the one hand, and their deviant or criminal behaviour (and even character), on the other'. In the Irish section of the report, the authors noted that during the early years

> the media began to develop a common vocabulary for issues related to racism and ethnic minorities. It was generally negative in tone and usually based on volume, such as refugees flooding Ireland, waves of immigrants and armies of the poor. According to the mainstream media, in 1997-1998 Ireland was being swamped, invaded and conned on an almost daily basis.

Examples abound of stigmatisation of foreigners. From the start, Nigerians (often portrayed as criminals and scam artists) and Romanians (gypsies, opportunists, spongers and freeloaders) were the butt of the most vicious stories. In May 1997 *The Sunday World* reported that 5,000 asylum seekers would arrive in the country that year. The article's strap-line – 'It's beg steal or borrow for the 20 illegal immigrants who arrive on our shores EACH DAY' – set the tone for what was to follow:

> The influx includes several hardened criminals and organised gangs of beggars, particularly Romanian gypsies.

> On a daily basis gardai have to deal with cases of robbery and assault involving asylum seekers.

> Earlier this week the situation took a more sinister turn when a refugee was lifted for an alleged rape.

It was breath-taking stuff, replete with suggestive language and innu-endo that also managed to avoid naming one attributed source. As a smear on a whole class of vulnerable people, it was staggering in its inclusivity. More was to follow:

> The influx of immigrants – some of whom are fleeing horrific oppression in their home countries – has given rise to all sorts of tension.

> In many cases shopkeepers, publicans, hoteliers and street traders are refusing to serve them.

---

[9] *Racism and Cultural Diversity in the Mass Media: An overview of good practices in the EU member states, 1995-2000,* Vienna, February 2002, p. 46.

Some retailers bitterly complain that many of the 'street refugees' are actively engaged in crime, picking pockets, shop-lifting and harassing their regular customers.

The two most egregious examples during 1997 and 1998 appeared in *The Star* and *The Wexford People*. In a story headlined 'Refugee Rapists on the Rampage' *The Star* quoted top Garda sources (which later turned out to be an individual member of An Garda Síochána) as saying that women should stay away from refugees because of a number of sex assaults perpetrated by Romanians and Somalians. *The Wexford People* article was written by its editor, Ger Walsh, and quickly assumed notoriety.[10] The two central allegations were – as were so many of the stories stigmatising refugees – unsupported by any evidence:

There is also the fear that some young male asylum-seekers are intent on striking up deep personal relationships with impressionable young local girls, fully aware that a baby would ensure a passport to permanent residence in this country.

Walsh's concluding sentiments on the new arrivals were not unique to him – the same baseless allegations had become the nightly fodder of phone-in shows of the two commercial Dublin radio stations.

The annoyance of many ordinary Wexford people who are struggling to make ends meet is understandable when they see new arrivals dressed in the latest designer shirts and jeans, eating their meals in a down-town restaurant and relaxing on the balcony of their apartment in an exclusive block, with the bills for their entire way of life being picked up by the Irish taxpayer.

As an argument it was jaw-dropping in its generality and absurd untruths. It could never be argued that it reflected – even *in extremis* – the Government stance, which was predicated primarily on economic considerations as well as upholding the integrity of the asylum-seeking process.

In his book, *Refugee and Asylum-Seekers in Ireland, Irish Times* journalist Paul Cullen described the situation that pertained at the time as frenzy.

The response of the Irish media to the arrival of large number of asylum-seekers in recent years has been characterised by inconsistencies, inaccuracies, exaggerations and generalisations … The sensitivity that usually applies in stories about Irish people have been lacking in many articles journalists have written about asylum-seekers. Emotive language has been widely used to whip up widespread fear of the new arrivals. Journalists have based many of their stories on the word of a single anonymous source, usually a Garda, without seeking any independent verification.[11]

---

[10] *The Wexford People,* 29 July 1998.
[11] Cullen, P., *Refugees and Asylum-Seekers in Ireland,* Cork University Press, Cork, 2000.

The more inflammatory articles seemed to tap into something that went far beyond any government policy intent on restricting numbers and upholding the integrity of its own asylum procedures. Their stigmatisation and vilification of refugees seemed designed to appeal to a perceived populist fear that somehow foreigners – deeply undeserving ones at that – presented a threat to the moral, social and economic order. The spectre of the Irish being racist, xenophobic and subject to *uberfreundung* (the fear felt by Europeans that somehow their identity will be erased through saturation by foreigners) became a subject of considerable debate in the national media.

Reporting and racism

Racial taunts had become a commonplace reality for immigrants by 1998 and there were several instances where casual insults had developed into racially-motivated assaults in Dublin. In an article on political and public reaction to immigrants in May 2000, *Magill* catalogued a number of assaults that took place during the spring and summer of 1998.

> In April 1998 four assailants left 17-year-old Landu Kalabutule curled in a pool of blood beside the Ha'penny Bridge. He needed 27 stitches. Two weeks later three men took a break from their work on a building site off Dominic Street to beat-up a passing African asylum-seeker in broad daylight. Shortly after, two Nigerians were stabbed on sunny O'Connell Street at teatime rush-hour. A heavily pregnant Angolan woman was savagely attacked leaving a maternity hospital. A dog was set on another pregnant Congolese woman.

While the incidents remained relatively isolated, there was political concern expressed that the cage-rattling tactics of some media outlets was inimical to the guidelines on anti-racism, drawn up by the National Consultative Committee on Racism and Interculturalism, a body that was set up by the Minister for Justice, Equality and Law Reform. At the Department of Foreign Affairs Third Annual NGO Forum on Human Rights in July 2000 the Progressive Democrat Minister of State at the Department of Foreign Affairs, Liz O'Donnell, asked journalists to display sensitivity:

> Sensational headlines, misleading statistics, unsourced claims and demonising of the refugee community can, and have, contributed negatively to public opinion and fuelled misinformed intolerance of asylum seekers and refugees.

Ms O'Donnell said that numbers seeking asylum had reached unprecedented levels, 'but that does not justify simplistic, knee-jerk analysis which presents their arrival as relentlessly problematic, disruptive and divisive'. She also referred to broadcasts where 'people can phone in and express outrageous views'. One of the difficulties was that her own government was continuously drumming home the message that the situation was a crisis caused by economic migrants or bogus asylum seekers abusing the system. The notion that the country was inundated and that authorities were struggling to cope in the face of such vast numbers entering the country gained further currency during 1999, leading up to the government announcement of a new dispersal policy. What the government implied by 'bogus' was widely interpreted by some sections of the media as 'spongers', 'scam-artists' and 'criminals'.

A notable feature in government pronouncements on the asylum issue was the lack of context presented to countervail the emphasis on numbers and costs. However, the media itself did supply some – albeit inconsistent – correction here. One of the paradoxes of media coverage in Ireland has been that news stories often portrayed asylum seekers in negative terms when describing them as an amorphous mass but when portraying individual asylum seekers – in profiles of a 'typical' asylum seeker or in reports on racist-motivated attacks – they were invariably described in sympathetic terms fleeing from persecution in their own country. Another anomaly is that tabloids – which have often led the charge against 'bogus' asylum seekers, including detailing generic stories on Nigerian drug dealers and Romanian conmen – have frequently interviewed the victims of racist attacks or abuse in the most sympathetic terms. Invariably they are portrayed as fleeing from persecution. An *Evening Herald* lead article from March 2003 is typical. It described the terrifying new life for an Algerian refugee family whose house in Dublin has been attacked.

> A terrified family this evening told how their new life here has been made hell by racist thugs. The young family fled war torn Algeria to suburban violence, including petrol bombings and stonings, at their Dublin home.

In an authoritative contribution to the debate in 1999, *Irish Times* journalist Andy Pollak identified the Independent Newspaper Group as having fuelled antipathy to asylum seekers in its coverage.[12] Much of its news coverage was written by its security correspondent, who strongly reflected in his coverage the views of the Department of Justice, Equality and Law Reform and An Garda Síochána that the asylum issue was a 'crisis'. According to Pollak

> There were far too many sensational headlines, misleading statistics, unsourced claims and other plain demonising of asylum-seekers. Refugees, a small, frightened and powerless group in Irish society had no comeback against the big guns of the country's most powerful media combine.

---

[12] Pollak, A., 'An invitation to racism? Irish daily newspaper coverage of the refugee issue', in *Media in Ireland: The search for ethical Journalism,* Damian Kiberd (ed.), Open Air, Dublin 1999.

In an interesting paragraph, Pollak acknowledged that journalists, like politicians, were gradually beginning to grasp that this new phenomenon of immigration was a complex, multi-faceted and unfamiliar one.

> The issues of refugees and racism are relatively new to Irish journalists. We have much to learn about the potentially dangerous nuances of language in this situation, about being aware that a careless phrase, a sensational headline, an insufficiently checked source can reinforce prejudice and ignite racial hate. My impression is that most of us were more conscious of the sensitivities involved at the end of 1997 than we were at the beginning.

One side of the story

Coverage of the asylum issue had undergone a transformation since the early 1990s. The scrutiny of government procedures and policies – a feature of the coverage in the early and mid-1990s – had been replaced by a deluge of 'crisis and cost' stories. A corollary of that was that the news media latterly paid disproportionately less attention to the conditions in which refugees lived or the causes that impelled them to flee or depart from their countries of origin than they did in the early 1990s. More often than not, the media has relied wholly on government or garda sources without accessing spokespeople for asylum seekers or others who might provide an alternative view. Ten years ago, the efficacy and basis of the government's own policies were scrutinised to an inordinate degree but in the latter phase such scrutiny became sporadic and infrequent. Only when leading public figures like Peter Finlay (one of the first to be appointed to deal with asylum appeals) and the Minister of State at the Department of Foreign Affairs made pointed criticism of the process (at a time when it was in a headlong rush towards system failure) did such criticism outweigh 'refugee numbers' stories on the news agenda. Nor was the basis for the findings that over 90% of applicants failed ever adequately challenged – too few reports drew comparisons with the higher success rates of asylum applications in other EU countries.

The Centre for Migration Studies at University College Cork maintained an internet-based press digest during 2000 and 2001. Predominantly drawn from only three newspapers (*The Irish Times*, *The Irish Independent* and *The Irish Examiner*), there were 922 stories posted during 2000. Less than 600 stories were posted the following year, suggesting that the 'furore' over the issue had peaked notwithstanding the fact that there was no significant decrease in the number of asylum seekers arriving into Ireland. Content analysis under various headings was carried out by Teresa Wyndham-Smith on 105 articles from the site, all of which related to nationally elected politicians.[13]

---

[13] Wyndham-Smith, T., 'A Study of Political Leadership and asylum issues in Ireland', MA Thesis, University of Limerick, 2002.

In analysing the themes of the stories, entry of asylum seekers unsurprisingly comprised the dominant theme (34%), with stories on the large numbers entering the country as well as the methods of entry predominating (the bodies of eight people were discovered in a container in Wexford during the period of the survey). The second most reported theme was racism (21%) – which included coverage of racist attacks as well as the government's much-publicised 'Anti-Racism Awareness Campaign'. Legal infrastructure stories, which examined the development of legislation as well as the asylum process in its totality, made up 18% of the stories.

Wyndham-Smith also conducted an ideological analysis that found a slight surplus of negatively-toned articles over positively-toned articles. When further broken down, a decisive majority of stories in relation to accommodation and entry to Ireland were negative. Her findings were revelatory.

> The pattern which emerges from analysing the stories is that comment from Irish politicians about asylum-seekers and refugees is rarely free from negative connotations. The most frequently occurring themes in the articles were contentious issues such as the number of asylum-seekers entering the country and the way in which they obtain entry; racism; legal infrastructure issues pertaining to the difficulties of processing asylum claims; and accommodation problems surrounding the pressure on accommodation in Dublin and consequent dispersal of asylum-seekers to other parts of Ireland along with suggestions of alternative forms of accommodation.
>
> Among the stories analysed there were none which sought to outline exactly what asylum-seekers are entitled to nor did any politician attempt to explain the circumstances in the home countries that they came from. Admittedly this may have been a theme of stories in previous years.

That is astounding. The number of articles that have investigated claims of persecution that asylum seekers may have faced in their countries of origin (and their difficulties in travelling to the host country) are negligible. Too seldom in my experience are the sometimes desperate lives of asylum seekers in Ireland covered. A report on the initial needs of the much derided Roma community in Ireland painted a sobering picture of the reality of the dispersal and direct provision policies.[14]

It noted the stress of living in camp style environments and the confined spaces of hostel rooms, the depressing routines of the institutions where they were housed, the dependency on set menus, the boredom of days with nothing useful to do, the fact that those in direct provision are entitled to a paltry €19.10 per week. The other old canard, that the

[14] *Roma in Ireland: An initial needs analysis,* Roma Support Group and Pavee Point, March 2002.

majority of asylum seekers are 'scroungers' who want to benefit from
Ireland's 'generous' welfare system has not been borne out by a single
asylum seeker of the scores I have interviewed in the course of my
work – all to whom I have spoken want to work, bar none.

Wyndham-Smith's analysis of articles in which the then Minister for
Justice, John O'Donoghue, was quoted found that he had shown some
leadership in relation to racism in his remarks, but that the overall
tenor of his public comments in the period covered was negative.

> So often when he has commented on refugees and asylum-seekers, he
> problematises the issues by making reference to illegal immigrants, to
> bogus asylum-seekers and to there being a crisis. Thus even when a
> positive comment is made the reader is left with the impression of crises.
> When the Catholic bishops called for a compassionate attitude to asylum-
> seekers and refugees, including giving them the right to work, he
> responded that this would send the message that people were 'entitled to
> come here and abuse the asylum process and pretend to be refugees and
> be actually considered to have the same rights as Irish citizens'.

The current minister Michael McDowell has adopted a stance that, on
some readings, is even more granite-hard than his predecessor. In a
lecture to the Merriman Summer School in 2002, NUI Galway lecturer
Donncha O'Connell argued, *inter alia,* that the previous minister
(O'Donoghue) had 'talked the talk' but this one (McDowell) walks the
walk as well.[15] In a reference to the much publicised Operation Hyphen
whereby gardaí effected a co-ordinated series of arrests around the
country – ostensibly to deport people whose applications for asylum
had failed – O'Connell stated that the operation was

> [A]nalogous to what Nigel Harris (*Thinking the Unthinkable: The
> Immigration Myth Exposed*, IB Taurius 2002) calls the 'drama of the borders'
> whereby governments play on popular paranoid fantasies about alleged
> 'illegals'. According to this dramaturgical analysis the excitement of the
> hunt neutralises what little compassion previously existed for the pathetic
> hunted when their status was less defined. While governments argue that
> tough measures are necessary to avoid outbreaks of racism or xenophobia
> what they really fear is an outbreak of compassion.

In a passage that could be seen as a summation of the general
approach of the media to the issue as much as that of the political
class, O'Connell goes on to argue:

> The rhetoric used to legitimise this policing gimmick is predictable to the
> point of being clichéd. Thus, Mr McDowell has taught us all that he is

---

[15] O'Connell, D., 'The Politics of Immigration and Asylum in Ireland: Justice Delayed or
Injustice Expedited?', paper delivered at the Merriman Summer School 2002,
Ennistymon, Co. Clare.

simply enforcing the law; that the incidents of genuine asylum applications are extremely rare (especially if you are from Nigeria or Romania); that most asylum seekers are merely economic migrants; that the integrity of the asylum process has to be protected at all costs; that the Irish system for processing asylum applications is one of the fairest in the world and that even the UNHCR hold to this view. Lest there be any doubt about the minister's layered assertions we are warned that if woolly-minded liberals like myself, who dare to question any of the foregoing assumptions, are listened to, the primary beneficiaries of our self-indulgent ideology of charity will be human traffickers and people smugglers. In other words, the minister is simply being cruel to be kind and anyone who cannot see this is misguided, naïve or plain wrong.

Using the media to win political points

There has been a distinct type of political self-projection that has received a disproportionate amount of coverage. That has occurred when individual politicians have gone on solo-runs to adopt populist and controversial stances on the asylum-seeker issue. This is inevitable – the media will always weight its coverage in favour of a controversial politician rather than a reasonable one. Noel O'Flynn and Jackie Healy-Rae both made divisive remarks about asylum seekers in the run-up to the 2000 general election – critics argued that the remarks were designed to stoke up support from anti-immigrant voters in their constituencies. O'Flynn, invoking the crisis theme, claimed that the country was being held hostage by 'spongers' and 'freeloaders' and 'intimidators',[16] and Healy-Rae continued a theme he had developed in May 2000 that they don't want to work and that 'some of them are misbehaving around the country at the present time'.[17] In terms of disproportionate coverage, there is none to surpass that given to Áine Ní Chonaill and her political vehicle, the Immigration Control Platform. Ní Chonaill was the focus of widespread national and international coverage during the May 2000 election campaign. A review of articles on Ní Chonaill and the Immigration Control Platform shows that the coverage ranged from neutral to openly hostile and derisive, with first references invariably describing her party as controversial and anti-immigration. The antipathy of the media to the Immigration Control Platform was shared by the voters – the party secured no more than several hundred votes.

The inconsistencies, inaccuracies and exaggerations to which Paul Cullen adverted in *Refugee and Asylum-Seekers in Ireland* are still too prevalent in the media but the coverage has evolved and matured. It

---

[16] *The Irish Examiner,* 'We can't let free speech become a victim of our fight against racism', Damien Byrne, 14 February 2002.
[17] In an interview on *Morning Ireland,* RTE, May 2, 2000.

could be argued that the controversies over the government's dispersal policies in Clogheen, Co Tipperary, and Corofin, Co. Clare, during 2000 facilitated a robust and prolonged debate in the national media and on the airwaves that led to a greater awareness of asylum seekers as individuals and tolerance for them in society. The tragic death of eight people whose bodies were found in a container in Wexford also received extensive coverage and gave a jarring picture of the brutal and appalling conditions that asylum seekers undergo to seek refuge in the EU.

The evolution towards fair reporting is far from complete. The government's agenda is set implacably towards bringing in increased powers and restrictions to limit the numbers of asylum seekers coming to Ireland. The cost of maintaining asylum seekers in Ireland – approximately €300 million euro per annum – is a theme to which the minister frequently returns. The state official policy is widely reflected – more often than not without further context – in the media. And just in case anyone was under any illusion that the more provocative rabble-rousing stuff had been excised from the agenda of the Irish media, *The Irish Mirror* of 14 March 2003 provides a jolting reminder that it has not. Its headline reads 'Refugees: The Truth' and the introduction is a classic of its kind.

> Today the Irish Mirror reveals the shocking burden bogus refugees are putting on Ireland. In the past three years alone the state has spent €750 million on shelter, food and other services. Asylum-seekers from Romania and Nigeria are even provided with satellite channels to watch their favourite programmes from home.

There are a couple of grunts from Jackie Healy-Rae about illegal immigrants who had 'misbehaved in their own country'. The newspaper also kindly gives a guest column to Áine Ní Chonaill to give an unfettered airing of her views. 'Ireland has become a mecca for bogus refugees from around the world', the paper editorialises. 'Sadly there are scroungers who never did a day's work back home and now want to live off our backs.'

Where have we heard that line before?

CHAPTER 11

Complementary Protection and Temporary Protection

Ursula Fraser

Introduction

The primary legal instrument that deals with protection for people forced to flee their countries and in need of international protection is the 1951 Refugee Convention.[1] The Refugee Convention was drawn up to deal with the massive human displacement caused by World War II and it has since become the cornerstone of global refugee protection.

In order to qualify for protection under the Refugee Convention, the motives for flight must stem from particular situations. To be granted what is known as 'Convention refugee status', a person must prove persecution – or fear thereof – due to reasons of race, religion, nationality, membership of a particular social group or political opinion.[2] If natural disaster or economic deprivation prompts flight, protection under the Refugee Convention is not available. Nor is protection available under the Refugee Convention for people who are forced to

---

[1] 1951 Geneva Convention Relating to the Status of Refugees was signed on 28 July 1951 and entered into force on 21 April 1954. The Refugee Convention contained a limitation whereby it expressly covered events only occurring before 1 January 1951. This dateline accorded with the wishes of governments at the time of drafting to limit their obligations to refugee situations that had occurred, or might occur, based on events already known at that time. In 1967, a Protocol was annexed to the Refugee Convention, which abolished this temporal limitation (1967 New York Protocol relating to the Status of Refugees, signed 31 January 1967 and entered into force on 4 October 1967).

[2] Article 1(A)(2) of the Refugee Convention. Paragraph 28 of the UNHCR *Handbook on Procedures and Criteria for Determining Refugee Status* reads: '[a] person is a refugee within the meaning of the 1951 Convention as soon as he fulfils the criteria contained in the definition. This would necessarily occur prior to the time at which his refugee status is formally determined.' In this chapter 'Convention refugee status' or 'refugee status' is used to describe the set of rights and obligations that flow from the recognition of a person as a refugee *after* he or she has undergone assessment in the asylum determination procedure of a host country.

flee the indiscriminate effects of violence which arise in situations of armed conflict, for example, if no specific element of persecution on one of the five above-mentioned grounds can be shown.

In less developed regions of the world, the scope of protection afforded to people forced to flee is wider than the Refugee Convention. The Organisation on African Unity (OAU), for example, includes as bases for refugee protection in its 1969 refugee treaty aggression, occupation and domination by foreign forces.[3] Similarly, the Organisation of American States (OAS) in its 1984 *Declaracion de Cartegena* extends its refugee definition to people who flee generalised violence, foreign aggression, internal conflicts and massive violations of human rights.[4] In spite of the extended groups of people that can benefit from the OAU and OAS instruments, however, most refugees in the developing world may be offered little more than space in a refugee camp with poor sanitary conditions and limited security. By contrast, if a person is granted Convention refugee status in an asylum state of the industrialised world, such as Ireland, he or she normally receives a full range of social and economic rights, akin to those of a citizen. Therefore, refugee status is not something that is granted lightly by states and it has become something of a 'Holy Grail' for contemporary asylum seekers.

As a result of the gap between the protection that states are legally obliged to offer under the Refugee Convention and the diverse protection needs that have evolved since the Convention was drafted in 1951, a number of compensatory protection policies and practices have emerged. For example, the United Nations High Commissioner for Refugees (UNHCR) has extended its mandate on occasion to protect a range of individuals who have had to flee their homes because of general disasters or massacres but whose profile does not match that of a Convention refugee.[5] Similarly, states of the industrialised world that receive significant numbers of asylum seekers are beginning to grant protection to a wider range of people whose reasons for flight do not fall under the scope of the Refugee Convention. The terminology used to describe such extended protection is varied. Terms such as complementary, ancillary or subsidiary protection, humanitarian or

[3] OAU Convention Governing the Specific Aspects of Refugee Problems in Africa 1969.
[4] Cartagena Declaration on Refugees 1984.
[5] See United Nations General Assembly Resolution 1388, 14th Sess. UN Doc. A/4354 (1959) which dealt with Chinese nationals entering Hong Kong; United Nations General Assembly Resolution 1673 16th Sess. UN Doc. A/5100 (1961) which dealt with civilians fleeing African countries engaged in independence struggles and United Nations General Assembly Resolution 2039, 20th Session, UN Doc. A/6104 (1965) which blurred the distinction between refugees strictly within UNHCR's mandate and those outside it.

temporary leave to remain, and *de facto* refugee status are used interchangeably. In this chapter, the term 'complementary protection' is chosen to describe the legal protection offered to asylum seekers whose cases fall outside the strict terms of the Refugee Convention.

The first part of this chapter explains the legal and political background to the development of complementary protection. Part I also describes the limited form of complementary protection that exists in Irish law. Part II of the chapter sketches the evolution of 'temporary protection'. This term, although sometimes used to signify a form of complementary protection, has progressed in a particular manner in the European Union (EU) and it is this evolution that is discussed. Temporary protection at the EU level describes the protection regime which can be activated if the EU is faced with a sudden mass influx of asylum seekers as a result of war or large-scale massacre.

PART I Complementary protection

1) Scope of the refugee definition

According to Article 1A(2) of the Refugee Convention, the term 'refugee' applies to a person who

> [o]wing to a well-founded fear of being persecuted for reasons of race, religion, nationality, membership of a particular social group or political opinion, is outside the country of his or her nationality and is unable or, owing to such fear, is unwilling to avail himself of the protection of that country; or who, not having a nationality and being outside the country of his former habitual residence as a result of such events, is unable, or owing to such fear, is unwilling to return to it.[6]

This represents the full extent to which signatory states could reach agreement on the categories of people to whom they were willing to offer asylum in 1951. However, even at that time, delegates were aware of the limits of the Refugee Convention and, in a supplementary statement, wrote:[7]

> [T]he Conference expresses the hope that the Convention relating to the Status of Refugees will have value as an example exceeding its contractual scope and that all nations will be guided by it in granting so far as possible to persons in their territory as refugees and who would not be covered by the terms of the Convention, the treatment for which it provides.

---

[6] The definition of a refugee in Irish law is found in Section 2 of the Refugee Act 1996 which, in a progressive step, extends the Refugee Convention definition to include three extra grounds for protection: gender, sexual orientation and membership of a trade union.

[7] Recommendation E of the Final Act of the 1951 UN Conference of Plenipotentiaries on the Status of Refugees and Stateless Persons, U.N.T.S. Vol. 189, p. 37.

206 SANCTUARY IN IRELAND

This envisages a situation whereby reasons for flight may not strictly attract Convention refugee status but where there may nevertheless be other situations, of equal gravity, where the protection provided by the Refugee Convention should be afforded. UNHCR has also advocated stretching the refugee definition to cover as many flight scenarios as possible, rather than introducing new forms of protection, such as complementary protection, which invariably carry more restrictive social and economic rights than those offered to Convention refugees. UNHCR's view is that people fleeing or remaining outside a country for reasons 'pertinent to' refugee status can be considered as falling within the Refugee Convention definition.[8] No matter how broadly the Refugee Convention is interpreted, however, it cannot be stretched to cover all modern forced migration movements due to factors such as political instability, poverty and natural disasters.[9]

2) *Legal protection for asylum seekers outside the Refugee Convention*

A number of human rights legal instruments have been drawn up since the adoption of the Refugee Convention in 1951, with the result that the Convention is no longer the only source of legal protection for asylum seekers. The most important legal protection for asylum seekers is the principle of *non-refoulement,* which is enshrined in a number of legal instruments. According to the Refugee Convention this principle forbids return of a person to a country if he or she may face persecution based on nationality, membership of a social group, political opinion, race and/or religion.[10] The principle of *non-refoulement,* although originating in the Refugee Convention, can be found in a number of other human rights treaties. The principle of *non-refoulement* is also considered to form part of customary international law, which means that states are bound by it regardless of their adoption of relevant international human rights treaties.

In this respect, Article 3 of the European Convention on Human Rights 1950 (ECHR) has been the most influential in the European context. It provides that 'no one shall be sent back to torture, or to inhuman or degrading treatment or punishment'. The European Court of Human Rights in Strasbourg has invoked Article 3 to prohibit the return of individuals to a country where there are substantial grounds to believe that a real risk of such treatment will take place (*Chahal v. UK,* see below).[11] Article 3 protection has also been interpreted to

---

[8] Kourula, P., 'Broadening the Edges: Refugee Definition and International Protection Revisited', 1997, *Kluwer Law International,* p. 110.
[9] See Hailbronner, K., 'Temporary and local responses to forced migrations: A Comment', 35 *Va. J. Int'l. Law,* p. 81.
[10] Article 33 of the Refugee Convention.
[11] *Chahal v. UK* (1996) 23 EHRR 413.

cover prohibition on return in the event of a civil war where the governmental apparatus has broken down,[12] and where a person faces certain and painful death due to ill-health because of lack of health facilities in the country of origin.[13]

The Chahal case has particularly interesting implications for the present day fight against terrorism. Chahal was issued with a deportation order on the basis that his presence in the UK posed a threat to national security. Chahal, an Indian Sikh, had been arrested for alleged involvement in a conspiracy to kill the Indian Prime Minister, Rajiv Ghandi, but was released for lack of evidence. He was also convicted of assault and affray in the UK but the conviction was set aside because of procedural irregularities. While in detention awaiting deportation, Chahal claimed asylum on the basis that he would be persecuted if returned to India. His asylum claim was turned down and he brought his case to the European Court of Human Rights. The Court, after reviewing the factual evidence on India, decided that the risk of ill-treatment was very real and to send him back would contravene Article 3 of the ECHR. The court ruled against Chahal's return regardless of the threat to national security that he allegedly posed in the UK. In Irish law, Section 5 of the Refugee Act 1996 anticipated jurisprudence of this type and does not place any national security qualifications on the obligation not to *refoule* an individual.[14]

The UN Convention against Torture and Other Cruel, Inhuman or Degrading Treatment 1987[15] and the International Covenant on Civil and Political Rights 1966 (ICCPR) also place limitations on a state's right to return an individual to potential harm.[16] Although it is not a legally binding instrument, but rather one of political persuasion, the

---

[12] *Ahmed v. Austria* (1997) 24 EHRR 278; *HLR v. France* (1998) 26 EHRR 29.

[13] *D v. United Kingdom* (1997) 24 EHRR 423. This case does not relate to asylum. The plaintiff involved was dying of AIDS.

[14] Section 5(1) of the Refugee Act states, 'A person shall not be expelled from the State or returned in any manner whatsoever to the frontiers or territories where, in the opinion of the minister, the life or freedom of that person would be threatened on account of his or her race, religion, nationality, membership of a particular social group or political opinion'. According to Section 5(2), 'Without prejudice to the generality of subsection (1), a person's freedom shall be regarded as being threatened if, *inter alia*, in the opinion of the minister, the person is likely to be subject to a serious assault (including a serious assault of a sexual nature).'

[15] Ireland has ratified the UN Torture Convention by virtue of the Criminal Justice (UN Convention against Torture) Act 2000. Section 4(1) of the Act reflects the *non-refoulement* obligation: '[a] person shall not be expelled or returned from the State to another state where the minister is of the opinion that there are substantial grounds for believing that the person would be in danger of being subjected to torture'.

[16] Article 7 ICCPR provides that 'no one shall be subjected to torture or to cruel, inhuman or degrading treatment or punishment'. The UN Human Rights Committee, to which individuals may lodge a complaint about an alleged human rights abuse under the Covenant, has developed similar jurisprudence to that of the European Court of Human Rights.

Charter of Fundamental Rights of the European Union is also relevant for asylum seekers. It guarantees the right to asylum and specifically states that no one can be removed to a state where there is a serious risk that he or she would be subjected to the death penalty, torture or other inhuman or degrading treatment or punishment.[17] The drafters of the Constitutional Treaty for the European Union[18] envisage that the Charter of Fundamental Rights be incorporated into the Treaty and thereby assume a legally binding character. If this does not happen, the Charter will remain a document of political persuasion and a guiding instrument for EU legislation.

3) Reluctance to extend the refugee definition

There is some merit in the proposition that the Refugee Convention should be revised to reflect modern reasons for flight but states providing asylum have shown consistent reluctance to do so. This is partly due to the principled stance that political asylum should remain sacred. But it is also due to the political obstacles governments face in granting Convention refugee status to an excessively broad range of people. Convention refugee status must be accompanied – at a minimum – by access to the courts and administrative authorities, adequate housing, social assistance or access to the labour market, healthcare, primary and secondary education and family reunification. Lesser social, legal and economic rights tend to be granted to beneficiaries of complementary protection. As a result, granting complementary protection instead of refugee status is a more attractive option for states that are subject to a citizenry that expresses unrest at apparent generous policies towards refugees, asylum seekers and immigrants generally.

The Refugee Convention simply defines a 'refugee' and refugee status determination is left entirely to the discretion of individual states. This renders the decision as to who receives refugee status vulnerable to the pressures of national political interests. Balancing refugee protection obligations and legitimate state interests is a difficult task. Often the latter interests prevail, especially around election times when tough stances on asylum and immigration become bountiful sources of votes.

Particularly in the EU there is growing anti-immigrant sentiment and pressure on governments to get tough on immigration. This has resulted in clampdowns on asylum seekers who are believed to gain entry to countries through the asylum channel without a legitimate case

---

[17] Articles 18 and 19 of the Charter.

[18] *Draft Treaty establishing a Constitution for Europe*, CONV 820/1/03 REV 1, Brussels 27 June 2003. Part One, Title II (Articles 5 – 7) 'EU citizenship and fundamental rights'. Copies of the draft text are available from the European Parliament Office, Molesworth Street, Dublin2, www.europarl.ie.

for refugee status. Reflections of public support for tough measures on asylum and immigration are apparent in the success of right-wing movements in France, Austria, Belgium, the Netherlands and the UK. In April 2003, for example, the far-right British National Party won sixteen council seats, weeks after it was announced that the UK had received a record number of 110,700 asylum applications in 2002. In February 2003, the Blair administration made an undertaking to halve the number of asylum seekers entering the UK by September 2003.[19]

Refugee organisations have cautioned against the excessive use of complementary protection measures when Convention refugee status should be granted. For example, people fleeing indiscriminate violence and disorder that accompany a conflict situation may be granted complementary protection instead of Convention refugee status, even if the persecution alleged is linked to a specific Refugee Convention ground of persecution. According to UNHCR,

> [e]xperience shows that most civil wars or internal armed conflicts are rooted in ethnic, religious or political differences which specifically victimise those fleeing. War and violence are themselves often used as instruments of persecution.[20]

Bearing this in mind, UNHCR and other refugee organisations warn that the Refugee Convention could be undermined by unjustified recourse to complementary protection.[21] But the value of complementary protection schemes, however imperfect from a legal human rights point of view, should be emphasised. The impact of unduly narrow interpretations of the Refugee Convention can be substantially offset by complementary protection schemes, which can strike a balance between legal protection obligations and domestic political pressures. As a senior UNHCR figure has acknowledged, '[r]efugee protection takes place in a highly politically-charged atmosphere'.[22]

Extension of protection to individuals who flee their countries for non-Refugee Convention reasons has been somewhat *ad hoc* but most EU states have by now established some form of complementary protection scheme. For example, Sweden has comprehensive legislation

---

[19] BBC news report *Blair's Asylum Pledge Rubbished,* 20 February 2003 http://news.bbc.co.uk/1/hi/uk_politics/2739453.stm.

[20] UNHCR's Observations on the European Commission's proposal for a Council Directive on minimum standards for the qualification and status of third country nationals and stateless persons as refugees or as persons who otherwise need international protection (November 2001), para. 35.

[21] For example, see European Council on Refugees and Exiles (ECRE). Position on Complementary Protection, September 2000, www.ecre.org. Refugee Protection Policy Group, *The Case for the Provision of Complementary Protection Status in Irish Law,* May 2000.

[22] McNamara, P., *UNHCR and International Refugee Protection,* Refugee Studies Programme Working Group Paper no. 2, University of Oxford, June 1999.

to protect people who have compelling reasons to remain even though
they do not meet the classic refugee definition criteria. If able to satisfy
this test, they may be granted the same rights as Convention refugees.
For years the United Kingdom has granted 'Exceptional Leave to
Remain' (ELR) to those who fall outside the Refugee Convention definition but who nevertheless need protection. ELR is normally granted
for one year and is generally renewable for a further three years. After
four years, a person may apply for 'Indefinite Leave to Remain'. ELR
may be granted for various reasons but most commonly it is based on
compassionate or humanitarian grounds. The UK Home Office, as of
1 April 2003, will replace ELR with 'humanitarian protection'. This
new status is intended specifically for people who do not fulfil the
requirements of the Refugee Convention but who are at risk of the
death penalty, unlawful killing or torture or inhuman or degrading
treatment.[23]

Other EU states offer varying levels of protection for those who fall
under complementary schemes of protection. Finnish authorities may
issue a residence permit on strong humanitarian grounds, such as ongoing civil war or natural disaster, and a stronger legal status may be
granted to a person falling outside the Refugee Convention definition
but who shows a clear need for protection. Portugal may also grant
protection for a period up to two years to persons displaced from their
country due to serious armed conflict.[24]

4) Complementary protection in Ireland

a) Section 3 of the Immigration Act 1999

Ireland does not operate a formal system of complementary protection, as exists in other states. However, Irish legislation does provide a
limited means for unsuccessful asylum seekers to remain in the state
where they show a need for protection (or some other basis which
justifies permission for them to remain) but have not met the Refugee
Convention requirements. The Refugee Act 1996 and the Immigration
Act 1999 set out this means.

Section 17(5) and (6) of the Refugee Act 1996 reflects in statutory
form, as it relates to unsuccessful asylum seekers, the minister for
Justice, Equality and Law Reform's power to control the stay in and
removal from the state of non-nationals. Section 17(5) of the Refugee
Act creates a link with Section 3 of the Immigration Act 1999, which
sets out the deportation process. That process gives an unsuccessful

---

[23] See http://www.westminster.gov.uk/socialservices/lasc/news/Exceptional-Leave-to-
Remain.cfm.
[24] For an analysis of complementary protection offered in EU member states, see Egan
S. and Costello K. (1999), *Refugee Law: Comparative Study*, Dublin: Stationery Office.

asylum seeker an opportunity to put forward reasons as to why he or she should be allowed to remain in the state.

The origins of Section 3 of the Immigration Act 1999 are worth out-lining prior to a description of its practical application. Before the Act was passed in 1999, the Minister for Justice's[25] inherent power to deport non-nationals was reflected in the Aliens Act 1935 and the Aliens Order 1946.[26] The Supreme Court in the *Laurentiu* case found that the Oireachtas, in 1935, devolved to the Minister for Justice a subsidiary legislation-making power in respect of deportation that was inconsistent with the provisions of the 1937 Constitution.[27] Accordingly, the relevant section of the Aliens Act 1935 was declared *ultra vires* (beyond the scope) of the minister's powers.[28] Although Mr Justice Geoghegan in the *Laurentiu* case remarked that the inherent power of the minister to deport exists without further need for legislative regulation, the government of the day decided to regulate by statute in detailed manner the deportation process.[29] Section 3 of the Immigration Act 1999 established a comprehensive deportation procedure, which largely reflects the principles of constitutional and natural justice.

Unsuccessful asylum applicants are liable to be deported in the same manner as every person who is illegally in the state. Section 3 of the Immigration Act 1999 gives the person, who has been notified of a proposal to deport him or her, fifteen days within which to make representations in writing to the minister as to why he or she should not be deported.[30] In this notice, the person is also offered a chance to leave the State voluntarily or consent to the making of a deportation order. The Department of Justice, Equality and Law Reform considers Section 3 representations. Eleven factors must be taken into account 'so far as they appear or are known' when deciding whether to issue a deportation order and they are as follows:

(a) the age of the person;
(b) the duration of residence in the State of the person;
(c) the family and domestic circumstances of the person;
(d) the nature of the person's connection with the State, if any;
(e) the employment (including self-employment) record of the person;

---

[25] As the office was then described.
[26] Section 5(1)(e) of the Aliens Act 1935 and Article 13 of the Aliens Order 1946, made under the Aliens Act 1935.
[27] The constitutional provisions relating to the role of the *Oireachtas* as law-maker.
[28] *Laurentiu v. Minister for Justice* [1999] 4 IR 26.
[29] *Ibid*. Geoghegan J: '[T]he power to require an alien to leave and to remain thereafter out of the State if a minister deems it to be conducive to the public good is not in any sense a purely regulatory or administrative matter though of course it is that also ...'
[30] Section 3(3)(a) of the Immigration Act 1999.

(f)   the employment (including self-employment) prospects of the person;
(g)   the character and conduct of the person both within and (where relevant and ascertainable) outside the State (including any criminal convictions);
(h)   humanitarian considerations;
(i)   any representations duly made by or on behalf of the person;
(j)   the common good; and
(k)   considerations of national security and public policy.[31]

Section 3 of the Immigration Act 1999 is not designed to act as a scheme of complementary protection. In the absence of such a scheme in Ireland, the compulsory deliberations of 'humanitarian considerations' and, to an extent, 'family and domestic circumstances of the person' have assumed this role. The Section 3 process is explicitly subject to the principle of *non-refoulement*,[32] insofar as it is defined in Section 5 of the Refugee Act.[33] Therefore an unsuccessful asylum seeker could, theoretically, be protected from return to a particular country by the Section 3 process. However, in the words of a senior Department of Justice, Equality and Law Reform official, '[i]n many cases the question of possible *refoulement* will have been answered by the negative asylum decision'.[34] It appears from this that the need to deliberate upon *non-refoulement* considerations is minimised at the deportation stage in the case of people who have failed the asylum process. This does not, however, absolve the minister from giving due consideration to the class of *refoulement* described, for example, in Section 4 of the Irish Criminal Justice (UN Convention against Torture) Act 2000, which has equal application in its own terms regarding potential removal from the state. Ireland is also bound by the jurisprudence pertaining to Article 3 of the European Convention on Human Rights and any other legal instruments, which the minister would be obliged to consider under humanitarian considerations. Therefore, situations that might give rise to a successful case for complementary protection in other jurisdictions could also yield a positive result in Ireland under Section

---

[31]   Section 3(6) of the Immigration Act 1999.
[32]   Section 3(1) states: 'Subject to the provisions of Section 5 (prohibition of *refoulement*) of the Refugee Act, 1996, and the subsequent provisions of this section, the minister may by order (in this Act referred to as a 'deportation order') require any non-national specified in the order to leave the State within such period as may be specified in the order and to remain thereafter out of the State'.
[33]   Section 5(1) of the Refugee Act states, 'A person shall not be expelled from the State or returned in any manner whatsoever to the frontiers of territories where, in the opinion of the minister, the life or freedom of that person would be threatened on account of his or her race religion, nationality, membership of a particular social group or political opinion'.
[34]   Ingoldsby, B., 'Leave to Remain Other Than Through the Regular Migration Process', paper delivered at the Incorporated Law Society Seminar: Rights to Reside in Ireland, 14 May 2002, at Blackhall Place, Dublin, p. 4.

3 of the Immigration Act 1999. This would include an instance where, for example,

> ... the individual can show that there is a situation of general lawlessness in the individual's country of origin which gives rise to indiscriminate violence, that is clearly a matter which the minister would have to consider, coming as it does within the 'humanitarian considerations' factor and, possibly also, in particular cases, under 'family and domestic circumstances'.[35]

In practice, most people who succeed in obtaining leave to remain following the Section 3 process do so on the basis of such factors as parentage of Irish children or marriage to an Irish or an EU national. During 2002, the total number granted leave to remain under Section 3 of the Immigration Act was 6,896. The number of people granted leave to remain during 2002 on humanitarian grounds was 159.[36] Regardless of the precise basis for granting leave to remain in Section 3(6) of the Immigration Act 1999, leave is granted for one year, with the possibility of subsequent annual renewals.

b) Shortcomings of Section 3 as a complementary scheme of protection

Section 3 of the Immigration Act 1999 offers a last chance for unsuccessful asylum seekers, and other potential deportees, to formulate a claim to stay in Ireland. It is described by the Department of Justice as a

> [r]easonably transparent means, with well-defined procedural steps, whereby any residual claim to remain in the State which the failed applicant may have can be thoroughly examined, where the individual's input into the decision-making process is guaranteed and the nature of the factors to be taken into account is clearly set out.[37]

However, Section 3 lacks the components of a fair and comprehensive scheme of complementary protection for three main reasons. Firstly, leave to remain under Section 3 is granted at the discretion of the minister and decision-making is not, therefore, independent of popular

---

[35] *Ibid.* p. 4.

[36] Dáil Questions to the Minister for Justice, Equality and Law Reform, 12 March 2003. The number granted leave to remain during 2002 on the basis of parentage of an Irish child was 3,123, on the basis of marriage to an Irish national 86, and on the basis of being a dependant of an EU national 138. The number of applications for leave to remain in the state during 2003 up to 31 March 2003 was 1,095. The number granted leave to remain in 2003 up to 31 March 2003 on the basis of parentage of an Irish child was 172, on the basis of marriage to an Irish national was seven and on the basis of dependants of an EU citizen was twelve. The number granted leave to remain on humanitarian grounds was thirty. (Dáil Questions to the minister for Justice, Equality Law Reform, 13 May 2003).

[37] Note 34, p. 6.

or political concerns. The composition of the asylum decision-making apparatus in Ireland is carefully crafted to operate independently of political interests and so has the freedom to act without regard to popular sentiments about immigration when fulfilling the state's important protection obligations. Similar standards need to apply to decision-making in a formal complementary protection regime. Secondly, there is no requirement under Section 3 for the decision-maker to hold an interview or have any personal interaction with the failed asylum seeker. This lacks the transparency and rigour that legal protection obligations require. Thirdly, the phrase 'humanitarian considerations' is more commonly associated with compassionate concerns, which more appropriately belong in an immigration code. Compassionate concerns pose moral issues for decision-making authorities whereas human rights concerns, such as refugee status or complementary protection, are born of nationally assumed international human rights obligations.

c) Incorporation of EU law

The Irish government has decided to participate in the EU subsidiary protection Directive that is under discussion in Brussels (EU legislators have chosen the term 'subsidiary' instead of 'complementary').[38] The proposed Directive lays down a framework for an EU policy on qualifications for refugee status and complementary protection in the context of the EU's greater harmonisation project. One of the stated aims of the proposed Directive is to limit the secondary movement of asylum seekers due to diverse refugee and complementary protection determination processes in different member states. By opting into this Directive the Irish government is committed to introducing a scheme of complementary protection into domestic law by 30 April 2004, the timeframe stipulated in the proposed Directive.

The proposed Directive does not purport to create new classes of persons that member states are obliged to protect but is based instead on existing international and Community law and the current practices of member states. The proposed Directive affirms the concept of a refugee as a person who has a well-founded fear of persecution based on race, religion, nationality, membership of a social group or political opinion, in accordance with the Refugee Convention.[39] The drafters of the proposed Directive consider that the Refugee Convention remains sufficiently full and inclusive to guarantee adequate protection to a significant number of people in need. Subsidiary protection, as set out

---

[38] Proposal for a Council Directive on minimum standards for the qualification and status of third country nationals and stateless persons as refugees or as persons who otherwise need international protection [COM (2001) 510 final Official Journal C51 E, 26.02.2002].

[39] Chapter III, Articles 11 to 14, deal with qualification for refugee status.

in the proposed Directive, is intended to complement the Refugee Convention by offering a minimum standard of protection for those who show a clear need for international protection but who fall outside the scope of the Refugee Convention.

Under the proposed Directive, 'subsidiary protection status' can be granted to people who show that they cannot return to their country of origin due to a well-founded fear of being subjected to

- torture, inhuman or degrading treatment (reflecting Article 3 ECHR)
- serious unjustified[40] violations of their human rights (systematic or otherwise)
- a threat to life or liberty, safety or freedom as a result of indiscriminate violence arising in armed conflict.[41]

According to the Directive, the social and economic rights granted to those with subsidiary protection status must be largely the same as those granted to Convention refugees due to the fact that the needs of all beneficiaries of international protection are broadly similar. However, the proposed Directive elevates Refugee Convention status over subsidiary protection:

> [t]he regime of subsidiary protection starts from the premise that the need for such protection is temporary in nature, notwithstanding the fact that in reality the need for subsidiary protection often turns out to be more lasting.[42]

To this end, beneficiaries of subsidiary protection status are entitled to lesser benefits than those granted Convention refugee status in three

---

[40] The term 'unjustified' was added to take into account the fact that some types of harm are considered justified, such as in the event of a public emergency. Although such instances are rare, according to the proposed Directive, '[i]t would be contrary to human rights instruments such as the European Convention on Human Rights and Fundamental Freedoms to exclude the possibility that some proportionate derogation from human rights standards may, in limited and particular circumstances, be justified, most commonly in the interests of the wider common good'. (Proposed Directive, *Commentary on Articles*).

[41] Article 15 of the proposed Directive. Chapter IV, Articles 15 to 17, deal with qualification for subsidiary protection status. UNHCR, in its commentary on the proposed Directive, states: '[i]n most cases the type of threats that are enumerated in Article 15 may indeed indicate a strong presumption for Convention refugee status, except perhaps for those fleeing the indiscriminate effects of violence and the accompanying disorder in a conflict situation, with no element of persecution or link to a specific Convention ground. And it is for the latter category of persons that subsidiary protection indeed fulfils an important function. Against this background, the elements listed under Article 15 would need to be revisited to ensure that the applicability of the 1951 Convention and the 1967 Protocol is not in effect undermined by resorting to subsidiary forms of protection' (UNHCR's Observations on the European Commission's proposal for a Council Directive on minimum standards for the qualification and status of third country nationals and stateless persons as refugees or as persons who otherwise need international protection, Geneva, November 2001, para. 42).

[42] Explanatory Memorandum to the proposed Directive, Section 2 *Scope of the Proposal*.

main respects: employment, residence permits and integration. Under the Directive, those granted refugee status must be authorised to work immediately. In contrast, the right to work for those with subsidiary protection status may be withheld for six months after status has been granted. Similarly, those with refugee status are entitled to access employment-related educational opportunities for adults, vocational training and practical workplace experience on the same basis as nationals in the state of asylum. Those with subsidiary protection status are only entitled to such rights one year after being granted protection.[43] Those with refugee status are entitled to a residence permit for five years, as opposed to one year for beneficiaries of subsidiary protection.[44] Finally, in terms of integration, those with refugee status are granted automatic entitlement to avail of full integration facilities in the host member state. In contrast, beneficiaries of subsidiary protection must wait one year before such rights accrue.[45] It is important to note that the proposed Directive sets out minimum standards and that member states are free to be more generous.[46]

5) *Conclusion*

When a complementary protection scheme is formalised in Irish law, the recognition rate for people deemed in need of protection will most likely be higher than it currently stands (in 2002, refugee status was granted in 14% of cases where recommendations were made – 10.67% at first instance and 20.3% at appeal stage).[47] How much higher is a matter of speculation but the experience of other countries is helpful. In the UK, the overall recognition rate for protection of both Convention and non-Convention asylum seekers for 1997 was 24%. In Sweden the figure was 45%, in Denmark it was 55% and in Canada it was 52%. The figures for Australia were significantly lower however – 15% for the 1997-98 period.[48]

    To be both useful and efficient, the terms of a complementary protection scheme must be concise and include clear definitions of the rights of potential beneficiaries. From a practical point of view, asylum

---

[43] Article 24 'Access to Employment'.

[44] Article 21 'Residence permits'.

[45] Article 31 'Access to Integration Facilities'.

[46] Article 4 'More favourable provisions'.

[47] It is a broadly held view – in Ireland and elsewhere – that asylum seekers are attracted to industrialised countries mainly, and sometimes exclusively, for the social and economic benefits. In Ireland, there has been ample commentary about the motives of asylum seekers. Although a scheme of complementary protection, which would increase the recognition rate of asylum seekers, would quell this criticism to an extent, a significant proportion of asylum seekers will continue to be found unworthy of the state's protection and would be better served by gaining access to the state through other immigration channels.

[48] Australian Refugee Council Position on Complementary Protection, May 2002.

seekers arriving to Ireland should be able to make claims for Convention refugee status and complementary protection simultaneously from the outset.[49] Indeed, the latter option might discourage unfounded claims for refugee status.[50] The most efficient and just model of complementary protection is one whereby protection claims are submitted to one appropriate body to consider all aspects of protection. In Ireland, the Refugee Applications Commissioner and the Refugee Appeals Tribunal are the most obvious candidates for this task, given their existing functions and expertise. These bodies could decide whether to grant Convention refugee status, or refuse it and offer complementary protection instead. A recommendation of the Commissioner that a person should not be entitled to refugee status or complementary protection should be capable of appeal to the Tribunal. In other words, at all stages of the refugee determination procedure, a simultaneous assessment for refugee status and complementary protection should take place to provide a just, speedy and cost-efficient service.

PART II Temporary Protection in the Event of Mass Influx

1) Temporary protection in the EU

The term 'temporary protection' has developed in the EU context to describe emergency protection granted by member states in the case of a mass influx of asylum seekers, which normally occurs in the event of war or large-scale massacres. Temporary protection has evolved into a distinctive and sophisticated tool for protection at the EU level.

Temporary protection may be distinguished from complementary protection insofar as it is strictly an emergency measure designed to cope with situations of mass influx where normal asylum determination systems cannot handle the large numbers of people involved. Complementary protection, on the other hand, is an ancillary protection scheme that has a permanent co-existence with the Refugee Convention regime. Also in contrast to complementary protection, temporary protection is granted on a group basis and does not require individual case assessment. It assumes that all members of a group in an emergency situation have a need for instant protection, at least for the crisis period.

The war in former Yugoslavia presented the international community and, in particular, Western Europe with a mass influx of people in need of protection. In total, some half a million people from former Yugoslavia were received in European countries during this

---

[49] Alternatively, claims for protection could be based on either status, depending on a particular protection need. This is one of the possibilities envisaged by the proposed EU Directive on subsidiary protection (Article 2(g)).

[50] Given the mixed reasons for flight and the overlap between Refugee Convention protection and complementary protection, shrewd legal advice would most likely encourage asylum seekers to apply for both statuses.

period, mostly on a temporary basis. UNHCR's approach at this time was in favour of temporary protection for the people from former Yugoslavia largely due to the fact that this was the maximum that states were prepared to offer when faced with so many people in need.[51] Given the large numbers of victims that were fleeing to the EU (because it was the nearest safe region) the most practical way to solve what was becoming a very difficult humanitarian and political problem for member states was to act collectively. Further incentives for the EU to act decisively were the geographical proximity of the conflict, which posed a threat to regional stability, and the extensive media coverage of the conflict, which produced a strong moral pressure to assist victims.

Although many victims of the Balkans war were granted refugee status in member states, these tended to be people who arrived on an individual basis or in small numbers rather than in large groups. Member states did not show a willingness to grant Convention refugee status to large numbers of Yugoslav victims arriving *en masse*, even though most of those who fled former Yugoslavia did so because of persecution due to religion, nationality and/or ethnicity – clear Convention grounds of persecution.[52] This undermined the Refugee Convention protection to which some people were technically entitled, but *realpolitik* dictated that such a contradiction existed. The alternative – granting refugee status to large groups – was perceived as politically untenable.

On 20 July 2001, the EU formally adopted a Directive on temporary protection.[53] It is made clear that a temporary protection regime is not intended to be an alternative to the Refugee Convention.[54] Rather,

---

[51] UNHCR's Background Note on Temporary Protection (1992) stated that 'persons fleeing from former Yugoslavia who are in need of international protection should be able to receive it on a temporary basis', U.N. Doc. HCR/IMFY/1992/Y. As far back as 1980, UNHCR stated that in cases of large-scale influxes, it is acceptable that persons seeking asylum receive temporary protection,' EXCOM Conclusion No 19 (XXXI) 1980 (Temporary Refuge).

[52] Human Rights Watch, *'Ethnic Cleansing' continues in Northern Bosnia,* November 1994 at http://hrw.org/reports/world/b-h-pubs.php.

[53] Four legal instruments relating to temporary protection have been tabled at the EU level. Each varies considerably in its level of detail. The first EU temporary protection initiative was in 1993 and took the form of a set of guidelines to cater for the victims of the war in former Yugoslavia. The second temporary protection instrument was drafted in 1997 and is more complex than its predecessor. The 1997 instrument included a provision on burden sharing which proved hard to get agreement upon and so was ultimately abandoned. A revised draft was tabled in 1998 which is broadly similar to the 1997 proposal but was relieved of any details on burden sharing. In order to address this, a separate burden sharing proposal was simultaneously presented. Finally, after the adoption of the Treaty of Amsterdam in 1999, a Directive on temporary protection was drafted and presented in June 2000. It was adopted on 20 July 2001: Council Directive on minimum standards for giving temporary protection in the event of a mass influx of displaced persons and on measures promoting a balance of efforts between Member States in receiving such persons and bearing the consequences thereof ([2001] OJ L212/12).

[54] Article 3 of the Directive.

temporary protection is a practical device that meets urgent needs during a mass influx situation when individual case assessment is not practicable under the normal asylum process.[55] In practice, a qualified majority vote by the Council, on the basis of a Commission proposal, can trigger a temporary protection regime.[56] The Directive imposes a time limit of three years on a temporary protection regime.[57]

Given the express recognition in the Directive that beneficiaries of a temporary protection regime might otherwise be entitled to Convention refugee status, the socio-economic rights afforded to them are broadly equivalent to recognised Convention refugees. Beneficiaries of temporary protection are entitled to work[58] and to appropriate accommodation, healthcare and social assistance.[59] Extensive provision is made for family reunification.[60] Beneficiaries of a temporary protection regime may apply for refugee status in the normal asylum determination process, but this is left to the discretion of member states who may refuse to allow concurrent claims for asylum with temporary protection status.[61] Financial support for member states in the event of a temporary protection regime being triggered comes from the European Refugee Fund.[62]

2) Is temporary protection necessary?

As can be seen from the Balkans example, the Refugee Convention and the traditional asylum procedures based upon it were not considered by the EU as the appropriate formula to deal with a mass influx of people. There are three main reasons why, generally speaking, the Refugee Convention is not regarded as useful in such circumstances, which have varying degrees of persuasion.

a) Individual persecution requirement

The Refugee Convention is deemed unsuitable for large-scale influxes because of its insistence on individually targeted persecution. Technically, to qualify for refugee status one must show a personal fear

---

[55] Article 2 of the Directive.
[56] Article 5(1) of the Directive.
[57] Article 4(1) of the Directive. The initial time period is one year with the possibility of two extensions, each for a six-month period. Article 4(2) allows a further extension of one year, on the basis of a Commission proposal, if the reasons for temporary protection persist.
[58] Article 12 of the Directive. Article 12 also states that '[F]or reasons of labour market policies, Member States may give priority to EU citizens and citizens of States bound by the agreement on the European Economic Area and also to legally resident third-country nationals who receive unemployment benefit'.
[59] Article 13.
[60] Article 15.
[61] Article 19.
[62] Article 24.

of persecution as well as an objective basis for that fear. The logical conclusion is that individual case-by-case assessment is necessary and this is not practicable in a mass influx situation.

This effectively excludes from Convention protection a person who has fled general war or violence and who cannot show that s/he was individually targeted. It is difficult to concede that the drafters of the Convention intended this. Hathaway, a leading writer on refugee law, doubts the need to show personally targeted harm or persecution in order to qualify for Convention refugee status. He makes the much-overlooked point that

> [t]he very persons of concern to the drafters of the Convention – Jews and other Second World War persecutees and those in flight from the rise of Communist states – were themselves the victims of broadly based risk.[63]

He points out that the central question is the gravity of the harm feared and asks

> [i]s the person who faces torture because [he or she] is black really more deserving of protection than the person who faces torture because his [or her] whole country is in the grip of a brutal dictator who punishes citizens indiscriminately?[64]

UNHCR has also doubted the individual persecution requirement and contends that it leads to a dilution of the object and spirit of the Refugee Convention.

> Some states contend that if warring parties terrorise a whole community-even as part of ethnic, religious, racial, social or nationality-based violence – none of the victims is a refugee unless he or she has been singled out for special treatment … in our view, the spirit and object of the Convention is seriously undermined when people with a well-founded fear of persecution based on race, religion, nationality, political opinion or membership of a social group are not afforded international protection just because […] the persecution is not individually targeted.[65]

In sum a narrow interpretation of the refugee definition is sometimes used by states to avoid the expense and political fallout from granting

---

[63] Hathaway, J.C., 'Is Refugee Status Really Elitist? An Answer to the Ethical Challenge', in *Europe and Refugees: A Challenge? L'Europe et les Refugies: Un Defi?* (eds. Carlier, J.Y., Vanheule D.) 1997, Kluwer Law International, p. 82.

[64] *Ibid.* p. 84

[65] McNamara, D., *UNHCR and International Refugee Protection*, RSP Working Paper number 2, Refugee Studies Programme, University of Oxford, June 1999, p.7. See also UNHCR, *Information Note on Article 1 of the 1951 Convention*, March 1995. In the view of UNHCR, indiscriminate shelling or bombardment, torture or arbitrary punishment against sectors of society may be considered as giving rise to refugee status under the Refugee Convention. This implies that people in such situations do not have to be targeted individually but if they prove that they belong to a class of targeted persons they may construct a Convention claim.

refugee status to large numbers fleeing all manner of abuse and turmoil from around the world.[66]

b) Group recognition under the Refugee Convention

According to UNHCR, states remain free to grant *prima facie* refugee status under the Refugee Convention to a group of people where it is generally accepted that the majority of their claims would be recognised under the Refugee Convention.[67] If it appears that a large group of people is fleeing for similar Convention reasons it may be expedient and fair that group recognition is granted in the early stages. This UNHCR policy position releases states from the technical burden of having to examine cases individually where a mass influx would overburden the asylum system – at least during an emergency phase. It also avoids the need to set up new *ad hoc* procedures, such as temporary protection regimes, to deal with emergencies.

Despite its feasibility under the Refugee Convention, however, group recognition has found little support among states. This is partly attributable to the political and economic concerns of states that might arise if refugee status, with its attendant set of rights, were granted automatically to large numbers. Another concern is the potential for blanket group recognition to allow the infiltration of unmerited or abusive claims to go unchecked. People who would ordinarily be excluded from Refugee Convention protection due to atrocities they may have committed can benefit from protection in the confusion of large groups,[68] as happened in the Democratic Republic of the Congo in 1994 when thousands were fleeing the genocide in Rwanda. How to exclude the undeserving in such situations is a difficult but necessary task.

Instant group recognition under the Refugee Convention is intended for emergency situations only. There are ways of sifting through the group in the aftermath of the emergency to establish who remains in need of protection. For example, states may formulate screening-out processes after the panic that accompanies a mass influx has subsided.

---

[66] See for example ECRE (1998), 'Position of the European Council on Refugees and Exile on temporary protection in the context of the need for a supplementary refugee definition'.

[67] UNHCR Report of the Sub-Committee on International Protection (UN Doc. A/AC.96/613, para. 33).

[68] Article 1(F) of the Refugee Convention contains the so-called 'exclusion clauses,' whereby 'The provisions of the Convention shall not apply to any person with respect to whom there are serious reasons for considering that: (a) he has committed a crime against peace, a war crime, or a crime against humanity, as defined in the international instruments drawn up to make provision in respect of such crimes; (b) he has committed a serious non-political crime outside the country of refuge prior to his admission to that country as a refugee; (c) he has been guilty of acts contrary to the purposes and principles of the United Nations'.

An example of how screening-out procedures have operated is found in the treatment of the large outflow of protection seekers from Southeast Asia. As will be seen, however, such procedures are not as straightforward as they may appear.

The exodus of people from Cambodia, Vietnam and Laos in the late 1970s gave rise to a situation where it was not practical for receiving states to examine asylum claims individually under the Refugee Convention. Yet the international community felt compelled to deal with the enormity of the Indo-Chinese refugee movement, in particular the US due to its part in the Vietnam War (and an element of political opportunism to offer exile to people from a communist regime). During the next few years, receiving countries, UNHCR and countries of resettlement[69] persevered with the task of finding durable solutions for the Indo-Chinese.

In 1989, the so-called 'Comprehensive Plan of Action' (CPA) was drafted. One of the CPA's most decisive measures was to agree upon a cut-off date after which Indo-Chinese nationals who had received protection were to be automatically deemed 'economic migrants'. The attempt to filter the tail end of this large refugee movement proved more difficult than expected however. In theory, those who were screened out were obliged to return to their country of origin. In practice, they were treated over the years as if they had been granted refugee status, or a relatively permanent form of protection. This appeared inconsistent and unfair to some of the Indo-Chinese and was attributed to the cause of violent reactions in the camps.[70] Protection for the Indo-Chinese that was supposed to be temporary spanned almost fifteen years in many cases. The CPA screening-out process took over six years to implement. This prolonged period raised expectations that refugee status would be granted and the fact that such expectations proved to be false made repatriation almost impossible to achieve.[71]

c) The permanence of refugee status

It is not uncommon for recognised refugees to be granted permanent immigration status sooner or later in the state of asylum. This may be due to a prolonged need for protection or by virtue of immigration rights, such as citizenship, that apply to all persons. It is lawful however for refugee status to be temporary and the Refugee Convention

---

[69] Resettlement refers to the situation where asylum seekers are given protection in one country on a temporary basis with a view to permanent resettlement in another state of asylum.

[70] Southeast Asia Resource Action Centre, *From Irac to Sireac: the Story of an Evolving Ethnic Organisation,* www.searac.org/iractosea.html.

[71] Steering Committee of the International Conference on Indo-Chinese Refugees, meeting March 1996. See also the report, *Return of Persons not in Need of International Protection,* EC/46/SC/CRP.36, 28 May 1996.

reflects this. The Convention contains important limitations on protection, known as 'cessation clauses', which make it clear that protection may be revoked in the event that it is no longer necessary or justified.[72] The cessation clauses can be invoked, for example, if there are positive political changes in the country of origin or where a refugee has secured protection or residence elsewhere. As cessation clauses are limiting in nature, they should be interpreted restrictively according to UNHCR, not least because a mistaken application could prove fatal for a returned person.[73]

Although refugee status does not have to be permanent the Refugee Convention system has developed, in practice, a right for refugees to be granted permanent residence, frequently resulting in eventual citizenship. Indeed, Article 34 of the Convention encourages states to facilitate the naturalisation of recognised refugees.[74] As a result, the Convention system has been regarded as unsuitable for granting protection on a more flexible and temporary basis.

Even if a cessation clause might technically apply to a recognised refugee, it is unlikely that he or she would be sent home if he or she has developed family or other connections to the state. But leave to remain based on links to the host country is regulated by immigration law and not asylum law. Therefore, the fact that states, including Ireland, might allow recognised refugees to stay permanently when the country of origin situation has improved is not as a result of legal protection obligations under the Refugee Convention. Nor is it due to the inapplicability of the cessation clauses. Leave to remain in such circumstances normally rests with the discretionary power of immigration authorities (in Ireland this is the Department of Justice, Equality and Law Reform). If refugee status evolves into permanent residence it is due to domestic immigration practices, not legal obligations.

3) Burden Sharing

Burden sharing is an ideal whereby countries work together to share refugee-related responsibilities. In the event of a mass influx of asylum

---

[72] Article 1(C) of the Refugee Convention provides that protection may cease to apply to a person if he or she has (1) voluntarily re-availed him or herself of national protection; (2) voluntarily re-acquired his or her nationality; (3) acquired a new nationality; (4) voluntarily re-established themselves in the country where persecution was feared or (5) the circumstances in connection with which he or she was recognised as a refugee cease to exist in the country of nationality or of former habitual residence.

[73] UNHCR, *Handbook on Procedures and Criteria for Determining Refugee Status*, Geneva, January 1992, p. 27, paras. 114-116.

[74] Article 34 states: 'The Contracting States shall as far as possible facilitate the assimilation and naturalization of refugees. They shall in particular make every effort to expedite naturalization proceedings and to reduce as far as possible the charges and costs of such proceedings'.

seekers to a country or region, provision for equitable burden sharing is a matter of collective choice, which works in the interests of everybody involved. Negotiations on the nature of burden sharing have produced various ideas, such as financial pooling, compensation and physical distribution of people. At the EU level, temporary protection is inextricably linked with burden sharing.[75] The provision for burden sharing in the proposed Directive on temporary protection allows for both financial pooling of resources and physical distribution of people.[76]

Although a state acting alone, or a small number of states, cannot deal with unreasonably large numbers of asylum seekers there is no legal obligation to step in and share the responsibility in a crisis situation. It is generally out of a sense of neighbourly relations or mutual interest that joint efforts arise. The Refugee Convention was drafted with the objective of distributing the responsibility for the protection of World War II refugees but no express provision for burden sharing was included. Regional agreements have endeavoured to introduce burden sharing policies and some bilateral agreements have come to fruition.[77]

Receiving a large share of the refugee population can take its toll on a state's economy and political situation and can often lead to 'compassion fatigue'. This is the term used to describe when a population becomes weary of giving humanitarian assistance and it is particularly exacerbated when a state offers disproportionate levels of assistance compared to other states. This in turn may result in the closure of borders and policies of *non-entrée* (restrictions on the admission of asylum seekers). There is no international financial structure to provide compensation to governments who take on a disproportionate share of the refugee burden but the European Refugee Fund was set up to be drawn upon if a temporary protection regime were invoked by member states.[78]

States tend to show greater willingness to engage in burden sharing when the flow of asylum seekers is controlled or when an international

---

[75] In the EC Treaty, as amended by the 1999 Treaty of Amsterdam, there are two provisions, contained in Title VI, on burden sharing. Although asylum measures under Title VI of the EC Treaty are subject to a timeframe for adoption, of five years from the date of the Treaty, provisions on burden sharing are not subject to any timeframes (see Article 63(2)(b) EC Treaty).

[76] Proposed Directive, Chapter VI Articles 24 – 26.

[77] Although not engineered for a sudden mass influx situation, the Dublin Convention is one example of an attempt at burden sharing: *Convention determining the State responsible for examining applications for asylum lodged in one of the Member States of the European Communities,* signed in Dublin on 15 June 1990.

[78] According to the explanatory memorandum to the proposed Directive on temporary protection, financial solidarity will be accomplished by drawing on a central fund to finance emergency measures in the event of a mass influx of displaced persons to the EU. On 28 September 2000, the Council adopted a Decision (2000/596/EC) establishing a European Refugee Fund as a solidarity measure to promote a balance in the efforts made by member states in receiving and bearing the consequences of receiving refugees and displaced persons.

organisation has asked for help in specific situations.[79] In such circumstances, burden sharing usually takes the form of individual governments' participation in refugee protection and assistance programmes, orchestrated by agencies such as UNHCR, the Red Cross, Medicins sans Frontières etc, by offering financial and human resources. Other measures taken by governments have included preparation for emergencies and resettlement schemes.

d) Ireland's response to large-scale refugee emergencies

Since 1956, the year when Ireland acceded to the Refugee Convention, the state has responded to various emergency situations by accepting people as so-called 'programme refugees'. A programme refugee is someone who has been invited to Ireland on foot of a formal government-sponsored scheme, normally in response to humanitarian requests from international agencies such as UNHCR. Programme refugees do not need to go through an asylum determination process and they are automatically granted more or less the same entitlements to public services as Irish citizens.[80] Under such arrangements, Ireland accepted a group of 530 Hungarian refugees in 1956. The majority of this group was eventually resettled in the USA and Canada.[81] Between 1973 and 1974, 120 Chilean refugees arrived, most of whom returned to their home country when democracy was restored. In 1979, 212 Vietnamese refugees were resettled in Ireland.

In 1991 the Refugee Agency was established under the aegis of the Department of Foreign Affairs to co-ordinate the admission, reception and resettlement of programme refugees. In September 1992, a group of 178 refugees from Bosnia was accepted and they were subsequently joined by other groups and family members. In September 1998 the government agreed to admit a further 350 relatives of Bosnians and 200 relatives of Vietnamese already in Ireland under family reunification arrangements for programme refugees.[82] Aside from assisting the Bosnians to settle in to Ireland, the Refugee Agency sought to enable refugees under its care to become self-sufficient and to ensure that their culture and specific needs were respected. As the situation in

---

[79] For example, during the Vietnam war, the Japanese government accepted very few people who needed protection but offered financial assistance for camp facilities, resettlement schemes and general maintenance, see Suhrke, A., 'Burden-sharing during refugee emergencies: the logic of collective versus national action' (1998), *Journal of Refugee Studies* , Vol. 11, p. 396 at p.405.

[80] Section 25 of the Refugee Act 1996.

[81] *Integra Review,* Issue 6, Summer 1999, 'Ireland: A Multi-Ethnic Society', http://www.iol.ie/EMPLOYMENT/integra/6refugee.html.

[82] Address by the Minister for Justice, Equality and Law Reform, John O'Donoghue TD at the launch of the UNHCR/EU Refugee Integration Campaign, Wednesday, February 3, 1999. See: http://www.justice.ie/80256996005F3617/vWeb/wpJWOD4TFJM3.

Bosnia improved, the Refugee Agency supported Bosnian refugees who wished to voluntarily return home. To this end, in 1997, forty-two Bosnians were repatriated and, subsequently, three Bosnians availed of the right to return to Ireland.[83]

The most recent group to arrive in Ireland was 1,032 Kosovar refugees who were invited under a government programme between May and June 1999. The Kosovars were granted 'temporary protection'.[84] Legislative developments at the EU level on temporary protection were very advanced at this point in time and so there existed a well-considered framework for the construction of such a scheme at the domestic level. In practice, the Kosovars who came under the temporary protection programme were granted the same socio-economic rights as the Bosnians and the Refugee Agency looked after their needs. During 2000, most Kosovars returned home on a voluntary repatriation programme with the aid of a grant, and approximately 150 remained in Ireland.[85]

It is most likely that the next serious refugee situation that Ireland faces, due to a mass influx to the EU, will be regulated by the EU Directive on temporary protection. The Oireachtas Joint Committee on Justice, Equality, Defence and Women's Rights formally welcomed the Directive in February 2003. The Minister of State at the Department of Justice, Equality and Law Reform described it as '[a] useful instrument that allows states to deal with a Kosovo type influx'.[86]. In his remarks to the Committee, the minister of state made it clear to concerned deputies that Ireland has the right not to opt in to an EU temporary protection regime in the event of a mass influx and that a refusal to take part would not breach Ireland's international obligations. However, in an encouraging remark, the minister of state said that

> An international response is necessary to address the international factors which give rise to asylum claims and migration movements. It is important that EU member states work together to share their experiences and develop a common approach in addressing these matters. It is important, therefore, that Ireland should participate in this measure.

EU member states did not need to invoke a temporary protection regime during the Iraqi crisis of 2003. However, UNHCR issued

---

[83] Ireland Aid, 1997, *Partnerships, Support and Co-operation*, The Refugee Agency, http://www.irlgov.ie/iveagh/irishaid/1997report/sect7-2.htm.

[84] Department of Justice Press Release, 10 May 1999, *O'Donoghue welcomes Kosovar Refugees to Ireland,* http://www.justice.ie/80256996005F3617/vWeb/wpJWOD4TFL66

[85] Address to Joint Committee on Justice, Equality, Defence and Women's Rights by Minister of State at the Department of Justice, Equality and Law Reform, 3 February 2003. Motion of the Minister of State concerning the exercise by the state of the option provided under the Fourth Protocol to the Treaty of Amsterdam in respect of a the Council directive on temporary protection.

[86] *Ibid.*

requests to governments in March 2003 to offer temporary protection to newly-arrived Iraqi asylum seekers or to those already in the asylum system. Governments were also urged by UNHCR to suspend normal asylum determinations for Iraqis and to ensure that none were returned forcibly.[87] During the crisis period, UNHCR kept open the possibility of putting a proposal to the European Union to activate a temporary protection regime under the Directive.[88] Although the anticipated mass influx of Iraqi asylum seekers did not materialise, the instability in places like West and Central Africa may yet trigger an EU temporary protection regime.

Conclusion

Complementary protection and temporary protection schemes have evolved to fill the gaps due to the limits, whether perceived or real, of the Refugee Convention. Critics of such schemes caution that they may undermine the Refugee Convention and deprive people of their rights under international law. This may be so, but in a world of widespread economic migration and terrorist threats, states are no longer willing to grant Convention refugee status without watertight assurances that a person fits the classic profile of a political refugee. States are experiencing growing pressure about abuse of the asylum system and are unable to overcome adverse media coverage that refers to asylum policies as 'soft'. In Ireland, it is estimated that approximately €350 million was spent in 2002 sustaining the asylum system. Current statistics show that the majority of asylum seekers coming to Ireland do not have a legitimate claim for refugee status. Even if Ireland had a complementary system of protection whereby greater numbers were presenting with an undisputed protection need, it is hard to ignore the possibility that a large swathe of the asylum seeking population continue to be undeserving of international protection. Nonetheless, this does not relieve the state from maintaining a fair and efficient system for all asylum seekers.

Between 2001 and 2002, the asylum figures for Europe dropped by 3%, but many individual states, such as Ireland, witnessed an increase during this period. Ireland's asylum experience is part of a global problem and it would be short-sighted to treat it as merely a domestic concern. UNHCR has embarked on a re-structuring of global refugee management. Its latest consultative process, known as 'Convention-plus', was launched in September 2001. UNHCR seeks all states, political

---

87 See www.unhcr.ch, UN Humanitarian Briefing on Iraq, 20 March 2003, and also see Relief web: http://www.reliefweb.int/w/rwb.nsf/0/08AEE5FA3D34872985256CF5006 A8709?OpenDocument&Start=1&Count=1000&ExpandView&StartKey=Iraq

88 The Directive states that UNHCR must be consulted on the establishment, implementation and termination of a regime of temporary protection (Article 5).

and legal players, and any other body with an interest in refugee issues to input to this momentous process. As the title suggests, UNHCR intends to safeguard the Refugee Convention as the cornerstone for international protection, while examining other methods. The 'Convention-plus' negotiations will examine methods of international burden sharing, including support for asylum states, and durable solutions in regions of origin. The outcome will affect all states, including Ireland.

Reality dictates that we allow complementary and temporary protection policies to develop but law and justice insist that we ensure that they respect human rights obligations and principles. The introduction of a complementary protection scheme in Ireland is likely to increase the protection recognition rate figures. By how much is a matter of speculation but it is crucial that all people in need of international protection are identified. Temporary protection, which is a useful expedient for emergency situations, should be *temporary*. If the country of origin situation does not improve then solid protection from return must be assured. This may entail granting refugee status or complementary protection. Whatever the mechanism, the legal principle that no person should ever be sent back to a country where his or her life could be threatened is paramount and should remain above politics.

CHAPTER 12

Citizenship and the Irish Constitution

Donncha O'Connell and Ciara Smyth

Introduction

For a document infused with the language and values of natural law – in both its constitutive and fundamental rights provisions – the 1937 Constitution appears to make certain rights contingent on citizenship, in the positivist sense, and makes specific enabling provision for legislation governing nationality and citizenship. The new Articles 2 and 3, eventually introduced after the 1998 Belfast Agreement referendum, are a model of inclusive rhetoric and progressive aspiration in contrast to the rather more controversial text contained previously in those articles.

In recent years the Irish courts have been drawn into acutely controversial areas of public policy concerning non-citizens (asylum-seekers and immigrants), as this group has attempted to benefit from the inclusiveness of the new Article 2. In particular, non-national parents of Irish-born children[1] have sought to assert a choice of residence in Ireland as a by-product of their child's citizenship/ residence rights, coupled with the constitutional guarantee that children are entitled to enjoy the company and care of their parents. Article 2 of the Constitution states:

> It is the entitlement and birthright of every person born in the island of Ireland, which includes its islands and seas, to be part of the Irish nation. That is also the entitlement of all persons otherwise qualified in accordance with law to be citizens of Ireland …

Even before the new Article 2 was inserted, with the effect of placing the *jus soli* principle (whereby citizenship is acquired by place of birth) on a constitutional footing, citizenship as a birthright was already provided for in ordinary legislation.[2] For as long as Ireland remained a

---

[1] It is probably more correct to refer to such children as 'Irish citizen children' but the phrase 'Irish-born children' is used to reflect its common usage in public discourse on this topic.

[2] Section 6 of the Nationality and Citizenship Act 1956.

country of outward migration, this posed little problem, though a portent of future difficulties was provided as early as 1990 in the Supreme Court case of *Fajujonu v. Minister for Justice.*[3] In that case, a family of illegal immigrants including three Irish-born children successfully resisted deportation on the basis that the Minister for Justice had failed to give adequate weight to their residence and family rights under the Constitution when making the decision to deport them, as he was entitled to do under immigration legislation. This case led to a government policy not to seek to deport non-national parents of Irish-born children which lasted for more than ten years.

In the interim, Ireland changed radically from a country of net emigration to a country of net immigration, with a large non-citizen population composed of migrant workers, illegal immigrants, asylum seekers and refugees. The trend of inward migration was already well established by the time the government concluded negotiations on the Belfast Agreement of 1998 and it is not yet entirely clear why the new Article 2 of the Constitution was not more narrowly drafted so as not to give such a strong constitutional expression to the *jus soli* principle. Such an approach would have posed no threat to the entitlement to Irish citizenship of persons born in Northern Ireland.

However, this was not done and, as a result, by the late 1990s increasing numbers of immigrants were seeking leave to remain in Ireland on the basis of parentage of an Irish-born child. Many such applications were made by asylum seekers who had withdrawn their applications for asylum. This was clearly problematical for a government which had invested heavily in establishing an immigration and asylum system, with institutions, rules and procedures for determining who is to stay, under what conditions and for how long, and, critically, who is to leave.

The 'Irish-born child' phenomenon effectively bypassed all of that and appeared to do so by allowing the asylum process to be used for the purpose of accessing the territory. A perception emerged that many non-nationals claimed asylum on arrival in order to gain entry into Ireland, whereupon they had an Irish-born child, applied for temporary leave to remain on that basis and then withdrew their asylum applications (or not, in some cases). The question of whether or not asylum applications were withdrawn on official advice is contested.

Thus, the government was in a bind: it was too late and politically impracticable to change the rules relating to citizenship which had been copper-fastened in the Belfast Agreement; but it was too much to allow the carefully constructed immigration and asylum system to be undermined by procedural bypass. Therefore, a policy decision was made to begin to refuse leave to remain on the basis of parentage of

---

[3]   [1990] 2 IR 151.

an Irish-born child, in the knowledge that inevitably a court challenge would be mounted on the basis of the *Fajujonu* principle. When this occurred, the minister would attempt to distinguish *Fajujonu* on the facts and hope that the deference displayed by the superior courts to the Executive in the area of asylum and immigration policy,[4] would lead to an endorsement of the minister's position. The test case was *Lobe and Osayande v. Minister for Justice, Equality and Law Reform.*[5]

In this chapter, we look at that decision and analyse it both from a refugee protection and constitutional law perspective. Our point of departure in considering *Lobe* must be its predecessor – the *Fajujonu* decision.

Fajujonu v. Minister for Justice [6]

Facts

The first- and second-named plaintiffs were a Nigerian and Moroccan husband and wife who had come to Ireland in 1981 as illegal immigrants. In 1983 their first child, the third-named plaintiff, was born. The couple was given a house by Dublin Corporation (as it was then known) and subsequently two further children were born. Mr Fajujonu was offered a job and his prospective employers sought a work permit from the Minister for Labour. This was refused on the basis that he was an illegal immigrant. The Minister for Justice then refused him permission to reside in the state, thereby confirming his status as an illegal immigrant because he had been refused permission to work. In 1990, before a deportation order could be made, the Fajujonus instituted proceedings in which they claimed orders restraining their deportation and declarations that they were entitled to reside in the state and that the provisions of the Aliens Act 1935 under which the minister was empowered to deport them were inconsistent with the Constitution. By this time they had lived in the state for eight years.

High Court decision

There were two essential questions for resolution before the High Court: 1) whether by virtue of Articles 40, 41 and 42 of the Constitution, a citizen of Ireland had a right to remain resident within the state and to have preserved the family of which she was a member as a unit of society within the state so that she could be parented by her parents within the state; and 2) whether this was an absolute right which could

---

4   Such 'hope' was based on the decision of the Supreme Court in the Article 26 reference of the Illegal Immigrants (Trafficking) Bill, [2000] IR 360, and on a number of successful (from a state perspective) judicial review applications in the High Court.
5   Decision of the Supreme Court of 23 January 2003.
6   [1990] 2 IR 151.

not be defeated or infringed by a deportation order made by the minister pursuant to the Aliens Act 1935.

On the first question, Barrington J acknowledged both the existence of a right of residency of an Irish citizen and a child's right to the society of its parents. However, he denied that these together formed a composite right of the child to the society of its parents in the state:

> I am prepared to accept that the child has, generally speaking, a right as an Irish citizen, to be in the State. I am also prepared to accept as a general proposition that the child has the right to the society of its parents. But does it follow from this that the child has the right to the society of its parents in the State?[7]

He continued:

> In the present case the parents never had a right to live or to work in Ireland. The child clearly has a certain right to be in Ireland. She also has the right to the society of her parents. But it does not follow from this that she has a right to the society of her parents in Ireland. I do not think that the parents can by positing on their child a wish to remain in Ireland in their society confer upon themselves a right to remain in Ireland, such as could be invoked to override legislation passed by the Irish parliament to achieve its concept of what the common good of Irish citizens generally requires.[8]

From the following extract, it is clear that Barrington J's response to the second question (as to whether the rights asserted were absolute) was also negative. He said:

> The rights of the family are declared to be 'inalienable' which means that they cannot be surrendered or given away. They are also declared to be 'imprescriptible' which means that they cannot be lost of forfeited through the wrongful act of a third party over a period of time. One is therefore driven to the conclusion that the Constitution reserves to the family a certain sphere of authority and that within the sphere it has inalienable and imprescriptible rights. But this does not mean that the sphere of authority is unlimited or the rights absolute. There are certain matters which are outside and beyond the competence of the family, for example, issues such as peace or war of the foreign policy of the State.

Supreme Court decision

The case made by counsel for the appellants before the Supreme Court was slightly different to that made before the High Court. It was not contended that the rights at issue were absolute and incapable of

---

[7]   at p. 156.
[8]   at p. 157.

being affected by immigration legislation. Rather, it was argued that the primary right at issue was a constitutional right of very great importance which could only be restricted or infringed for very compelling reasons. In the Supreme Court, judgments were given by Finlay CJ and Walsh J, the other members of the court concurring.

The appellant's alleged right to the care and company of her parents in the state

Finlay CJ confirmed that the appellant had a right to the care and company of her parents and accepted that this was a right exercisable within the State:

> I have now come to the conclusion that where as occurs in this case, an alien has in fact resided for an appreciable time in the state and has become a member of a family unit within this state containing children who are citizens, that there can be no question but that those children, as citizens, have got a constitutional right to the company, care and parentage of their parents within a family unit. I am also satisfied that prima facie and subject to the exigencies of the common good that that is a right which these citizens would be entitled to exercise within the State.

> I am also satisfied that whereas the parents who are not citizens and who are aliens cannot, by reason of their having as members of their family children born in Ireland who are citizens, claim any constitutional right of a particular kind to remain in Ireland, they are entitled to assert a choice of residence on behalf of their infant children, in the interests of those infant children.[9]

Walsh J also confirmed that the appellant, as a citizen, had residency rights and therefore could not be deported. He considered that if the appellant's parents were deported, this would lead to a violation of the child's family rights because if the parents elected to leave the child behind, this would lead to enforced separation of the child from the family, and if the parents elected to take the child with them, the child would cease to benefit from the protection of the Constitution, and in particular the rights afforded to the family under Article 41:

> It is abundantly clear that citizens of this State may not be deported. The third plaintiff is one of three children of the first two plaintiffs, all of which children are citizens of Ireland. If the first two plaintiffs, being the parents of the infant children, are deported, the effect must be that their children who are Irish citizens are faced with the choice of remaining within this State as they are entitled to do and therefore being in effect compulsorily separated from their parents, or having to leave the State with their parents and thus ceasing to have the benefit of all the protection afforded

---

[9]   at p. 162.

by the laws and the Constitution of this State. In my view, the first two plaintiffs and their three children constitute a family within the meaning of the Constitution and the three children are entitled to the care, protection and the society of their parents in this family group which is resident within the State. There is no doubt that the family has made its home and residence in Ireland.

He went on to say:

In view of the fact that these children are of tender age, who require the society of their parents, and when the parents have not been shown to have been in any way unfit or guilty of any matter which makes them unsuitable custodians to their children, to move to expel parents in the particular circumstances of this case would, in my view, be inconsistent with the provisions of Article 41 of the Constitution guaranteeing the integrity of the family.

Circumstances under which the right could be restricted or infringed

The Chief Justice considered that the Minister for Justice could only infringe the constitutional right at issue if it was found to be necessary in the interests of the common good:

Having reached these conclusions, the question then must arise as to whether the State, acting through the Minister for Justice pursuant to the powers contained in the Aliens Act 1935, can under any circumstances force the family so constituted as I have described, that is the family concerned in this case, to leave the State. I am satisfied that he can, but only if, after due and proper consideration, he is satisfied that the interests of the common good and the protection of the State and its society justifies an interference with what is clearly a constitutional right.

He continued:

The discretion, it seems to me, which in the particular circumstance in a case such as this is vested in the Minister for Justice, to consider as to whether to permit the entire of this family to continue to reside in the State, on the one hand, or to prevent them from continuing to reside in the State, on the other, is a discretion which can only be carried out after and in the light of a full recognition of the fundamental nature of the constitutional rights of the family. The reason, therefore, which would justify the removal of this family as it now stands, consisting of five persons three of whom are citizens of Ireland, against the apparent will of the entire family, outside the State has to be a *grave and substantial reason associated with the common good.* (Emphasis added)

Similarly, Walsh J found that the state was obliged in such situations to do a balancing test between the important constitutional rights involved and the interests of the common good:

> In my view, [the Minister] would have to be satisfied, for stated reasons, that the interests of the common good of the people of Ireland and of the protection of the State and its society are so *predominant and overwhelming* in the circumstances of the case, that an action which can have the effect of breaking up this family *is not so disproportionate to the aim sought to be achieved* as to be unsustainable. (Emphasis added)

The Supreme Court did not overrule Barrington J's decision in the High Court, and did not find for the appellants. It did, however, invite the minister to revisit his decision on the deportation of the family in the light of its judgment.

Arising from the non-deportation of the Fajujonus a perception emerged that 'constitutional families', so-called, with Irish-born children were not amenable to deportation. The practice which ensued was, arguably, based on a misapprehension as to the true ratio of the decision but that did not become clear until the definitive Supreme Court ruling in *Lobe and Osayande v. Minister for Justice, Equality and Law Reform* ten years later following a dramatic change in the general profile of those seeking the benefit of policy founded on this rule.

Lobe and Osayande v. Minister for Justice, Equality and Law Reform

The situation of both families party to the proceedings was broadly similar. The Lobes were from the Czech Republic and the Osayandes were from Nigeria. The parents of both families had previously applied for asylum in the United Kingdom and then made applications for asylum in Ireland. The Lobes were accompanied by their three children, and the Osayandes by one child. Decisions were made under the terms of the Dublin Convention that both families should be transferred to the UK, the jurisdiction in which their original asylum applications were lodged. In each case those decisions were unsuccessfully appealed and deportation orders were subsequently issued.

Both families then instituted the present proceedings, applying for leave to apply, by way of judicial review, for *inter alia* an order of certiorari quashing the deportation orders. In the meantime, Mrs Lobe and Ms Osayande had each given birth to a baby in Ireland and were granted an adjournment to make submissions to the minister as to why each family should not be deported on account of the births. Those applications were refused, on the basis of a memorandum prepared for the minister by one of his officials, a Mr Lohan.

In respect of the Lobes, the Lohan Memorandum (as it came to be known) advised that in view of the fact that the deportation of the family could result in the removal of the minor applicant from the state in circumstances which could be interpreted as a 'constructive deportation', the minister should weigh up the rights of that Irish citizen against the needs of the common good. The rights of the Irish citizen were identified as including a possible right of residence and the right to the company, care and parentage of family/parents. The needs of the common good were identified as the preservation of the integrity of and respect for the state's asylum and immigration laws. In weighing the competing rights, Mr Lohan referred to the fact that the Lobes had only been in the state a short time and that their actions were designed to circumvent the operation of the Dublin Convention. He also referred to a presumption that they would preserve the family unit if deported by taking their Irish born child with them. A similar memorandum was prepared in respect of the Osayandes.

The High Court decision

In the High Court, the application for leave to apply for judicial review was treated as the application for judicial review itself. Smyth J (who, for some time had been dealing with most asylum matters on the judicial review list in the High Court) considered the decision of the Supreme Court in *Fajujonu v. Minister for Justice*. He held that it was distinguishable from the instant cases on the facts: the Fajujonu family had been resident in the state for a considerable length of time as compared with the Lobes and Osayandes; and in *Fajujonu*, there was no evidence that the minister had given careful consideration to the constitutional rights at issue in reaching his decision unlike the level of consideration averred to in the Lohan memorandum. Smyth J refused to quash the deportation orders.

The Supreme Court decision

Majority judgments

There were five majority judgments and two dissents. Attention will be given to the leading judgment of Keane CJ, with reference to the other majority judgments when they differ significantly.

The constitutional rights of the applicants

Citizenship

The majority judges differed on the issue of whether citizenship of the Irish-born child is derived from the Constitution or from ordinary legislation.[10] Keane CJ felt that it was unnecessary to determine the precise legal effect of the new Article 2 of the Constitution, since all parties were in agreement that the child applicants were citizens and therefore entitled to the full range of rights which flow from citizenship. Murray J went further and held that there was nothing in Article 2 to suggest that the rights of citizens had been either enhanced or diminished. However, he did seem to consider that the 'amplitude' of citizenship rights may be enhanced by the circumstances of the citizen, and in particular the length of his/her residence in Ireland:

> When the question of making a deportation in such circumstances [where a family has made their home and residence in Ireland] arises, the Minister is not dealing with the fact that an infant was born in Ireland as an abstract notion.

Hardiman J considered that the use of the terms 'nation' and 'citizen' in Article 2 were not interchangeable, and that it was at least questionable that Article 2 conferred, as opposed to acknowledged, any right of citizenship. However, this was an issue that did not need to be resolved in this case. Denham J was alone in her forthright assertion that the citizenship rights of the Irish-born child derive from Article 2 of the Constitution.

None of the foregoing statements form part of the *ratio* of the majority decision because the state never sought to question the principle of citizenship as a birthright. They do, however, raise questions of fundamental importance if the essence of the judicial role in this context is the balancing of competing *constitutional* as opposed to *statutory* rights. It may be the case that there is a hidden *ratio* in *Lobe and Osayande*.[11]

Residence and family rights

Keane CJ accepted that Irish citizens cannot be expelled or deported and that a corollary of the right to citizenship is a right of residence.[12]

---

[10] Keane CJ (pp 15-16) reproduces section 6 of the Irish Nationality and Citizenship Act 1956, as originally enacted, and says: 'This legislation was in force at the time when the minor applicants in these proceedings were born [4 October and 2 November 2001] and is still in force'. Denham J (p. 8) makes the same assumption, as does Mc Guinness J (p. 11), Hardiman J (pp 8-9) and Fennelly J (p. 15). However, since both applicant children were born after 5 June 2001, which was the date of enactment of the new Irish Nationality and Citizenship Act 2001, it was arguably the provisions of that Act that regulated their status. While this may not have a bearing on the central point about whether citizenship is a constitutional right, it is surprising that such an elementary point was overlooked by the Supreme Court.

[11] This is especially evident in the judgment of Hardiman J at pp 9-11.

[12] The rule that citizens cannot be deported is grounded in both municipal law and public international law.

However, he held that there is a distinction between the exercise by an adult citizen of his/her right of residence and the position of an infant citizen who is too young to effectively exercise the right and who must live wherever his/her parents decide. Thus, he said 'it may reasonably be regarded as a right which does not vest in them until they reach an age at which they are capable of exercising it and, it may be, of asserting a choice of residence different from that which their parents would desire'. Since a minor does not have a right to choose to reside in Ireland (as s/he is both factually and in law incapable of making such a choice), it follows that his/her parents cannot assert a right to reside in Ireland on his/her behalf. In situations where parents themselves *are* lawfully entitled to reside in Ireland, the right of their minor children to live with them is not derived from some nascent right to choose a residency, but from their constitutional right to be in the care and custody of their parents. And although in the present case, the minor applicants undoubtedly had the constitutional right to be in the care and custody of their parents, the parents were not lawfully entitled to reside in Ireland. Therefore, the minor applicants' right to be in the care and custody of their parents did not imply a right to exercise that right in Ireland.

But, Keane CJ's finding on this point is in direct conflict with that of Finlay CJ in *Fajujonu*. As the court in *Lobe* was not asked to overrule *Fajujonu*, and if Finlay CJ's statement on the issue in *Fajujonu* formed part of the *ratio decidendi* of that judgment, Keane CJ would be required to give effect to it. In order to avoid this, the Chief Justice found Finlay CJ's statement to be *obiter dictum*. He based this finding on the fact that Walsh J (in *Fajujonu*) did not rely on Finlay CJ's statement in reaching his decision and on the fact that the decision of Barrington J in the High Court (with its clear statement that parents could not 'posit' on their child a wish to remain in Ireland and thereby confer on themselves a right to remain) was affirmed, not overruled, by the Supreme Court.

In essence, Keane CJ was pointing to the decision of Barrington J as the true *ratio* in *Fajujonu*. This was precisely the corrective ruling sought by the state.

The right of the state to control immigration

In considering the origin of the state's right to control immigration, Keane CJ found that it is a power which inheres in the state by virtue of its sovereignty, and not because it has been conferred by statute on particular organs of the state, although it is regulated by statute. Indeed, the legislative context had changed radically since *Fajujonu* was decided, by the introduction of a complex of statutory provisions reflecting Ireland's obligations under international law.[13] The factual

---

[13] The Refugee Act 1996 as amended by the Illegal Immigrants (Trafficking) Act 2000, the Immigration Act 1999 and the Immigration Act 2003.

context had also changed, in terms of the numbers of asylum seekers and immigrants arriving annually. Keane CJ emphasised that the changed immigration environment could not be ignored when considering the state's right to control immigration. He also laid emphasis on the exclusive power of the Oireachtas and the Executive, subject to judicial review, to regulate immigration.

In ascertaining the breadth of the state's right, the Chief Justice considered a number of important cases concerning the impact of the exercise by the state of its power to expel non-nationals or refuse them entry when the constitutional rights of Irish citizens are involved.

The first case was that of *Pok Sun Shun and Others v. Ireland and Others*,[14] where a deportation order made pursuant to the Aliens Act 1935 was challenged on the basis that it interfered with the constitutional rights of a family, some of whom were Irish citizens. Costello J said:

> I do not think that the rights given to the 'family' are absolute, in the sense that they are not subject to some restrictions by the State and [as counsel for the State] has pointed out, restrictions are, in fact, permitted by law, when husbands are imprisoned and parents of families are imprisoned and undoubtedly, whilst protected under the Constitution, these are restrictions permitted for the common good on the exercise of its rights.

In fact Walsh J in *Fajujonu* had taken issue with the above passage, finding it to be a bad example of the non-absolute character of family rights under the Constitution. Counsel for the applicants in *Lobe* argued that Walsh J's criticism undermined the value of the statement and left open the question as to the absolute nature of family rights. However, Keane CJ rejected that interpretation, classifying Walsh J's criticism as *obiter* and pointing to other parts of his judgment where he made clear that family rights are susceptible to limitation.

The second case was that of *Osheku and Others v. Ireland*,[15] where again the Aliens Act 1935 and statutory instruments made thereunder were impugned as violating the guarantees in the Constitution for the protection of marriage and the family. In the High Court, Gannon J stated:

> ... The Constitution does not impose on the citizens a duty or obligation to remain resident within the State, nor does it impose on the State a duty to provide a place of residence within the State for every citizen.

And later in the judgment, he stated tautologously:

> An order made by the Minister for Justice deporting Mr Osheku, the first plaintiff, if made by him in the due exercise of the discretion vested in him

---

[14] [1986] ILRM 593.
[15] [1986] IR 733.

by the Aliens Act 1935, and the statutory orders made thereunder, would not infringe the constitutional rights of any of the plaintiffs.

Again, counsel for the applicants (in *Lobe*) argued that Walsh J had disapproved of this statement in *Fajujonu* by declining to comment on its constitutionality. However, Keane CJ found that Walsh J was actually distinguishing between the two cases factually, and therefore indicating that it was unnecessary to comment on the constitutional principles discussed in *Osheku*. In any event, Keane CJ pointed out that Gannon J's statement regarding the inherent 'right' of the State to control immigration into its territory (in *Osheku*) was approved by the Supreme Court in the case of *Laurentiu v. Minister for Justice*.[16]

Conflicting rights: the Fajujonu *test*

When considering the conflict of the applicant's constitutional rights with the state's right to control immigration (the common good) in *Fajujonu*, both judges appeared to set a high threshold for the requirements of the common good. Finlay CJ referred to 'a grave and substantial reason associated with the common good', while Walsh J found that the interests of the common good would have to be 'so predominant and overwhelming in the circumstances of the case' as not to be 'disproportionate'.

Counsel for the applicants in *Lobe* argued that this meant that the parents of Irish-born children could only be deported in *exceptional circumstances* associated with the common good. They claimed that it was clear from the judgments of Finlay CJ and Walsh J that the exceptional circumstances would have to *relate to the behaviour of the parents themselves,* such as criminal or anti-social activity, which would make their continued presence in the state inimical to the common good. It followed that a general desire to maintain the integrity of the immigration system would not constitute 'exceptional circumstances'.

There are actually two discrete points here: 1) that the reasons associated with the common good must be exceptional; and 2) that the exceptional reasons must be case-specific and not generic.

The response of the majority judges to this line of argument was to distinguish *Fajujonu* on the facts. Justice Murray, who is possibly most compelling on the first point, argued that the statements of both the Chief Justice and Walsh J in *Fajujonu* were patently facts-based. For example, the then Chief Justice premised his statements on the fact that the Fajujonus had resided in the state for an appreciable time and in ensuing paragraphs referred to the 'family concerned in this case' and the 'particular circumstances of a case such as this' and the justification for the removal of 'this family as it now stands'. In fact, the

---

[16] [1999] 4 IR 27.

correct (and much lower) standard for evaluating the common good was provided by the Chief Justice in *Fajujonu* when he said that the minister would have to be

> ... satisfied that for *good and sufficient reason* the common good requires that the residence of these parents within the State should be terminated, even though that has the necessary consequence that in order to remain as a family unit the ... children must also leave the state ... [Emphasis added]

Counsel for the applicants had argued in *Lobe* that it was absurd to contend that the constitutional rights identified in *Fajujonu* were facts-based, ie related to the length of residence in the state or the number of Irish born children in the family, as this would lead to the conclusion that the rights of citizens are dependent on the circumstances of other individuals. Murray J agreed that constitutional rights of citizens exist regardless of external determinate factors, but pointed out that the degree to which they were enjoyed, and indeed infringed, depended on the factual context:

> If ... a family has made its home and residence in the State for an appreciable period of time, the amplitude of the rights of the infant citizens would be affected and a deportation order of their parents may have a more intrusive or injurious effect on those rights than in the case of infant citizens whose parents had been in the country for some weeks or months.

As an aside, it is interesting to note that Hardiman J appeared to accept the 'grave and substantial' standard but considered this standard to have been satisfied in the present case.

The Chief Justice countered the second argument by pointing to the cases of *Pok Sun Shun*, *Osheku* and indeed *Fajujonu*, in which the behaviour of the applicants did not play a decisive part in the respective judgments. He also pointed to the absence of a nexus between the common good and any case-specific factors in Barrington J's judgment in *Fajujonu* in the High Court. It was significant that neither Finlay CJ nor Walsh J disapproved of Barrington J's statement of law on the issue. Keane CJ also rejected the notion that the non-deportation of a single immigrant family, in the absence of any specific negative behaviour, would not be detrimental to the common good – understood in this case as the maintenance of the integrity of the immigration and asylum systems. He said:

> While the Minister must consider each case involving deportation on its individual merits, he is undoubtedly entitled to take into account the policy considerations which would arise from allowing a particular applicant to remain where that would inevitably lead to similar decisions

in other cases, again undermining the orderly administration of the immigration and asylum system.

In summary, the majority position is that in each case in which a right of residence is claimed on the basis of the citizenship of an Irish-born child there must be an individualised consideration of the merits of the application. This right is still qualified by reference to the requirements of the common good but there is now a very different understanding of those requirements based on the altered immigration context in which such claims arise. The majority judges insisted on taking judicial notice of that context even in the absence of tendered evidence. It is clear, therefore, that claims which are more factually akin to the facts in *Fajujonu* will have a greater likelihood of success than those with similarities to *Lobe*. In practice this will be advantageous to those families seeking renewal of leave to remain originally granted on the basis of an Irish-born child but disadvantageous to newly-lodged applications by those not in the jurisdiction for an appreciable time.

The dissenting judgments

McGuinness and Fennelly JJ dissented from the majority and the bases of their dissents were slightly different.

Mr Justice Fennelly based his decision on the fact that *Fajujonu* could not be distinguished 'in any meaningful way' in the context of *Lobe*. Regardless of the fact that both Finlay CJ and Walsh J had both referred to the duration of time spent by the Fajujonus in Ireland and the size of their family, he did not see that these matters constituted part of the *ratio* in that case. This was crucial because the minister sought to distinguish *Fajujonu* in *Lobe*, not overrule it.

In considering the provision of Article 2 of the Irish Constitution entitling those born on the island of Ireland, its islands and seas to be 'part of the Irish nation', Fennelly J was emphatic that this 'must have real content and should not be treated as a piece of empty sloganeering'. He rejected the notion of two-tier citizenship based on the 'fortuity' of a person's birth and went on to state:

> The State cannot expel an adult Irish citizen from the national territory. Nor can it expel a child citizen who has validly elected through his parents to remain in the State ... A child who is *de facto* deported from the State before his education commences cannot conceivably be *'part of the Irish nation'* or *'share its cultural identity and heritage'*.

Referring to a number of established authorities on the constitutional position of the family as moral institution with rights derived from the natural law which is superior to those of the state itself, Fennelly J highlighted the difficulty facing the minister in any attempt to establish that the common good might be served by compromising or qualifying family rights.

He then embarked on a consideration of the evolving jurisprudence under Article 8 of the European Convention on Human Rights emphasising the importance attached to considering each case on its own merits and signalling (*obiter*) the possibility of future problems for the state under the Convention in cases of family deportations based on generalised concerns about process integrity.[17]

Commentary

From a refugee law perspective, the judgment in *Lobe and Osayande* can be viewed in a positive light. Firstly, it will prevent the perceived abuse of the asylum process by removing the incentive for people to claim asylum solely for the purpose of accessing the country in order to have an Irish-born child. Secondly, it will remove a parallel process (automatic residency on the basis of an Irish-born child) which effectively circumvents a necessary outcome of the asylum process in respect of unsuccessful asylum applicants, namely, deportation. While the concept of deportation may be distasteful to many, if one accepts the basic premise of refugee law (ie *non refoulement* of refugees) then it follows that refugees must be distinguished from non-refugees, and the latter made amenable to deportation.

Refugee status must be preserved as a *status-conferring protection* for those in genuine need of such protection under the terms of the Geneva Convention relating to the Status of Refugees 1951 as incorporated by the Refugee Act 1996 (as amended). A right of residence is neither status-conferring nor a form of protection (understood as Convention protection or complementary protection – whether on the basis of Irish law or the ECHR – as currently provided by the grant of temporary leave to remain on humanitarian grounds). In an ideal world, refugee protection would be a door through which those fearing persecution would walk with confidence. That is infinitely preferable to having them climb through the window of residency rights (bearing in mind the personal consequences for women in this process) as an inferior alternative.

A further possible consequence of the decision may be that asylum seekers/refugees and other persons seeking leave to remain for non-protection reasons will no longer be popularly categorised as one and the same group. This is vitally important from the point of view of developing a strong regime of *refugee* protection, which includes a well-informed public that understands the distinction between refugees and other groups of migrants. In this regard, it is regrettable that some popular misconceptions about asylum seekers as a class,

---

[17] at p. 19.

were reflected in *Lobe*. For example, in a passage of the judgment of Mr Justice Hardiman, tellingly entitled 'Asylum and immigration: a digression', the following comment is made:

> It must however be recalled that asylum seekers are a small minority of potential immigrants to Ireland. The great bulk of immigrants are people who come here in possession of work permits and their families ... They work in thousands of enterprises and manage some of them. They make a much needed contribution to Irish life by their skills and industry, just as Irish emigrants in the past made a valued contribution in their new homelands. This orderly process of immigration seems likely to continue, bringing further welcome and productive newcomers to Ireland. This case is not concerned with that large group of people which, however, constitutes the great bulk of immigrants to Ireland.

While it is undoubtedly true that the majority of immigrants are economic migrants who contribute on many levels to Irish society it is noteworthy that the learned judge made no reference to any equivalent positive contribution made by asylum seekers/refugees in their countries of asylum. It is worth pointing out that amongst asylum seekers are refugees (the status is declaratory not constitutive) who are not just victims of persecution but also survivors, and who throughout history have contributed enormously to their countries of asylum. And even those asylum seekers whose applications are subsequently rejected (a fact that does not make them 'bogus'), also have a contribution to make to their host communities. It is equally noteworthy and, perhaps, ironic that Mr Justice Hardiman makes no acknowledgment in the course of this digression of the fact that many of the Irish emigrants who made a 'valued contribution in their new homelands' were, in fact, illegal immigrants.

In an earlier part of his judgment, Mr Justice Hardiman displayed a less than complete understanding of the mechanics of the asylum process – again reflective of popular misunderstandings. He spoke about the fact that asylum claims are 'typically ... made by persons who arrive in the State for that purpose rather than applying from abroad, even from a safe country'. This is a classical confusion of resettlement (an option for some *recognised refugees* who cannot remain in their first country of asylum) and asylum. It is simply not possible to make an asylum application in the manner described.

From a constitutional law perspective there are a number of issues of concern arising from the reasoning of the majority. It is well established that the natural law basis of family rights (under Article 41 of the Constitution) does not confer absolute rights on families as institutions or on individuals within family units. However, when the courts permit the qualified application of such rights in deference to an Executive-centred view of the common good based on process integrity – in this case, the integrity of the asylum-seeking process – compelling reasons are called for.

The majority in *Lobe* acknowledge the importance of a child's right to the care and company of its parents but do not accept that this right must be exercised within the jurisdiction of Ireland. In other words, they explicitly accept that certain Irish citizens are amenable to deportation by virtue of the non-Irish citizenship of their parents and the age of the citizens in question.

It would appear that the analogous (and, indeed, unanimous) principle established by the Supreme Court in the extradition case of *Finucane v. McMahon*,[18] that citizens should not be extradited where there is a probable risk of a violation of their constitutional rights in the receiving jurisdiction, was not given due consideration by the Supreme Court majority in *Lobe*. It is clear that the majority took the view that, in exercising his/her discretion in relation to applications for leave to remain on humanitarian grounds, the Minister for Justice, Equality and Law Reform was best charged with the task of assessing any risk to the constitutional rights of citizens about to be deported. On a strict view of separation of powers that may well be correct but it remains to be settled definitively by the Supreme Court what level of judicial scrutiny ought to be applied in applications for judicial review of decisions to deport. Although a number of the majority judgments in *Lobe* indicate a satisfaction with the so-called *O'Keeffe*[19] test of reasonableness these comments are *obiter* because the point was not argued in the case. Contrary opinions were, however, expressed by McGuinness and Denham JJ with the latter judge forming part of the majority. This is a matter which will, undoubtedly, be settled in a later case.

While there was apparent satisfaction at government level with the majority decision in *Lobe* there still remains a 'problem'. Ireland is the only country in Europe that confers an automatic birthright of citizenship. It is clear that this does not create an immunity from deportation but there is still an incentive for those who wish to acquire Irish (and, ultimately, EU) citizenship for their children. Perhaps this matter will eventually be settled by means of a constitutional amendment. In the meantime, a political consensus will have to be carefully constructed in order to avoid an opportunistic reduction of the complex issues involved in such a referendum to one of race.

---

[18] [1990] 1 IR 165.
[19] *O'Keeffe v. An Bord Pleanála* [1993] 1 IR 39.

Table of Cases

Index